DISCARD

Iran Today

Iran. Cartography by Bookcomp, Inc.

Iran Today

AN ENCYCLOPEDIA OF LIFE IN THE ISLAMIC REPUBLIC

—— VOLUME TWO: L–Z ——

Edited by Mehran Kamrava
and Manochehr Dorraj

Greenwood Press
Westport, Connecticut • London

Library of Congress Cataloging-in-Publication Data

Iran today: an encyclopedia of life in the Islamic Republic / edited by
Mehran Kamrava and Manochehr Dorraj.

   p. cm.

  Includes bibliographical references and index.

  ISBN: 978-0-313-34161-8 ((set) : alk. paper)

  ISBN: 978-0-313-34162-5 ((vol. 1) : alk. paper)

  ISBN: 978-0-313-34163-2 ((vol. 2) : alk. paper)

  1. Iran—Encyclopedias. I. Kamrava, Mehran, 1964– II. Dorraj, Manochehr.

  DS253.I69 2008

  955.05′403—dc22   2008019488

British Library Cataloging in Publication Data is available.

Library of Congress Catalog Card Number: 2008019488

ISBN: 978-0-313-34161-8 (set)

     978-0-313-34162-5 (vol. 1)

     978-0-313-34163-2 (vol. 2)

First published in 2008

Greenwood Press, 88 Post Road West, Westport, CT 06881

An imprint of Greenwood Publishing Group, Inc.

www.greenwood.com

Printed in the United States of America

The paper used in this book complies with the
Permanent Paper Standard issued by the National
Information Standards Organization (Z39.48–1984).

10 9 8 7 6 5 4 3 2 1

For
Melisa, Dilara, Kendra, Farah, Katayoun, and Maryam

Contents

✦

Alphabetical List of Entries

✦

Topical List of Entries

✦

L

✦ LAW, ISLAMIC

The Iranian version of Islamic law is based on Shïite jurisprudence (*fiqh*). According to the traditionalist version of this body of law, Islamic law regulates both the public and private aspects of life. *`Ebādāt* (acts of worship), and *möāmelāt* (human interactions), have the same status in this version of Islamic law. This approach does not resort to political authority to enforce Islamic laws. Traditional jurists do not see any causal relationship between enforcing Islamic laws and having access to political power. While reformist and liberal readings of Islamic law in Iran emphasize the legal and charismatic authority of religious leaders, the traditionalist approach gives priority to (traditional authority) of Muslim leaders. This does not mean that the traditionalist jurists believe in separation of state and religion, but it means that they do not resort to the state for accomplishing their mission.

The ideological version of Islamic law presented after the Islamic Revolution of 1979 and the subsequent establishment of the Islamic Republic of Iran claims that all public and private aspects of human life should be regulated by Shïite jurisprudence as provided in the Quran, *hadith*, and texts of Shi'ite jurisprudence, from early jurists to the contemporary sources of emulation. According to this approach, establishing an Islamic government is necessary for executing Islamic laws. Ideological *shari`a* deals with every aspect of day-to-day life, including politics, economics, banking, business law, contract law, sexuality, and social issues. This approach elevates *`ebādāt* to the level of public affairs; individuals are evaluated, judged, rewarded, and punished based on their observation of Islamic ordinances in the area of worship. Ideological recruitment for public offices and the necessity for qualification by the jurists to run for elected bodies based on the private lives of individuals have their roots in this perspective of Islamic law.

The third reading of Islamic law in contemporary Iran belongs to reformists, who believe *shari`a* is a changing body and should be interpreted according to the new needs and demands of the changing society. They believe that Islamic law has been interpreted differently across times, places, and scholars. Reformist jurists assert *mòāmelāt* is not as sacred as *`ebādāt,* and (they) have and can be changed over the centuries. Reformists believe that new Islamic legal theories can lead to the creation of a modernized Islamic law and a democratic state that may adapt to the social and political demands of the modern world. They want to resolve incompatibilities between democracy and Islamic law by recognizing pluralism in the political sphere and religious freedoms in the religious domain, due process in judicial affairs, upgrading the legal status of women, and limiting the ways *shari`a* intervenes in all spheres of private and public life. A minority among the reformists still believe that the principles of *shari`a* are fully compatible with democracy and human rights.

The totalitarian reading of Islamic law emphasizes the comprehensive nature of *shari`a* law. This reading states that the law must provide all that is necessary for a person's spiritual and physical well-being. This fact, that all possible actions of a Muslim are divided (in principle) into five categories, i.e., obligatory, meritorious, permissible, reprehensible, and forbidden, is presented as a proof for totalitarians' maximalist approach to law, although these categories can be found in any system of law. The totalitarian approach puts more emphasis on *`ebādāt* due to its emphasis on controlling the personal lives of believers and non-believers in an Islamic state.

The liberal approach to Islamic law questions the relevance and applicability of *shari`a* in modern times. Liberals believe that the political reality in most Islamic states contradicts the compatibility of *shari`a* with democracy and human rights. According to this approach, *shari`a* law was created and deliberated during the first centuries of Islam and Islamic empires, and this body of law was responding to the questions and demands of the time. This approach infringes upon the principle of non-discrimination between individuals regarding their enjoyment of public freedoms. Death penalty for conversion and homosexual acts, stoning for adultery (for women), amputation for theft, lashing and flogging for adultery (for men), fornication, and intoxication, and other harsh and cruel punishments are outdated in our time, and enforcing such punishments is no longer fair and effective. The core of *shari`a* in this reading is *`ebādāt,* which is sacred and shapes the relationship between a

Muslim and her/his God. *Mòāmelāt*, in this approach, is considered a secular and worldly law that may be changed in any capacity. This point of view draws a line between sin and crime: to violate certain ordinances in acts of worship or private matters is sin and should not have any consequences in public life. To violate secular public law is a crime that should have consequences for the violators in their lifetime, while violation of *shari`a* laws in the areas of worship will have consequences for believers in another world.

In all of these approaches to Islamic law, certain laws, for private or public life, are considered as divinely ordained, concrete, and timeless for all relevant situations. Muslims believe that Islam ought to regulate the sphere of law as well. The reformists have a minimalist, and the totalitarians have a maximalist, theory in this regard. Totalitarian, traditional, and ideological readings of Islamic law believe that enforcing cruel and harsh punishments serves as a deterrent to crime. Reformist and liberal readings emphasize preventive policies rather than punitive ones. Liberal readings of Islamic law accept the enforcement of *shari`a* law if both sides of the case believe in this body of law and are willing to be judged according to it.

The different approaches to Islamic law came about as a result of various interpretations meant to deal with the realities of contemporary life. Ideological and totalitarian versions were created in reaction to other ideologies, especially liberal democracy and Marxism, while the reformist version was created to help decrease tension between the Muslim world and the West. From the thirteenth century, after the golden age of Islamic civilization, almost all Muslim societies have been in decline; calls for reform have gone different ways and tremendous effort has been put on Islam to bring it up to date.

Shi`ite scholars in general accept *shari`a* as the body of precedent and legal theory established and deliberated between the tenth and early twentieth centuries. Traditionalist jurists look at this body of law as a static entity that should be protected from new and secular interpretations; reformist and liberal jurists, though in the minority, view this body as a dynamic entity that has and will be changing throughout the centuries based on new social and political necessities and possibilities. Totalitarian and authoritarian versions put emphasis on political issues when the dynamism of Islamic jurisprudence is considered.

The sources of Islamic law in Shi`ite tradition are the Quran, *sunnah* (sayings, actions, and confirmations of the prophet Mohammad and Shi`ite Imams), consensus (*ejmā`*: the unanimity of prophet Muhammad and Shi`ite Imams' disciples on a certain issue), and reason or intellect (`*aql*). In Sunni tradition, these sources are Quran, *sunnah*, consensus, and analogy (*qiyās*: drawing analogy from the essence of divine principles). The "reason" that Shi`ite jurists talk about is completely different from the "reason" or "intellect" that is discussed in enlightenment tradition. This "reason" in traditional and ideological approaches is bound to the ordinances of God. Totalitarian, reformist, and liberal approaches have a modern perspective of "reason" and its role in human life. The totalitarian approach is open to the exigencies of reason only for strengthening the power of Islamic government, while reformist and liberal approaches let reason have more say in human affairs, even allowing for questioning of the traditional readings of Islamic texts. Like justice and freedom, reformists and liberals believe that Islamic law should be evaluated according to the human intellect, while traditionalist and ideological versions believe that everything in *shari`a* is just and rational and if enforced will lead to human freedom. Whenever the Quran, *sunnah,* and a consensus of experts are silent about an issue, Muslims can refer to reason to find God's ordinance. Later in the history of the Muslim world, local customs (`*orf*) that did not contradict *shari`a* ordinances became part of the Islamic body of laws in both the Shi'a and Sunni communities.

Six social processes have influenced the pace and direction of change in Islamic law in contemporary Iran: urbanization, secularization, social differentiation, modernization, increase of literacy rates, and transformation of Shi`ite authority. The renowned contemporary thinker Morteza Motahhari discussed two different readings of Islamic law: urban and rural. First, urbanization has led clerics to have more of an urban reading of Islamic *shari`a.* This reading focuses on the necessities and demands of an industrial and service-based society, while the rural reading focuses on the needs and necessities of an agricultural society. Next, secularization during the Pahlavis dynasty led to transplantation and codification of Islamic laws and gave priority to the state law rather than jurist law. Through the pressure of Western educated elite, codified state law started replacing the role of scholarly legal opinions of Islamic jurists. Western countries were the source of inspiration, pressure, and force upon the Iranian state to change its laws. Secularist elites pushed for laws deviating from the opinions of the Islamic legal scholars. Islamic legal scholarship remained the sole authority for guidance in matters of rituals, worship, and spirituality, while they lost authority to the state in areas such as transactions, contracts, penal law, and judicial procedures. The third process, social differentiation, has led to powerful appeal for pluralism and toleration toward alternative lifestyles (*degarbashi*) and alternative thoughts (*degarandishi*). Next, modernization of social, cultural, economic, and political organizations created a new world that Shi`ite clerics at first completely rejected. This has been the story of traditional reaction to modernity in different stages of encountering the Islamic world and the West. An increase of literacy rates changed the traditional relationship between the emulators and sources of emulation. Now the emulators could use the catechisms and did not need to be in a face-to-face relationship with `ulemā` to ask their religious questions. The sixth process is the transformation of Shīite authority from a pluralistic structure to a monopolistic one under the absolute power of the ruling jurist. The authoritarian structure of the polity in the Islamic Republic of Iran has facilitated this process.

Islamic law in Shīite tradition is neither a common nor a civil law system, although it has some elements from both systems. Muslims are bound to the Quran and *sunnah,* while there is no sacred element in common or civil law system. Islamic law of Iran is not based on Iranian customs, as opposed to common law system, although its roots go back to customary law of Medina and other Muslim societies of pristine Islam. Some customary laws were codified in areas of private law, similar to civil law, but legislation is not the primary source of law in Iran. Similar to common law system, cases presented to *mujtaheds* (Islamic jurists) could be the primary sources of law in Shīite tradition, but decisions on these cases have usually had a very limited impact on the body of Islamic law. The system of *velāyat-e faqih* (guardianship of the jurist) has not left any room for these decisions.

Suggested Reading

Gerber, H. 1994. *State, society, and law in Islam.* New York: State University of New York Press.
Hallaq, W. B. 2001. *Authority, continuity and change in Islamic law.* Cambridge, UK: Cambridge University Press.
Mallat, C. 1993. *The renewal of Islamic law: Muhammad Baqer as-Sadr, Najaf and the Shîi International.* NY: Cambridge University Press.
Maududi, S. A. A. 1960. *The Islamic law and constitution,* trans. & ed. by Khurshid Ahmad. Lahore: Islamic Publications LTD.
Motahhari, M. 1989. *Āshnā'e bā `Olum-e Eslāmi,* Vol. III, *Osul-fiqh va Fiqh (An introduction to Islamic sciences,* Vol. III, *The principles of jurisprudence and Islamic jurisprudence).* Qom: Sadrā.
Rosen, L. 2000. *The justice of Islam: comparative perspectives on Islamic law and society.* Oxford: Oxford University Press.
Schacht, J. 1984. *Introduction to Islamic law.* Oxford: Clarendon Press.
Schiller, A. A. 1958. Jurist's law. *Columbia Law Review,* Vol. LVIII.

MAJID MOHAMMADI

✦ LEGAL SYSTEM

There are three levels of law in Iran: constitutional law, statutory law, and executive circulars and regulations. The Constitution operates on two levels: on one hand, it codifies the Shiite major theory of Islamic government, and on the other hand, it establishes and confirms a new nation-state with people's sovereignty and rights, separation of powers, and minimal checks and balances. According to the Constitution, the government represents the fulfillment of the political ideal of the Iranian people who supposedly bear a common faith and common outlook. This position is considered the foundation of the Islamic state. It intends to establish an ideal and model society on the basis of Islamic norms, and within this lies the realization of a holy government upon earth. The mission of the Constitution, as presently interpreted by regime conservatives, is to realize the ideological objectives of the regime and allow the clerics to keep their absolute power.

Courts

Iran's legal system consists of several courts under the Head of the Judiciary with a duality in court system that weakens the control of the Head of the Judiciary. It includes a myriad of courts which, in many cases, stifle public debates and freedom of the press and repress dissidents and reformists. The State Supreme Court is the highest judicial authority in the country; it is supposed to supervise the proper enforcement of laws by the courts of justice, to make judiciary precedent, and to revise judgments delivered by the Military Court and the significant judgments of the Public and Revolutionary Courts. According to section 10 of Article 110 of the Constitution, this court is competent to investigate miscarriages committed by the President in discharging his duties. The main seat of the Supreme Court is in the capital, Tehran, but it is composed of various branches. The Head of the Judiciary may establish branches of the court in other cities. The Supreme Court does not determine the laws, but it is the court of last resort; the Supreme Court is the highest judicial court that implements the laws.

The Supreme Court acts as a court of appeals to hear issues concerning heavy punishments such as the death penalty, amputation, body retaliation, confiscation and release of property, imprisonment for more than ten years, judgments pertinent to patronage, endowments, marriage, and divorce, and judgments that amount to a remedy exceeding 20 million rials. The provincial court (*dādgāh-e ostān*) shall act as court of appeal for all other cases. Decisions of the authorities in charge of reinvestigations shall be valid when adopted by votes of at least two of its three judges. Should there be an error in judgment delivered by a court of first instance, or if the judgment is issued in contradiction with the laws or the Islamic ordinances, it will be rejected. In all other cases it will be affirmed by the Supreme or Provincial Court.

Appellate courts stand between the Supreme Court and Public Courts in the judiciary chart. The judgments of the Public Courts and the Revolutionary courts shall be final except for those which are subject to rejection or revision. The following rulings are subject to rejection and revision: if the judge who issued the decision becomes aware of his mistake in the decision; if another judge becomes aware of the mistake in a court decision and makes it known to the judge who has issued it; and if it is proved that the issuer of the decision lacked the qualification. In addition to the mentioned cases, the losing party of each case has the right to request that the State Prosecutor General revise the case within one month from the date the decision is served. The Appellate Court has the right to reinvestigate a case even if no party having an interest in the lawsuit had requested it, in case the judge of the primary court does not notice an erroneous decision or lack of qualification for the investigation, or in case another judge notices an error in the judgment. Should the State Prosecutor General find the judgment evidently contradictory to the Islamic rules or laws, he will request the State Supreme Court to revise the judgment. If the Supreme Court rejects the decision, it shall assign another court of the same category to reinvestigate the case. For the most part, these legal provisions are not followed in practice, and the gap between reality and the existing law is huge.

The decisions that fall within cognizance of reinvestigations are those delivered for the death penalty, imprisonment for more than six months, lashes, penances, retaliation (talionis), confiscation and appropriation and release of property, and the judgments for relief of one million rials or more. The revising authorities are not allowed to increase the discretionary punishments awarded by the courts of first instance. The primary court must specify in its decision the eligibility of the judgment for reinvestigation. The elimination of the offices of the public prosecutor on the basis of the General Court Law of 1994, which was supposed to increase direct access to judges and accelerate litigations, led to a huge increase of appeals.

The Public Courts are divided into Civil and Criminal Courts. Investigations of all civil, criminal, and non-litigious cases are within the jurisdiction of the public courts. Civil Courts settle disputes in the areas of transactions and contracts, damages, marriage and divorce, and inheritance. Penal Courts deal with adultery and sodomy, robbery, burglary, murder, and assault. The extent of the jurisdiction of such courts is comprehensive and general, except for the cases which fall under the jurisdiction of the Revolutionary Courts.

There are four special courts in the IRI's judiciary system: Military Courts, Revolutionary Courts, Clerical Courts, and the Disciplinary Court of Judges. Military Courts are established to investigate crimes committed in connection with military or security duties by members of the armed forces (Article 172 of the Constitution). Revolutionary Courts were established by the new revolutionary regime to try the members of the earlier regime in a speedy manner. Later, the jurisdiction of this court was expanded to include all the crimes which are considered to be a threat to the establishment and survival of the new regime. This court's jurisdiction includes all offenses against the internal and external security of the country, behaving in a corrupt manner on the earth, slandering the founder of the Islamic Republic of Iran and the leader, conspiracy against the country or carrying arms, engaging in acts of terrorism, destruction of state property, engaging in espionage for aliens, and all crimes involving smuggling and the use of narcotics. Almost all political acts could be prosecuted based on this list of allegations. Special Clerical Courts were set up in 1987 to try clerics that commit offenses like counter-revolutionary and anti-clerical crimes. The Disciplinary Court for Judges investigates violations by judges working for the Ministry of Justice, of whatever rank or position.

See also Judiciary.

Suggested Reading
Schirazi, A. 1997. *The constitution of Iran: politics and the state in the Islamic Republic.* New York: I. B. Tauris Publishers.
Zerang, M. 2002. *Tahavvol-e Nezām-e Qazā'i in Iran (The development in Iran's judiciary system)*, Vol. I & II. Tehran: Markaz-e Asnād-e Enqelāb-e Eslāmi.

MAJID MOHAMMADI

✦ LIBERALISM, ISLAMIC

LATE QAJAR ERA AND THE CONSTITUTIONAL REVOLUTION (1794–1925)

Liberalism was introduced in the West as a cluster of interrelated ideas that included individual autonomy in political, economic, and cultural life; limits on the exercise of political power; and transparent, responsive, and responsible government. The first appearance of liberalism in Iran was in the guise of political aspirations against the corrupt and absolutist monarchy and the foreign domination of Iran. Islamic liberalism in Iran is traceable to the Constitutional Revolution (1905–1909). Like its secular counterpart, Islamic liberalism advocated the ideals of individual rights and limited government. However, it adduced theological and scriptural reasons to justify the cause. These arguments revolved around God's justice and mercy, his approval of a benign and fair government, and his displeasure with corruption and arrogance of autocratic rule. In its frequent references to the divine purpose of creation and its ultimate commensurability with human laws, Islamic liberalism resonates with its Western counterpart in the seventeenth and eighteenth centuries.

Early advocates of Islamic liberalism were Iranian and Azeri expatriates traveling to or residing in neighboring territories of India, the Ottoman Empire, or Transcaucasia. Thinkers such as Seyed Jamal al Din Asad Abadi (1838–1897) and Ahmad Aghayev (1865–1939) proposed various versions of Islamic liberal democracy in their widely circulated essays and articles. The most well known Persian document devoted to the defense of the principles of Islamic liberalism, however, is Mohammad Hossein Na'ini's prolegomenon: "Tanbih al Ommah va Tanzih al Mellah; ya Hukumat az Nazar i Islam" (Exhortation of the Faithful and Purification of the Nation; or Islam's View Concerning the Nature of Government). Na'ini published this essay in 1909 in defense of the grand Ayatollahs of Najaf who had actively advocated and issued explicit edicts in support of the Constitutional Revolution. The essay challenged the clerical allies of the renegade anti-constitutionalist monarch, Mohammad Ali Shah, who had opposed the notion of limited government on allegedly religious grounds. In his "exhortation to the nation," Na'ini mustered theological, traditional, and modern arguments concerning the affinity of the notions of divine and social justice. He envisioned their culmination in the idea of conditional government and political civil liberties. Nai'ini summarized his arguments in the preamble to his pamphlet in five propositions. The most theologically innovative were the first two:

> First: The foundation of government in the religion of Islam and in other religions, as well as in the cogitations of non-religious philosophers: the sages of the yore and thinkers of recent times, is that degeneration of the conditional government to the absolutist dominion is among the apostasies of the tyrannical rebels in all periods and epochs of history.

> Second: During the time of the occultation of the Imam, when we are deprived of the divine stewards, as well as their public representatives … should one allow the tyrannical government compounding injustice and usurpation to take hold or is it incumbent upon Muslims to reduce the degree of injustice and usurpation?

The triumph of the Constitutional Revolution established the historical profile of the pamphlet as a manifesto of Islamic liberal aspirations and that of his author as a fervent Muslim nationalist. Iran's Constitutional Revolution, then, its Western sources of inspiration notwithstanding, was a religiously supported experiment with the idea of limited government. As the first such attempt in the Islamic world, it stood in sharp contrast to the customary Western perceptions of Islamic politics as ineluctably despotic and absolutist. Luminaries such as Voltaire, Francis Bacon, and Ernst Renan, who had espoused such views, would have been surprised by a revolution advocating constitutional monarchy in an Islamic country—a revolution headed by high-ranking clerics such as grand Ayatollahs Khorasani, Mazandarani, and Tabataba'i. Ironically, it was Montesquieu, himself one of the Western believers of Islam's propensity toward tyranny, who eventually influenced the Islamic world and inspired emancipatory religious tracts. There is incontrovertible evidence that the Italian author Vittoriao Alfiri's rendition of Montesquieu's critique of "Tyranny," recounted by the Syrian cleric Sayyid Abd al-Rahman al-Kawakibi in a book entitled *The Characteristics of Tyranny and Destruction of Enslavement* (1899), influenced and inspired Naini's seminal essay on limited government. The subsequent enfeeblement of the constitutional checks and balances and the parliamentary system during the Pahlavi dynasty, on the other hand, would appear to corroborate Western distrust of the viability and longevity of democratic and liberal institutions in the Islamic world. This, however, cannot be attributed to any "conceptual incoherence" between Islam and liberal democracy but to the absence of social and economic formations such as a strong and autonomous middle class.

Pahlavi Era

Liberal (as opposed to radical) Islamic politics was pursued by two distinct factions during the Pahlavi period: parliamentarian clerics and political lay intellectuals. The clergy, the political progeny of the clerical leadership of the Constitutional Revolution, played a salient, if fractious, role during the reign of both Pahlavi monarchs. Representative figures during each Pahlavi monarch's rule are, respectively, Seyed Hassan Modarres (1870–1937) and Ayatollah Abolghasem Kashani (1886–1961). The parliamentarian clerics could be considered de facto liberal insofar as they advocated limited and responsible government and the legitimate practices of the representative democracy. The fall of Mossaddegh's government in 1953 marked the closing of the era of independent parliamentarian clerics. The lay intellectuals, most prominently Mehdi Bazargan (1907–1995) and Yadollah Sahabi (1905–2002), however, were liberal both in theory and in practice. Both descended from traditional middle-class backgrounds and came of age in the relative openness during the allied occupation of Iran that marked the hiatus between the two

Pahlavi kings followed by two subsequent eras of nationalist politics in the first decade of the second Pahlavi monarch and the post coup d'état clamp-down. Liberal Islamic intellectuals also witnessed, with mounting alarm, the looming hegemony of the (pro-Soviet) Marxist ideology as the main voice of opposition—hence the appeal of Western liberal ideas bolstered by Islamic precepts concerning the dignity of individuals, value of civil rights, and virtues of limited government.

It is possible to divide the history of Islamic liberalism in the decades before the Islamic Revolution into four distinct periods: 1941 to 1953 were the inchoate formative years during which the first generation of Islamic liberal lay intellectuals returned from Europe with graduate degrees and occupied teaching and managerial positions in Iran's fledgling universities and industries. The paramount challenge for the Islamic liberal opposition was the near monopoly of the ubiquitous Tudeh party in organization and outreach. The founding members Bazargan and Sahabi collaborated with likeminded, albeit traditionally trained colleagues, Taleghani and Shariati (the elder), to found three civic associations: "Islamic Society" ("Kanun e Eslami"), "The Islamic Engineers Association" ("Anjoman e Eslami ye Mohandesin"), and "Muslim Student Association" ("Anjoman e Eslami ye Daneshjouyan"). These formations and similar political activities continued until the heady years of nationalist politics ushered in by Prime Minister Mohammad Mossaddegh and his "National Front." Mehdi Bazargan was entrusted with the management of the newly nationalized oil industry and, later, with Tehran's water and electricity authority. With the downfall of the Mossadegh government and his trial and internal exile, the second period of the political activity of the Islamic liberals commenced. From 1953 to 1961, the leading Islamic liberals first joined the "National Resistance Movement" and then the "Second National Front," but the political phase aspect of their activities was overshadowed with cultural and intellectual work aimed at reconciling traditional Islam with modernity and gaining a substantial audience among the religious masses. Sherkat e Enteshar, a publishing house with offices in Tehran's Bab Homayoun street, was founded to publish original contributions and translations of works that reflected the Islamic liberal outlook. Eventually, in 1960, the Second National Front faced increasing government suppression, alienation of its youths, and fractious internal disputes among its leaders, and the Islamic liberals began deliberating on the possibility of creating their own political organization. This signaled the third period in the life of Islamic liberalism in Iran: 1961 to 1963. In March of 1961, Islamic liberals announced the promulgation of a new organization called "Nehzat e Azadi ye Iran" ("The Freedom Movement of Iran") with twelve founding members who had nationalist credentials and a general (albeit varying degrees of) commitment to Islam as guiding principles in politics. While affiliated with the second National Front, this newfangled organization was, for all intents and purposes, an embryonic autonomous political party. These potentials were never realized as the organization, despite the new Prime Minister Amini's attempts to guarantee some freedoms for it, was shut down in January of 1963, and most of its leaders were arrested and later tried. In the nineteen months of its open activities, the movement did not move in the direction of establishing a nationwide organization or overt electoral politics. Instead it organized an influential public lecture series entitled the Monthly Talks Society (Goftar e Mah), which foreshadowed later institutions such as Hosseinieh Ershad. It also proved effective in organizing assistance to the victims of a major earthquake in Lar" near Ghazvin. In its few internal publications, the movement criticized the increasing domestic repression and the highly unpopular alliance of the regime with Israel. During the trials of the movement's leaders in 1963, Bazargan accurately predicted that theirs would be the last legal opposition to be silenced under the Shah's autocratic rule, implicitly warning that resistance from that point on would take a violent path. When the lawyers who were appointed by the government to defend the movement's leaders were themselves tried for treason, it was a sure sign of the increasing repression in the "Sultanistic-style" government of the Shah toward the end. The next period covers 1963 to 1979, during which time the jailed leaders of the movement were gradually freed and resumed (mostly intellectual) activities. The bulk of the organized political opposition went into exile to form the Third National Front, the confederation of Iranian Students, and the Organization of Islamic Students in Europe and in the United States. Ibrahim Yazdi, the most prominent figure of the Freedom Movement, went on to lead the sprawling Islamic Student Organization in the United States. Bazargan and Yazdi served in the first government of the Islamic Revolution as Prime Minister and Foreign Minister, respectively.

Intellectual Leadership of Mehdi Bazargan

The theoretical, theological, and political writings of Mehdi Bazargan are essential for understanding the nature and trajectory of the Freedom Movement and its cognates. Bazargan himself is clearly indebted to the classical liberal political philosophy of the West. In his first publication, "Religion in Europe" (1978), penned while the author was still a graduate student abroad, he praised the liberal principles that undergird the material and moral assent of the Western European civilization. However, his approach to the West, even at this early stage, reveals his synchronistic ambitions to combine liberal European ideals with native Islamic and Iranian values: "Unlike the early generation of Iranian students ... some of us no longer thought that we should imitate Europeans. We believed that we should follow the principles, which are universal." Bazargan, a professor of thermodynamics in Tehran's technical faculty of the University of Tehran, was also an avid and talented student of Islamic law and philosophy and wrote a number of influential books indicating the compatibility of Islam with Western science, technology, ethics, and politics. Perhaps the most iconic is his book *Purifiers in Islam* ("Motahharat dar Islam"), in which he appraised the scientific validity of Islam's ritual regulations concerning purity and pollution.

On political matters, Bazargan mined a wide variety of Islamic sources in search of a coherent liberal political theory. In dozens of essays and speeches, he tackled complex issues of Shi'a casuistry concerning the sovereignty of God versus the agency of man, religious rules versus human responsibilities, and the optimal form of government from religious as well as secular perspectives. In mid-career, Bazargan published the text of one of his speeches entitled "Religion and Liberty," in which he argued, at length, that all religions affirm "individual rights," including "freedom, responsibility, and autonomy." In another significant essay, "Man and God," he asserted that the common denominator of religion and democracy is the "nobility of man," a principle from which all other rights and responsibilities of human beings in society are derived. He was not merely paying lip service to these principles. Throughout his political career he actively advocated these values, citing both universalistic moral principles and their Islamic textual corroborations. Bazargan's last published article, "The Prophets' Mission," exemplifies his life-long project of weaving the principles of liberal governance into the tapestry of native and local values:

Politics ... is an issue about which people can reason and find their own way.... Prophets were not directly concerned with politics, although in fulfilling their mission, they sometimes had to address political issues. Therefore, politics is not a domain where specific divine guidance should be sought.

These views were only strengthened in the last year of Bazargan's life. He felt vindicated in his political liberalism, given the results of the country's predicament after his resignation. He was also disheartened at the "deception" of the Islamic liberals at the hand of the clerical leadership of the country in the first years of the revolution. In questions of ethical rationalization of everyday life and applications of religious precepts to routine and political matters, Bazargan was also influenced by the American "pragmatism" of philosopher William James and his colleagues.

Throughout its two decades of activity in the Pahlavi era, the Freedom Movement and its affiliated circles Islamic Association of Physicians, Islamic Association of Engineers, Islamic Association of Teachers, and Islamic Association of Students were subjected to periods of relaxation and restraint in their political and cultural activities. The Freedom Movement also witnessed the departure of younger members and the founding of the radical People's Mojahedin organization. Internally, the left wing of the Freedom Movement comprised mostly younger members represented by Ezat Ollah Sahabi, the son of one of the founders of the movement, Yadollah Sahabi. The faction was critical of the movement's benign acceptance of Western-style economic liberalism. Nevertheless, throughout his decades of activity under both Pahlavi and Islamic regimes, Bazargan remained steadfast in his defense of the ideas of limited government and civil liberties and in his general tolerance of both free enterprise and welfare state. He was, alternatively, praised and blamed for his refusal to compromise on those beliefs. It was in the service of these principles that within the first year of the Islamic Revolution's era he first wielded and later yielded political power. The influence of Bazargan and other religious/liberal politicians extends far beyond the organizations they created and the roles they played in the realpolitik of the Pahlavi and Khomeini eras. Above all, they advocated and (in contrast to their predecessors) explicitly articulated the idea of Islamic liberalism. This school of thought captured the imagination of a wide spectrum of religious and lay ideologues and inspired thinkers and activists during the first-generation Islamic liberals' lifetime and beyond.

Suggested Reading

Abrahamian, E. 1989. *The Iranian Mojahedin*. New Haven: Yale University Press.

Bayat, M. 1991. *Iran's first revolution: Shi'ism and the constitutional revolution of 1905–1909*. New York: Oxford University Press.

Chehabi, H. E. 1990. *Iranian politics and religious modernism: the liberation movement of Iran under the Shah and Khomeini*. Ithaca: Cornell University Press.

Enayat, H. 1982. *Modern Islamic political thought*. Austin: University of Texas Press.

Hairi, A.-H. 1977. *Shi'ism and constitutionalism in Iran*. Leiden: Brill.

Kurzman, C. 1998. *Liberal Islam: A Source Book*. New York: Oxford University Press.

Kurzman, C. 2002. *Modernist Islam 1840–1940*. New York: Oxford University Press.

Ali Taghawi, S. M. 2005. *The flourishing of Islamic reformation in Iran: political Islamic groups in Iran (1941–1961)*. New York: Routledge.

Web Sources
http://www.nehzateazadi.org/english/history.htm
http://www.nehzateazadi.org/english/tajik.htm
http://www.answers.com/topic/freedom-movement-nezhat-e-azadi-iran

MAHMOUD SADRI

✦ LITERATURE, DIASPORA

Although a handful of Iranian immigrants to North America were writing and publishing (fiction, poetry, nonfiction) prior to 1979, the principle oeuvres of Iranian–American literature have been penned in the past decade by those who left Iran after the 1979 revolution or by second-generation Iranian–Americans. Among the early Iranian expatriate and immigrant writers, Nahid Rachlin is the most widely recognized for her novel, *Foreigner* (1978). This semiautobiographical novel of immigration marked the first female Iranian voice to write and publish in English, and was suggestive of Rachlin's early attempts to identify some of the cultural schisms between the country of her birth and that of her adopted homeland. While Rachlin was among the earlier novelists and writers, she has continued to publish both fiction and memoir. Her later works of fiction include: *Married to a Stranger* (1983), *Veil*s (1993), *The Heart's Desire* (1995), and *Jumping Over Fire* (2006); she has also written a memoir, *Persian Girls* (2006). Other early expatriate Iranian writers include Bahman Sholevar, author of the novellas *Night's Journey* and *The Coming of the Messiah*, Taghi Modaressi, a novelist and psychiatrist married to American writer Anne Tyler, whose novels include *The Pilgrim's Rules of Etiquette* and *The Book of Absent People*, and Donné Raffat, whose works include *The Prison Papers of Bozorg Alavi*, *The Caspian Circle*, and *The Folly of Speaking*. Like many other Iranian immigrants, these early writers came to the United States at a time when the two countries' governments were more closely aligned; many of these writers initially came here seeking opportunities in higher education. The dramatic fallout of the Iranian revolution and the subsequent eight-year war with Iraq caused even greater numbers of Iranians to leave their home in the early 1980s. The period immediately following the hostage crisis in Tehran, the 444-day ordeal in which 52 Americans were taken and held hostage at the U.S. embassy, caused a kind of self-imposed silence and shame for the many Iranians living in North America. Many Iranians chose to publicly identify themselves as "Persian" in order to avoid any association with the government and policies of the Islamic Republic of Iran.

It was only after a period of approximately ten years, when Iran's international image improved with the election of the reformist candidate Mohammad Khatami and received positive and worldwide recognition for its cinema, that Iranians in North America gained more confidence to write and publish. The 1990s initiated the beginning of a more public and positive awareness of being "Iranian–American," and as such, created a greater impetus among writers to write about their experiences of revolution, war, immigration, exile, loss, and nostalgia. This period saw the publication of a series of memoirs that were nostalgic but that also articulated the early stages of what might be called "Iranian–American" immigrant narratives. Some of these early memoirs were penned, and in many cases, co-authored, with the assistance of professional writers, and represented an Iran that was "lost" to the revolution and to the extreme ideology of the newly established Islamic Republic. Two of the most notable of these memoirs were written by members of the Farmanfarmaian family—one of the families of the ruling dynasty of the Qajars, and as such these memoirs depicted a particular class and privilege. Settareh Farmfarmaian's memoir, *Daughter of Persia: A Woman's Journey from Her Father's Harem through the Islamic Revolution* (1992, co-authored with writer Dona Munker), and her brother's memoir, *Blood and Oil: Memoirs of a Persian Prince* (1997, co-authored with his daughter Roxane Farmanfarmain), are suggestive of the nostalgic vision of an Iran that no longer existed after the revolution.

More recent memoirs have complicated this view of Iran and have been largely written by women who have lived during their formative school years in Iran, but who have also benefited from the experience of immigration; for these writers the idea of going back to Iran evokes a complex set of questions and issues of belonging and non-belonging and of living between two cultures. Tara Bahrampour's *To See and See Again: A Life in Iran and America* (1999) and Gelareh Asayesh's *Saffron Sky: A Life Between Iran and America* (1999) were among the most literary of these early memoirs. Bahrampour's narrative evokes the disruptive and painful experience of leaving Iran during her adolescent years, while Asayesh depicts some of the experiences Iranian–Americans had after returning to Iran after a long absence (living in the United States) only to feel just as alienated in post-revolutionary Iran as they did as an Iranian in America.

During this same period, Gina Nahai, a Los Angeles-based fiction writer, also received acclaim for *Moonlight on the Avenue of Faith* (1999), a novel that depicts the Jewish ghetto in Tehran in the years before the overthrow of the Shah as well as the arrival of Jewish–Iranians in the United States. Salar Abdoh, the New York–based Iranian-born writer, published a very prescient and powerful spy novel, *The Poet Game* (1999). Abdoh's novel depicts the shadowy world of Islamic radicals and identifies New York, two years before the actual event, as "ground zero" as part of an international terrorist plot. The same year the first anthology of writing by Iranian–Americans, *A World Between: Poems, Short Stories, and Essays by Iranian-Americans* (1999), was published. This anthology mapped and articulated a collective, public literary discourse for the Iranian–American experience and for the first time identified the term "Iranian–American" as an ethnic literary category.

The Paris-based graphic novelist Marjane Satrapi, whose works include *Persepolis 1* and *Persepolis 2* (translated into English after they were published and serialized in France as *Persepolis* 1-4) has been enormously popular in both the Francophone and Anglophone worlds since 2000. The graphic novel has given Satrapi an international audience that has drawn from both Diaspora Iranians and non-Iranian readers. A film adaptation of *Persepolis* received the Grand Prize of the Jury at the Cannes Film Festival when it was shown there in 2007. Satrapi has also received numerous literary prizes in France, including the Angouleme Coup de Coeur award in 2001 for *Persepolis*.

September 11th and the subsequent attention focused on Iran after President George W. Bush's "Axis of Evil" speech in January 2002 generated new concerns about Iran and its regime. This negative attention on Iran laid the groundwork for renewed interest on the part of publishers and readers. At the start of the twenty-first century, a series of memoirs followed one after the other. These include the nationally acclaimed *Reading Lolita in Tehran: A Memoir in Books* (2003) by Azar Nafisi and Firoozeh Dumas's *Funny in Farsi: A Memoir of Growing up Iranian in America* (2003). Nafisi's memoir was on the *New York Times* National Bestseller list for more than a year but also received some of the sharpest criticism by some Iranian scholars (Hamid Dabashi of Columbia University and Negar Mottahedeh of Duke University) for her largely negative depiction of Iranian women's experience and of the repressive conditions surrounding her own experience as a university professor in Iran. Roya Hakakian's memoir, *Journey From the Land of No*, highlights the experience of a young Jewish–Iranian woman caught up in the revolutionary fervor of the 1970s and the particularly painful experiences that Jewish communities experienced after the establishment of the Islamic regime. Azadeh Moaveni, a journalist who has been reporting for *TIME* magazine, published *Lipstick Jihad: Growing Up Iranian In America and American in Iran* in 2005. Her memoir, based on her experience of going to Iran as an adult and learning to navigate there as a journalist, offers an interesting commentary on her own as well as other young people's disillusionment and frustration living in Iran in the post-Khatami period. Nearly all the memoirs published in the past decade and a half (with the exception of a rare few) are authored by women, which suggests that women of the Iranian Diaspora are vigorously engaged with writing and self-representation and with recreating the tradition of letters in Iran that has historically excluded women. Many of these memoirs echo each other in experiences and sentiments.

In addition to the memoir, poetry has been an important genre for expressing the emerging voice of Iranian–American writers. Because of Iran's rich poetic tradition, many writers have naturally gravitated towards poetry because it provides a point of continuity and connection for both Iranian and American-born writers. Among the best-known Iranian–American poets is the late Susan Atefat-Peckham, who in 2000, was selected by Victor Hernandez Cruz as the winner of the National Poetry Prize for her collection *That Kind of Sleep* (2001). Atefat-Peckham, who was born and raised in New York to Iranian immigrant parents, pays homage to her rich Iranian heritage and the truly bicultural nature of her upbringing. Atefat-Peckham's career was cut short by a fatal car accident while on a Fulbright teaching fellowship in Jordan in 2004. Other Iranian–American poets who have achieved some success include Katayoon Zandvakili, Zara Houshmand, and Sholeh Wolpé, all of whom have published widely in literary journals or have published individual collections of their work. A number of writers, including poets, have been successful at publishing their work through Iranian-based internet sites. The role of the internet generally, and the website *Iranian.com* particularly, have been critical to creating a literary voice for the Iranian Diaspora community. For many of these writers, publication on Iranian Diaspora websites has given them the confidence, exposure, and audience that they might otherwise not have had. As with the themes in many of the memoirs, the poetry of Iranian Diaspora writers has dealt with loss, separation from family, immigration, politics, culture, gender, and displacement. Women have been far more visible in poetry as well as in the genres of memoir and fiction. Many of these poets from the English-speaking world have been anthologized in a second collection, *Let Me Tell You Where I've Been: New Writing by Women of the Iranian Diaspora* (2006). This collection, like the first anthology, includes fiction, poetry, and nonfiction, and features the work of fifty-three writers from regions as disperse as North America, Europe, and Australia.

A new generation of writers of fiction has begun to emerge, which suggests both an oversaturation of the genre of memoir and the maturation of a literary voice that relies less on first-person narratives as part of a legitimate and intriguing landscape of world fiction. While Dalia Sofer's *Septembers of Shiraz* (2007) focuses on the experience of Jewish–Iranians and highlights the events of the Iranian revolution, both Gina Nahai's *Caspian Rain* (2007) and Anita Amirrezvani's novel *Blood of Flowers* (2007) highlight periods before the revolution. Amirrezvani's novel depicts a much earlier period in Iran's history; the novel is set in 17th century Iran and features a first person narrator who is young female carpet weaver in the city of Isfahan.

While the body of work that currently constitutes the literature of the Iranian Diaspora is not yet immense, it is suggestive of the important role that literature has played in developing a discourse and literary culture for Iranians outside of Iran. Many of the stories, memories, and narratives depicted in poetry, fiction, and nonfiction are indicative of a desire to reconcile with the tumultuous history of Iran's twentieth century history and the impact that events in Iran have had on those Iranians living outside of Iran. It is also suggestive of the importance of the desire and need to self-represent when Iran and Iranians have been so negatively portrayed in the Western media for the last three decades. While the number of memoirs by women indicates an interest and perhaps even a fixation on women's particular experiences (such as the veil, and the ways that women have been excluded in the context of Iran), on the part of publishers as much as on readers, it is significant that women writers of the Iranian Diaspora have paralleled the dominant role that women writers in Iran have played. Without a doubt, this is a reflection of women's altered experience in both Iran and the United States, and indicates a desire on the part of women to challenge, confront, and undermine the often singular or monolithic views of Iranian women depicted in both the Islamic Republic of Iran as well as in many countries in the West. The literature of the Iranian Diaspora reflects the often tense relationship between Iran and the countries that have played host to the largest number of Iranian immigrants (the United States, France, Canada, among them), and many of the themes of this literature are a reflection of this complicated and difficult relationship.

See also Literature, Persian; and Literature and Literary Figures.

Suggested Reading

Karim, P. M. 2007. *Let me tell you where I've been: new writing by women of the Iranian Diaspora*. Fayetteville: University of Arkansas Press.

Karim, P. M., and M. M. Khorrami, eds. 1999. *A world between: poems, short stories and essays by Iranian-Americans*. New York: George Braziller.

Milani, F. 1992. *Veils and words: the emerging voices of Iranian women writers*. Syracuse, NY: Syracuse University Press.

Naficy, H. 1993. *The making of exile cultures*. Minneapolis: University of Minnesota Press.

Rahimieh, N. 1992. The quince-orange tree, or Iranian writers in exile. *World Literature Today*. 66:1.

Sullivan, S. 2001. *Exiled memories: stories of Iranian Diaspora*. Philadelphia: Temple University Press.

PERSIS M. KARIM

◆ LITERATURE, PERSIAN

The literature of post-revolutionary Iran has developed along with the social changes in the country. This literature is defined in its approach to the familiar themes of piety, secularism, language, nationalism, war, dislocation, immigration, exile, discontent, tradition, youth-culture, family, and self-identity in relation to gender. These themes are elaborated through various mediums and styles in poetry, prose, drama, and journalistic prose.

A significant characteristic of this literature is the parallel coexistence that exists of works by authors who reside in Iran and produce their work in Persian, and the Iranian-born authors who live in Diaspora and write either in Persian or in the languages of their host-culture. These Diaspora writers include renowned literary figures who left Iran after the revolution and those who turned to professional writing abroad. A third group are second-generation immigrant authors who were born abroad. The works that are produced by all of these authors represent varied approaches to the aforementioned themes and to Persian language.

The delineations between the literature of natives and those in Diaspora are not exclusive to the developments of recent years. Many of the authors and writers of the Constitutional Revolution (1906–1911) shared a similar fate. The specific distinction of this generation of writers is their response to the 1979 revolution and the institution of theocracy which created unprecedented grounds for revisiting Iran's past and pondering the questions set forth by the recent events.

After the revolution, there were many who had a story to tell and felt compelled to express themselves in writing. This need led to the prevalence of prose over poetry as a medium more readily accessible to an author. The rise of the autobiographical narrative and memoir is a direct expression of this recent development. In contrast to the years prior to 1979, autobiography and memoir are no longer exclusive to important statesmen or men of stature whose lives are worthy of attention. In recent years, autobiographical writing has become a medium for ordinary people to express themselves and tell the extraordinary tales of their lives. The majority of these writers are women who reside outside of Iran, where they are not subjected to the state-regulated censorship. In fact, recent years have witnessed an unprecedented increase in the number of female Iranian authors. Prison and escape memoirs are other major productions in Diaspora. These are authored by former political prisoners and those citizens who had to illegally escape the country after the revolution or during the Iran–Iraq War. These authors discuss the trials and ordeals of imprisonment, immigration, and exile.

Journalism and journalistic prose is another prominent field in Persian literary studies. The censor of the Islamic Republic Ministry of Culture and Islamic Guidance closely scrutinizes authors working in this arena. Against this tumultuous background, journalistic prose is especially valuable in our understanding of the rhetorical dynamics of authorship under censorship. The growing number of periodicals and the unprecedented rise of journalism in Iran saw the eventual confrontation between the regime and the press in the 1990s and ended in massive arrests and persecutions of journalist, writers, editors, and their staff. Seen against the backdrop of this popularly involved enterprise, the journalistic prose style has left a permanent imprint on the authors writing in Iran today. In the same vein, web-based publications as well as satirical journalistic prose of the post-revolution era hold their own ground.

The fall of the Pahlavi monarchy and the advent of the revolution and its aftermaths have essentially changed the cultural and the literary life of Iran. The authors and writers of the post-revolution era are addressing questions and issues that grow out of a revolutionized society where the former categories of meaning are uprooted and replaced with new sets of definitions. Their work is a reflection of a self-conscious society that speaks assertively in the stark shadow of censorship.

See also Literature, Diaspora; and Literature and Literary Figures.

FIROOZEH PAPAN-MATIN

✦ LITERATURE AND LITERARY FIGURES

Literary and cultural figures often embody the movement of a culture through time. In that sense, the Iranian revolution of 1978–1983 provided a highly meaningful cultural turning point, which initially separated seemingly secular social leaders from deeply religious ones, setting them in binary opposition. The two groups were seen to hold divergent, even irreconcilable, visions of the past and the future of the country, its culture, and the direction in which it was or ought to be moving. Now, viewed from a thirty-year perspective, these pairs tend to be seen as figures in a variegated tapestry of an old culture in the grip of modernity, each figure capable of adding color, shade, and texture to varying degrees, some fading away considerably into barely noticeable silhouettes, others seen in bold relief, as if to demonstrate the staying power of certain abiding traits that can lie dormant for centuries but retain their potential to resurface at crucial times and in contexts that cast them in novel colors or in chiaroscuro hitherto unknown to illustrate the power of the ideas they embody.

The serious cultural rethinking that eventually led to the Iranian revolution began in the early 1960s. Many of the major figures in that intellectual process did not survive to see the fruits or ramifications of their ideas in the form of the political revolution that materialized in 1979. The lives, works and ideas of these men and women have been the subject of important studies in the last thirty years or so. By all accounts, Jalal Al-e Ahmad (1921–1967) is now seen as the principal popularizer of the notion of Gharbzadegi (Westoxication) as a social malaise in modern Iran. In a seminal 1962 work of the same title, he set forth the premise that blind imitation of the West had led Iran to an impasse from which no escape would be conceivable unless and until a genuine cultural about-face would return the culture to its authentic native dynamics and restore the precarious balance that has historically mediated between its twin pillars, namely pre-Islamic Iran and Iranian Islam.

Numerous major poets, playwrights, and novelists, chief among them Ahmad Shamlu (1925–2000), Mehdi Akhavan Saless (1930–1990), Forugh Farrokhzad (1935–1967), and Gholamhossein Saedi (1936–1985), carried that idea into the realm of literature, which by then had in the main adopted the goal of social relevance, which in the practice of the time meant a showy display of radical political opposition to the monarchical state and all that it stood for. Al-e Ahmad's wife, Simin Daneshvar (b. 1927), deserves special mention in this regard, as the leading woman fiction writer in modern Iran and as the writer whose best known 1965 novel *Savushun* proved hugely popular. In the all important empire of literature so central to the culture of the 1960s, the idea that the malady of aping the West was growing on Iran's culture like a cancer was extended, fleshed out, and cast in the form of a thousand concrete poems and stories lamenting the loss of the vitality and vibrancy of Iran's culture, increasingly viewed as its historic birthright.

Some of the luminaries of Iran's pre-revolution literary sky who survived the revolution but refused to be co-opted into the new Islamic state faced a variety of problems, which affected their lives as opinion makers in the post-revolutionary ea. Of those who are mentioned, Shamlu continued to write and publish in opposition to the despotic political system emerging from the chaos of the revolution but was soon reduced to silence; Saedi was driven into exile, eventually to die in Paris; Akhavan faced a variety of restrictions and an unsuccessful attempt at co-optation into the new literary discourse or cooperation with the new state. To these were added younger writers who had begun their careers in the decade before the revolution but owed much of their reputation and popularity to the new context and who tried desperately to retain their independent line of thinking. Poet and playwright Said Soltanpur was executed in 1962, Shahrnush Parsipur was imprisoned for six years, and Mohsen Yalfani, Esmail Khoi, along with a host of other writers fled the country to continue their careers in the spaces of Iran's expatriate communities, mostly in Europe and North America.

The generation of writers and poets who emerged with the revolution and who, in time, contributed to a new and different literary discourse are discussed here. A prime example is writer and filmmaker Mohsen Makhmalkbaf (b. 1957), a brilliant literary and cinematic artist whose 2001 film *Kandehar* has been selected by *Time* Magazine as one of the top one hundred films of all time. Born and raised in the slums of south Tehran in a devout Muslim family, Makhmalbaf was still a teenager when the revolution began. One can see the impact of revolutionary pageantry—of marches and strikes by the millions, of widespread torching of cinemas and banks, and of huge crowds chanting "God is Great" in mosques and on rooftops across the country. Images of this sort dazzled the world and launched or directed numerous careers in Iran's literature, cinema, and the arts.

Makhmalbaf began his career as a young functionary and apologist of the Islamic Republic's cultural policies, on literary communication and on the arts in general. In his first two books, *Notes on Fiction and Playwriting* (1981) and *An Introduction to Islamic Art* (1982), he postulated that the Qur'an holds before the Muslims the perfect aesthetic model of human edification for all time and that, therefore, all literature ought to do is use it as a guide to serve the cause of ennobling the human spirit and elevate humanity to its potential God-like perfection. As the rules concerning an "Islamic" dress codes were being drawn, it was Makhmalbaf who theorized that "Islamic Theater" would enable women to remain properly dressed even in the most intimate of settings and still remain true to the portrayal of realistic life. Such positions, with a little a pun on his family name, earned him the nickname of Mohsen the Nonsense-Weaver (Mohmalbaf) among the older literary intellectuals, still engaged in a rear-guard battle against the tide of the revolution and the Islamization of culture.

Later in the decade of the 1980s, as the war with Iraq was raging and the Islamic Republic's repression grew rampant, Makhmalbaf gradually matured into an artist with a vision of his own. He modified his earlier stances, largely rehabilitating himself as a genuine artist, and while remaining anchored in a strong sense of man's spiritual aspirations he began to write and publish works that marked the distance he had come in a decade from his early infatuation with the ideology of the Islamic Republic. This maturation was crystallized in his 1986 novel titled *Crystal Garden* and his 1987 film *The Wedding of the Blessed*. In these two works, Iranians began to see a new Makhmalbaf, an artist more interested in asking questions than supplying answers, displaying grave doubts rather than embracing dogmas. In sum, Makhmalbaf had succeeded in crossing the line that separates the state functionary to the artists in ways that his peers, men such as Morteza Avini in filmmaking and Reza Rahgozar (b. 1954) in literature, had not dared to even approach.

Crystal Garden is a notable work of fiction among many stillborn efforts by similarly situated figures, but more importantly it charts the course of the Iranian novel affected but not eclipsed by the course of the Iranian revolution. Dedicated to "the wronged women" of Iran and opening with the birth pangs of a woman named Layeh, the pain whose intensity comes to stand for the enormity of the wrong that Iranian women as a social group are subjected to, the novel features many of the ways in which the minds and bodies of Iranian women have come to be the battleground between patriarchy and individual aspirations for liberation, between spirituality and oppression cloaked in the garb of religion, between superstition masquerading as tradition, and Westernized alienation as the essence of modernity.

Makhmalbaf's impressive achievement in *Crystal Garden* has now been extended and elevated in several other works of fiction, chief among them *The Apple* (1998), *A Turn for Love* (1990), and *To See and Not To See* (2002). In recent years, Makhmalbaf, almost at the height of his artistic career, seems to be directing increasingly greater amounts of his intellectual acumen and creative energies to filmmaking rather than writing. To that extent he may be remembered ultimately as an artist working with moving images more than with moving words. To this day, he remains the sole artist, certainly the most notable novelist that has emerged from the revolutionary chaos of the late 1970s, in Iran to display his potential for a staying power far outlasting the specific historical dynamics that propelled him and so many others onto the literary scene, thus bridging the old and the new millennia.

Something resembling the reverse trajectory marks the artistic life of Abbas Kiarostami (b. 1940), the other notable figure with twin artistic careers as filmmaker and maker of literature—poetry in his case. He began in the decade of the 1960s as a filmmaker and is now known equally as a poet, at least on the international scene. Although he too manifests a strong spiritual dimension in his work, this has nothing to do with the revolution that took a religious character after it had happened or the theocratic state that has ruled Iran for the past thirty years. Initially a maker of commercials in the increasingly consumer-based emerging economy of Iran, he rose to prominence in 1987 with his film based on a poem by Sohrab Sepehri, a neo-mystic poet whose powerful presentations of a living nature has influenced many artistic genres in contemporary Iran.

It took another decade for Kiarostami to achieve international renown when his film *Taste of Cherry* won the Golden Palm in 1997 at the Cannes Film Festival, the highest honor ever accorded an Iranian director. The film highlights many paradoxical characteristics of Iran's living culture in the character of its protagonist, in the meaning and significance it assigns to nature and, above all, in the subtlety with which it tackles the moral question it raises about the efficacy of political change as a source of cultural rejuvenation. As Badii seeks help to have his corpse interred after he has committed suicide (which he has resolved to attempt), he comes across many others whose situations appear worse to him but who cling just as resolutely to hope and life nonetheless. One man in particular invites him to contemplate the joys of life, asking him at one point whether he has experienced the taste of fruits like cherry and mulberry under his teeth. As he is driven through scenes of sublime natural beauty next to the ugliness of urban sprawl, he hears the life stories of men who, as deeply in crisis as they are, still remain hopeful of the future of humanity. Certainly, there are states of the mind that can be preserved in the face of the cruelest treatment of fellow humans by men such as those who, having killed so many, are driving numerous others to desperation.

Such basic themes, expressed with an uncanny combination of simplicity and sophistication, were to prove central to Kiarostami's art as he extended his work into poetry. In 2000, he published a collection of poetry (English–Persian edition, 2002), which highlighted many of the same concerns with and responses to specific, often paradoxical, situations in modern life, clad in highly nuanced, extremely subtle, and strongly visual haiku-like poems. Each "poem" consisted of no more than a mere prosaic few lines without any outward trappings of meter or rhyme; they thus resembled nothing the culture would perceive as poetry. Still, they often set out to compare and contrast God, man, and animals with each other and one with the other, always working through a strong chiaroscuro that gave life a transcended shade of meaning observable only when life is lived to the fullest and with sufficient sense of awe and an acknowledgement of the world's mysteries. He has since published one more collection of poetry, *A Wolf in Wait* (English–Persian editions, 2004). By now, the two volumes have been translated into many languages and used as models for genuinely novel modes of perception and expression in many poetic traditions, East and West. Currently Kiarostami is raising the level of postmodern art in ways that are as exciting as they are unclassifiable.

Several of the older literary figures with well-established reputations before the revolution of 1978–1983 moved closer to the center of the literary scene and took important strides toward contributing to more recent trends in the general movements of literature in Iran, as outlined in the entry of Iran's literature. To begin with the most famous contrarians of the previous decades, when literature wore the mantel of social commitment, Yadollah Royai (b. 1931), now living the life of an expatriate poet in the suburbs of Paris, has continued to break new ground in the type of poetry that reaches to the lowest depths of the language for its artistry, using words and sounds as artifacts ultimately capable of producing poeticity.

Whereas in the decades preceding the revolution he dazzled Iran's literary elites with his startling images of seascapes and a central concern with the form of poetry, Royai now uses his unorthodox behavior with the language of poetry to drive more deeply into the aesthetic traditions of the past, in ways similar to how they were used in pre-modern times by non-Iranian Persian poets from Central Asia and India or from Caucasus and Anatolia. Two of his poetry collections, *Labials* (1990) and *Seventy Tomb Stones* (1999), did much to make Persian poetry once more visual and more form-conscious than anything any contemporary poet has produced. In the latter volume particularly, he demonstrates that poetry can be made to examine abiding features in the culture in ways that might help deep-seated cultural tendencies to create icons that display hitherto unnoticed patterns of thought.

A second poet with a firm reputation earned before the revolution, and a uniquely significant presence among Iran's literary figures, Simin Behbahani (b. 1925), now in her eighties, never chose life in exile; rather she continued to write and publish in Iran, at times in direct defiance of the restrictions imposed on women in general and more specifically on their literary expression. With the publication of *A Line of Speed and Fire* in 1982, Behbahani's poetry, almost exclusively in the millennium-old genre of the Persian ghazal, began to reveal a new dimension of her mastery as a wordsmith in drawing images and icons of a country in the grip of paralysis by an increasingly unpopular political establishment.

And then there are those whose careers reached its peak in the decades of the Islamic republic, but who did not in any way cease to advance their vision

of a secular society expressed in worldly poems of a philosophical or even pro-
fane or erotic poems. Manuchehr Atashi (1930–2005) and Mohammad Ali
Sepanlu (b. 1941) best exemplify this tendency. Atashi kept faith with what he
was known for, using the tribal and local images of his native southern coast to
express a burning desire for greater liberties, and ultimately reaching for a
deep-seated yearning for freedom from all restrictions, at times presented in
ways that tend to incorporate the human psyche and the power of memory in
the struggle for greater civil liberties. Sepanlu, on the other hand, constrained
his treatment of Iran's history as an arena for the display of emotions that
related the local and the topical to the universal and the eternal. Both poets
raised their profiles, and Sepanlu is still one of the best two or three poets
active in Iran.

Of special significance to Persian poetry of the turn of the 21st century are
the compositions of Mohammad Reza Shafii-Kadkani. A maverick poet as
well as an outstanding literary scholar, Shafii-Kadkani continues to write far
more than has been seen of him in print. His main struggle is for human dignity and a sense of spirituality that lies beyond all perception of religion perceived as a system of oppression, used by states such as the Islamic Republic.
While he shuns controversies of all type, his poems are well loved for the
simple reason that they clearly distinguish, in their content and through
rhetorical properties, between an understanding of religion as a singular relationship between humanity and the myriad mysteries that surround it, on
the one hand, and as a system of advocacy based on specific myths, rituals,
and observances with a claim to exclusive truth.

Moving on to the literary figures who have continued to produce works
of literature as exiles or expatriates, an even stronger sense is shown of the
movement of Persian literature toward greater involvement with social and
political realities of the homeland and of exile, as well as a more vivid
anchoring of literature, most visible in poetry, in a more imagistic and kinetic
aesthetic. The works of poets Nader Naderpur (1930–2000) and Esmail Khoi
(b. 1938) and of the novelist Shahrnush Parsipur (b. 1946) deserve particular
attention in this connection. Naderpur had always been known for his imagistic poetry. When pushed into self-imposed exile, first in Paris and eventually in Los Angeles, his talent seems to have moved him in the direction of
depicting a visually overwhelmed mind with a deepening sense of skepticism
brooding over a paralyzing sense of marginality, often leading poem after
poem to end up in a dark vision of a world wherein everything is seen as
plotting against the poet.

Khoi's reputation in pre-revolution times back in Iran was based essentially on his treatment of social and political issues in the context of a

philosophical worldview that bore witness to a profound sense of commitment and a contemplative poetic temperament. In the spaces of exile, first in Italy and later in London, the poet's deep dislike of all that the Islamic Republic stands for has worked in ways that have not always been commensurate with his poetic powers. The upshot of the tension between the poet and the political activist has led to a bifurcation in Khoi's poetry where in some compositions, mostly those written in the old forms and genres, such as the qasida and the robai, one sees in the speaker a persona of the poet who has no qualms sacrificing the aesthetic integrity and value of his works on the altar of naked, barren satire or lampoon. He does, at the same time, have love poems and other lyrical works in which the aesthetic imagination trumps the will to political activism, the poetic superseding the political.

Parsipur occupies a singularly precious position among the exiled Iranian writers working outside Iran today. She made herself quite a reputation with some fairly important narratives of dazzling storylines and profoundly controversial aspects in the decade before the Iranian revolution. Still, it is her work after the revolution, particularly those written in the past two decades outside Iran, that has radicalized her in ways unprecedented in Iran's modern literary canon. For one thing, despite being deeply steeped in Iran's native culture, Parsipur now seems to be directing her message to the entire world through works in which local and national concerns have to live side by side with universal concerns for the fate of humanity or give way to them. Her *Tuba and the Meaning of Night*, a historical novel written in Persian and based on Iranian history in the 20th century, is easily accessible to readers everywhere who may be interested in the machinations of patriarchy that stifles female creative energies and the spiritual fertility that the author believes is exclusively a property of the female spirit. Her *Women without Men*, a novella disguised as collection of short stories, remains a landmark of literary achievement in grafting the sense of native wonderment expressed in many pre-modern Persian narratives and poems to the magical realism of the Marquez type, resulting not just in endless academic discussions but in a greater integration of modern Persian literature into the body of world literature of the 21st century.

From the vagaries of the Iranian revolution to the anomalous achievements of Iranian literary elites, particularly the country's women writers and poets, Iran's literature continues to push the boundaries of its historical realm and modern territories, while fixing its gaze, with wonderment and awe, on one of the most repressive political systems to emerge from a genuinely liberating movement. Both at home and abroad, Iranian writers see themselves faced with situations that demand to be inscribed imaginatively, situations that have naturally been absent from the classical cannon of their predecessors, and experiences unprecedented in modern traditions. No end to the process of modernity appears in their sight over the perilous horizon beclouded by tribal and national rivalries, no point of arrival, where one might hope for some semblance of stability, visible to their naked eye.

In this twilight zone of literary creativity, where political and social situations remain in conflict with the free exercise of the human imagination, the expanse of the human imagination seems wide open, full of perils and possibilities. Writers and poets are often driven forth by a spirit of experimentation and an intuition that invite them to press forward on the path before them, even in the absence of a clear picture of what may lie ahead. In this, the vision that guides them appears akin to that of the old Sufi wayfarers who, even as they were not certain where their next step may take them, nonetheless clung to a vision of a borderless world lying in the distant future.

See also Literature, Diaspora; and Literature, Persian.

AHMAD KARIMI HAKAK

✦ LORS AND LORESTAN

One of Iran's western provinces, Lorestan, is situated amidst the Zagros Mountains. With a population of fewer than two million, Lors live in central and southern Lorestan, northern Khuzestan, and southern Hamadan province. Like many other ethnic peoples in Iran, Lors are one of the oldest ethnic peoples living in the country. The current people of Lorestan have intermingled with the neighboring ethnicities—such as Kurds, Arabs, and Bakhtyari nomadic tribes—who move between their summer abode in the high mountains of Zardakuh and their winter abode in the western foothills of Khuzistan. Bakhtyaris are Twelver Shi'ites and speak a Lori dialect. Their population is approximately 600,000. Recently there have been attempts to sedentarize Bakhtyaris. They live in towns and villages of Chahar Mahal, as well as in the Faridan district of Isfahan. Although the two dialects of Lori and Laki are known to be the major ones, there are different dialects such as Khorrmabadi, Borujerdi, Nahavabdi, and others as well. Lori is classified as an Indo–European language. However, the Kassites, the early settlers of the land, spoke an agglutinative language with no relation either to Indo–European or Semitic languages.

HADI SULTAN-QURRAIE

M

✦ MAJLES

The Iranian national struggle for political modernity and good governance started more than a century ago. The Constitutional Revolution forced Mozaffor o-ddin Shah Qajar to accept a Constitution and the establishment of a parliamentary system on August 5, 1906. The activities of the elected Majles parliament in curtailing the Shah's absolute power on one hand and the Anglo–Russian domination over the Iranian government's affairs on the other resulted in the bombing and suspension of its functions. For seventy-two years, from 1907 to the Islamic Revolution in 1979, *Majles Shoray-e Melli*, the National Consultative Assembly (the lower house), had to address issues such as the separation of powers, media law, and corruption.

At first, Majles deputies were divided into two groups. Half of the deputies represented different guilds, while the other half was a combination of passionate constitutionalists, liberal politicians, and members of the clergy. Deputies were divided into two main radical and moderate parties with fringe members representing despotic tendencies. Most progressive intellectuals, even those attracted to Western (European) politics and enjoying some social support, were drawn to the Democratic Party. Individuals from the middle class, landlords, members of clergy, and conservative and traditionalist aristocrats belonged to *Ejtema'iyoun*, or *E'tedalioun*, a moderate political party. However, the government gradually isolated the emerging political parties and they never transformed into effective, strong, and durable power brokers.

Mahmoud Ahmadinejad speaks as his picture is seen on giant screens at Parliament after his second nominee for Iranian oil minister withdrew his candidacy, 2005, Tehran. (AP Photo/Hasan Sarbakhshian)

To have better control over the political process in Iran, Mohammad Reza Shah Pahlavi decided to create an upper chamber, the Majles Sena. This Senate consisted of 60 members, 30 of whom were nominated by the Shah; the rest were elected by the populace: 15 senators in the provinces and other administrative regions and 15 in Teheran.

In the absence of any credible opposition party since the 1953 coup d'état against the nationalist Prime Minister Mohammad Mossadegh, the regime decided to divide its loyal servants into an artificial political structure. In the 1960s House of Representatives elections, three political groups confronted each other: the Iran Novin (New) Party, headed by the Prime Minister, Amir Abbas Hoveyda; the Mardom (People) Party; and the extreme right-wing Pan-Iranian Party. Not concerned by this up-to-bottom division of labor, about 65% of the electorate abstained. As expected, the victory went to the Prime Minister's Iran Novin Party. In order to introduce big reforms in Iran, the Shah allowed women to vote or run for office in the Majles in 1963.

After the revolution in 1979, the Senate was abolished. In an attempt to Islamize all aspects of life in Iran, "Islamic" adjectives replaced "national" (melli). Majles Shoray-e Melli became Majles Shoray-e Eslami (Islamic

Consultative Assembly). The Constitution of 1979 invests legislative power in the Islamic Consultative. Article 69 of the Constitution stipulates, "the deliberations of the Islamic Consultative Assembly must be open and full minutes of them made available to the public by the radio and the official gazette. A closed session may be held in emergency conditions, if it is required for national security, upon the requisition of the President, one of the Ministers, or ten members of the Assembly. Legislation passed at a closed session is valid only when approved by three-fourths of the members in the presence of the Guardian Council. After emergency conditions have ceased to exist, the minutes of such closed sessions, together with any legislation approved in them, must be made available to the public." Since 1980 the Majles open deliberations have been broadcast regularly.

All members of Parliament are elected by public vote for a four-year term. The Majles has a speaker, two deputy speakers who run the meetings in his absence, and nine secretaries and provisions administrators.

Article 64 (2) of the Islamic Republic of Iran's Constitution recognizes the political rights of religious minorities. "The Zoroastrians and Jews will each elect one representative, Assyrian and Chaldean Christians will jointly elect one representative, and Armenian Christians in the north and those in the south of the country will each elect one representative."

Articles 71 to 90 of the Constitution ascertain the powers and authority of the Majles. The Majles has the power to establish laws on all matters; interpret the ordinary laws; debate the motions tabled by the government upon the cabinet's approval, as well as bills tabled by at least 15 MPs; investigate all the national affairs; approve international treaties, protocols, agreements, and contracts; effect minor changes in the border lines by considering the national interests with a majority of 4/5 of MPs; agree to the cabinet's request for proclamation of martial law for no more than 30 days; table a motion of no confidence in the president of the Republic or any of the ministers; and cast a vote of confidence or no confidence in the government or in any of the ministers. Some recent debates and bills passed by the Majles establish new dress requirements for women and assert that the country's cooperation with the International Atomic Energy Agency be revised based on the interests of Iran and its people.

The Guardian Council of the Constitution, an arbitrary non-elected steering board, first decides who among the candidates is qualified to become an MP and who is not. Then, those women or men whose qualifications are approved run for elections. In addition, the Guardian Council is invested with the authority to interpret the constitution and to determine whether the laws passed by the Majles comply with the Iranian Constitution and conform to

Islamic law (*shari'a*). The Council has the legal power to veto the laws passed by the Parliament.

Chapter VI, "The Legislative Power," Section Two, "Powers and Authority of the Islamic Consultative Assembly," Article 91 of the Constitution defines the Guardian Council's authority in checking the Majles' work. The same Article establishes the number of members on the Council at twelve, elected to serve for a period of six years. Six members of the Council are Muslim faqihs (clerics), conscious of the needs and issues of the present day, and selected by the Supreme Leader. The other six members are the jurists specializing in different areas of law. They are proposed by the Head of the Judicial Power, himself nominated by the Supreme Leader, and voted in by the Majles. The Parliament can turn down the proposed jurists by the head of the Judiciary Power. The latter will then put forward new names.

The following section outlines key articles of the Constitution and their respective functions.

KEY ARTICLES OF THE CONSTITUTION

Article 92

Members of the Guardian Council are elected to serve for a period of six years, but during the first term, after three years have passed, half of the members of each group will be changed by lot and new members will be elected in their place.

Article 93

The Islamic Consultative Assembly does not hold any legal status if there is no Guardian Council in existence, except for the purpose of approving the credentials of its members and the election of the six jurists on the Guardian Council.

Article 94

All legislation passed by the Islamic Consultative Assembly must be sent to the Guardian Council. The Guardian Council must review it within a maximum of ten days from its receipt with a view to ensuring its compatibility with the criteria of Islam and the Constitution. If it finds the legislation incompatible, it will return it to the Assembly for review. Otherwise the legislation will be deemed enforceable.

Article 95

In cases where the Guardian Council deems ten days inadequate for completing the process of review and delivering a definite opinion, it can request the Islamic Consultative Assembly to grant an extension of the time limit not exceeding ten days.

Article 96

The determination of compatibility of the legislation passed by the Islamic Consultative Assembly with the laws of Islam rests with the majority vote of the fuqaha' on the Guardian Council; and the determination of its compatibility with the Constitution rests with the majority of all the members of the Guardian Council.

Article 97

In order to expedite the work, the members of the Guardian Council may attend the Assembly and listen to its debates when a government bill or a members' bill is under discussion. When an urgent government or members' bill is placed on the agenda of the Assembly, the members of the Guardian Council must attend the Assembly and make their views known.

Article 98

The authority of the interpretation of the Constitution is vested with the Guardian Council, which is to be done with the consent of three-fourths of its members.

Article 99

The Guardian Council has the responsibility of supervising the elections of the Assembly of Experts for Leadership, the President of the Republic, the Islamic Consultative Assembly, and the direct recourse to popular opinion and referenda.

RESPONSIBILITIES OF IRAN GUARDIAN COUNCIL

The Guardian Council of the Constitution holds veto power over all the legislation approved by the Majles. There are two reasons it is possible to drop a law: First, if a law is considered contradictory to Islamic law, and second if it contradicts the Iranian constitution.

In such cases when the Iranian Guardian Council rejects a law, it is passed back to the Majles for correction. If the Majles and the Guardian Council cannot decide on a case, it is passed up to another council called the "Expediency Discernment Council" for a final decision.

It is the Guardian Council who decides on the qualifications of all candidates of parliamentary elections, presidential elections, and candidates for the Assembly of Experts. If approved by the Council, they can run in the election.

However, the new Majles, which was inaugurated on May 27 and is dominated by reformers, has vowed to make new amendments to the press law and restore press freedom, which has been encouraged by President Mohammad Khatami since he took office in 1997.

An urgent motion for the plan was approved in a Majles open session on June 18 and was scheduled to top the agenda for the open session on Sunday.

Majles speaker Karrubi, however, announced at the start of the session that a decision had been made not to debate new amendments to the press law following an order by supreme leader Ayatollah Ali Khamenei.

The Islamic Republic News Agency reported that after the speaker made the announcement, a number of Majles members voiced strong protest, which disturbed the order of the Parliament to the extent that the live broadcast of the proceeding was interrupted. Some physical confrontation occurred between some Majles members, and the protesting legislators were later escorted outside the Majles hall by other members.

Parliament, or Majles, in post-revolutionary Iran, has been, for the most part, a conservative force, with the exception of the sixth Majles, which formed three years after Khatami's election in 1997. The sixth Majles (2000–2004) reflected the vote of 84% of the voting population, mostly comprised of reformists (dovom khordadis).

Women of the sixth Majles made history by standing up for women's issues, or at least discussing them in Parliament. Jamileh Kadivar and Elahe Kulayi were the two outstanding female reformists in the sixth Majles who pursued women's issues despite the opposition of the powerful right wing in the country. This was manifested in their struggle to lead the Majles to pass the bill on Iran joining the Convention on the Elimination of All Forms of Discrimination Against Women (CEDAW).

There are twelve women in the seventh Majles, but they exert no political power and actually represent the far right despite their occasional reformist rhetoric. The women in the seventh Majles are against the bill on Iran joining CEDAW, which the female reformists in the sixth Majles had fought for vigorously. So far, the women in the seventh Majles have exhibited conservative, right-wing tendencies, setting them apart from their counterparts in the preceding parliament.

On January 7, 2001, the Majles voted overwhelmingly to strike provisions of Article 3 of the 1986 Law on Sending Students Abroad that currently require the permission of a male guardian (father or husband) to allow adult women to study abroad and bar single women from receiving governmental financial aid for continuing their higher education in foreign universities.

Political struggles between reformers and the conservatives have stepped up since the February parliamentary election, in which President Khatami's reformist allies dealt a severe blow to their opponents. But the conservatives obviously have the upper hand in the struggle, because they are still controlling such powerful state organs as the judiciary and the military. Even though reformers have seized control of the Majles, any bill passed must be approved by the conservative Guardians Council. The press law has become one of the centers of the factional struggle. The conservatives tend to use the restrictive law to suppress reformist press, while the reformers, with the Majles as their tool, try to amend the law so that reformist papers can no longer be banned easily.

HOUCHANG HASSAN-YARI

✦ MANDAEANS AND MANDAEISM

Mandaeans are adherents of the Mandaean religion, which is Gnostic, and live primarily in southern Iraq and southwestern Iran. They are also known as *Sabian* (in the Qur'an) and *Subbi/Sobbi* (in Arabic). Iranian Mandaeans speak Persian (Farsi) in addition to a localized Arabic dialect similar to the Arabic spoken in the southern region of Iraq.

Early scholars of the 1920s debated the origin of Mandaeans, proposing them to be Jewish baptizing sects, Christian, or Babylonian—all originating in the Jordan area. More recently, Jacobsen Buckley (1993) argued that "... a consensus, based on linguistic and historical research, puts Mandaeism back into its original, 'heretical' Jewish baptist milieu." This argument is based on the linguist specialists' argument based on the language used in their religious texts and the time and religious environment of John's gospel. Buckley firmly believes that Mandaeism never had a Christian stage. Popular legends describe Mandaean migrations from the Jordan area. Buckley states that Mandaeans moved from their homeland under the protection of Ardban, the Parthian King in the first century AD, perhaps during the time of Ardban III.

Currently, Mandaeans live next to the Tigris and Euphrates rivers in Iraq as well as the Karoon River in the southern region of Iran (Khozestan), in the cities of Khorramshahr, Abadan, Ahvaz, Shushtar, Dezful, Shush, Chogha Zambil, and Howeizeh.

MANDAEAN RELIGIOUS BELIEFS

The Mandaean religion is mostly associated with Gnosticism, with certain elements such as *yarna* (running water), *Kushta* (truth), and *Manda* (knowledge) directly connected to the religion's Western origins. Mandaeans believe in Yahya, who is the prophet John the Baptist. In its early periods, as Mandaeanism was coming into contact with existing religions of the time—most notably Zoroastrianism, Manichaeism, and other belief systems prevalent in Babylon—it experienced some hostility from Christianity. These influences and contacts with various religions that existed at the time of the Mandaean migration to Iranian regions are evident through Manichaean hymns which directly translate Mandaean poetry. Mandaeans believe that Miriai (Mary, mother of Jesus) became pregnant by witchcraft or by another man who was not her husband. The Jewess Miriai is a Mandaean. Mandaeans believe that they are former Jews and that the language in the Talmud is the language of Babylonia, which is very close to classical Mandaic (the language of Mandaeans). Miriai is a heroine, but her son Jesus deviated from the truth of his Mandaean heritage. Mandaeans also believe that the punishment of the Jews is deserved.

The Mandaean holy book is called *Ginza* (treasure). It is separated into a right (*Ginza* Right/GR), and a left (*Ginza* Left/ GL). GR contains materials, mostly in poetic style, related to the soul's ascent to the Lightworld. GR is believed to be the oldest surviving text. When turning the *Ginza* upside down, one can read the GL, which deals with the fate of the soul when the body dies. Among other matters (such as the destiny of the soul, prayers), it contains the story of the first man who died, Adam's son Sitil.

The Mandaean story of creation has three different levels: the upper Lightworld, which is heavenly, known as *alama d-nhura* or "world of light," a middle world, which is the earthly world of human inhabitants known as *Tibil*, and the third world, which is the dark and gloomy underworld.

Most attention is paid to the Lightworld, where the supreme First Life lives and the true home lies above in the light. The supreme First Life is also known as the King of Greatness or the King of Light.

Mandaean scripture describes two models of creation of the world: the first is an emanation model of creation and the second model is based upon the opposing poles of the Lightworld and the Darkworld. While the creation model is by far more commonly held, there are too many variations in the creation mythology to accurately point to one as the original version. Inhabitants of the Lightworld are known as *utras* (angels, guardians), who were involved in creation of the dark and light worlds and continue to look after the earthly and Lightworld and keep in touch with Mandaeans of earth.

The Lightworld sends prayers and all forms of rituals by the forces of light to be taught to the Mandaeans. Thus, the human world and the rituals and prayers connect the Lightworld. Therefore, the Mandaean must be concerned with how to live his life in Tibil, the earth, and how to die in order to receive a proper ascent to the Lightworld. The rituals connected with the Mandaean religion are complex and time-consuming, and a number of them require the assistance of a priest and thus cannot be performed by a lay person.

STATUS OF MANDAEANS IN IRAN

Mandaeans enjoyed protection by the kings during the later part of the Iranian Dynasty of Ashkanian, who ruled from 248 BC until their overthrow by the Sassanid Dynasty in AD 224. However, during the reign of the Sasanid ruler Bahram I in AD 273, religious persecutions were carried out regularly. Mani, founder of the religion Manichaeism, was executed in the early stages of Bahram I rule, around AD 276. The Zoroastrian high priest Karter suppressed followers of other religions such as Mandaeans, Manichaeans, Christians, Jews, Hindus, and Buddhists. At the early stages of the Islamic expansion, Mandaeans showed the Muslim authorities their holy book *Ginza* and proclaimed that John the Baptist was their prophet. This was crucial for Mandaeans to receive protection by their Muslim rulers, because they were aware that a holy book and a prophet are essential to gain the status of "People of the Book" (*ahl al Kitab*). In addition, Mandaeans cite the Qur'an for their existence in the holy scripture of Muslims. They are mentioned by the name of Sabians (II: 62, and V:72):

> Those who believe (in the Qur'an),
> And those who follow the Jewish (scriptures),
> And the Christians and the Sabians,
> Any who believe in God
> And the Last Day,
> And work righteousness,
> Shall have their reward. (2:62)

According to *Commentary to The Holy Qur'an* by Yusuf Ali, 1983, p. 33:
Latest researches have revealed a small remnant of a religious community
numbering about 2,000 souls in Lower Iraq, near Basra. In Arabic they
are called *Subbi* (Plural: *Subba*). They are also called Sabians and Nasor-
aeans or Manaeans or Christians of St. Johan. They claim to be Gnostics
or Knowers of the Great Life. They dress in white and believe in frequent
immersions in water. Their Book Ginza is in a dialect of Aramaic. They
have theories of Darkness and Light as in Zoroastrianism. They use the
name *Yardan* (Jordan) for any river. They live in peace and harmony
among their Muslim neighbors. They resemble the Sabi-un mentioned in
the Qur'an, but are probably not identical with them.

Mandaeans enjoyed prosperity and freedom to practice their religion.
Many scribal activities and collections of Mandaean texts existed at this time
(mid 7th century).

The Mandaeans' status as "people of the book" has come into question
throughout history in Iran. For example, Mandaeans under Qajar rule in the
1780s experienced difficulties by the Shah's local representatives by throwing
them into wells where they drowned. In addition to loss of life due to the cru-
elty of the local authorities, later in 1830 half of the inhabitants of the city lost
their lives to the great cholera epidemic known as the Plague of Shushtar.

The most recent wars and crises in Iran and Iraq have caused migrations
of large numbers of Mandaeans from both Iran and Iraq to the Western
world. The Iran–Iraq War (1980–1988) as well the Gulf War of 1991 are responsible for a large population of Mandaeans dispersion around the world.

Varying statistics about Mandaean numbers range from 15,000–100,000,
with the largest population still living in Iraq. Claiming religious persecution,
non-recognition of their religion by the government of Iran, discrimination,
and exclusion from the normal protections of the law, a significant number
of Iranian Mandaeans have fled to Australia.

Religious persecution in Iran, based on measured assessments, is on record
by Amnesty International, including the following: in Iran all religious minorities, including Christians and Jews, suffer varying degrees of persecution, *vis-
á-vis* the Shi'ite Muslim majority. The State, for example, does not permit non-
Muslims to engage in government employment or to attend university. And
there are restrictions on the extent to which they can fully practice their religion, such as, for example, teaching it publicly. If injured or killed, Mandaeans

or their dependents receive less compensation than would the Muslim majority, and they may suffer in assessments of their credibility as witnesses before Iranian courts. In recent years, Mandaeans who worked in any business requiring direct contact with food (such as cooking or baking or selling food items) have lost their jobs because they are viewed as "unclean" people. The discrimination against Mandaeans has increased since the establishment of the Islamic Republic in 1979.

Suggested Reading

Ali, A. Y. 1983. *The holy Qur'an, text, translation, and commentary.* Brentwood: Amana Corp.

Buckley, J. J. 1993. The Mandaean appropriation of Jesus' mother, Miriai. *Novum Testamentum.* 35:181–196.

Buckley, J. J. 2002. *The Mandaeans, ancient texts and modern people.* Oxford: University Press.

FAEGHEH S. SHIRAZI

✦ MAZANDARANIS AND MAZANDARAN

The Mazandaran province of Iran, also called Tabarestan, covers the Caspian coastal plains, backed by the forested slopes and valleys of the Alborz Mountain ranges. The region is believed to have been populated as early as other parts of Iran. Due to its geographic isolation, Tabarestan partially preserved its pre-Islamic identity even many centuries after the Muslim conquest of Iran and other Central Asian regions. Along with its neighboring province Gilan, Mazandaran enjoys a highly favorable climate, with highly fertile and cultivated plains. With the central city of Sari, Mazandarani dialects are believed to be spoken by almost 3.5 million people. Mazandarani is classified as an Indo–Iranian language.

HADI SULTAN-QURRAIE

✦ MODERNITY

Iran's encounter with modernity began in earnest with its very first encounter with European progress in the seventeenth century, during the Safavid dynasty (1501–1736). But these developments were not initially considered to be significant. The Iranians had no reason to think in a manner different from their own, because at the time, they were the second most important actor in global politics after the Ottomans. They had a magnificent civilization and called their capital city, Isfahan, "half of the world," the other half being the heavens. It was only in the late eighteenth century and the beginning of the nineteenth century that they realized the value of these modern ways. In fact, the reforms initiated by Abbas Mirza (1789–1833), the crown prince who dispatched the first group of Iranian students to study abroad in 1811, marked the beginning of that realization. It is an irony of history, however, that despite two centuries of modernization, no ruling elite in Iran succeeded to modernize Iran as much as the very people who claimed commitment to creating a purely religious and Islamic state: the elite of the Islamic regime who came to power after the 1979 revolution.

What caused this paradox lies in the eventful history that characterizes the modernization of Iran in the past centuries. Like all human phenomena, modernization is Janus-faced—one side represents human freedom and reason, the other power and rationality. The early encounters between Iran and modernity resulted from the interaction of almost equal powers. Thus, it produced a sober response of studying, selecting, and borrowing. Soon, the progressive and dynamic Europe assumed the posture of imperialism, and Iran lost its confidence. This led to the emergence of a group of Iranians who repudiated slow and gradual change, and instead suggested wholesale and quick adoption of "Western ways." Thus, the encounter between Iran and modernity has gone in two trajectories, including the followers of a genuine yet modified Iranian self, and those who followed modernism, the hegemonic face of modernity. The result is the appearance of parallel polities regarding a modern worldview during the past two centuries of Iranian history.

Eras of modernization and reforms include: 1) modernizing the state, 1810s–1851; 2) parliamentary monarchy, 1890s–1921; 3) popular democracy, 1940s–1953; and 4) republican democracy, 1970s to the present. In each era, Iranians reconstructed their world by combining the demands of their eternal past (tradition) with the requirements of their eternal future (modernity). Each era became victim of an unholy alliance between various forms of "isms." For example, the conservatism and traditionalism of the Iranian oligarchy crushed the first moment, while the second fell victim to the forces of modernism and imperialism of the "great game" among the European powers who dominated the region at the beginning of the twentieth century. The discovery of oil changed the nature and the form of imperialism in the Middle East to economic capitalism, thus making the third era the subject of exploitation by forces of modernism and economic imperialism. Traditionalism and Islamism seemed to challenge the last era and continue to do so today.

The first phase identified with the figures of the aforementioned Abbas Mirza (1789–1833) and Mirza Taqi Khan Amir Kabir (1807–1852). The former paved the way for the coming of "Western civilization," notably by initiating army reform, dispatching students to Europe, and adopting new practices such as the wearing of modern attire. The latter became Prime Minister from 1948–1852 and followed a two-pronged reform policy. First, he tried to strengthen the existing state, and second, he introduced many ideas of modernity that changed the system forever. For example, he established order in the finances, administration, military, industry, agriculture, trade, mining, and public welfare in order to strengthen the state. On another level, his reforms included the establishment of a new institution of modern learning, the publication of a newspaper, and the translation of new Western works. His new school opened in 1852 posthumously, but it reoriented the frame of Iranian society from tradition to rationality and modernity. Amir Kabir reportedly planned to introduce a constitution with a parliamentary monarchy for Iran, but this had to wait for the next phase of modernization.

The tobacco concession to a British company in the early 1890s proved detrimental in all respects. It initiated a popular movement against the existing policies of the government. What was significant about it was that it involved all social classes and resulted in mass protest. The government had to retreat and cancel the concession, but the opposition gradually became a movement for the establishment of the constitution in 1906. In its own way, the Constitutional movement was a revolution in that all social classes of the time, the Ulama, the aristocracy, even the royal court, signed on and demanded popular sovereignty. In fact, the people's protests continued through the summer of 1906, demanding the establishment of "the house of justice" and a democratic constitution with people's representation. Finally, on August 5, 1906, Mozafaredin Shah issued an edict for the writing of a constitution that led to an interesting compromise. In that document, sovereignty remained God's only, and was delegated on earth to the people who, in turn, bestow it upon the monarch. The three branches of the government were responsible for governing the country, and parliament oversaw every action taken. The process was similar to what was happening in many European countries at the time, which explains why the Belgian constitution became the model in Iran. However, an unholy alliance of local modernism and European imperialism disrupted the natural course of historical development for the Iranian parliamentary system. From 1921 to 1941, Iran was ruled by the iron fist of a local autocrat supported by the British Imperialism. That came to an abrupt end with the onset of WWII.

The forces of Iranian genuine modernization took advantage of the chaos and tried to revive constitutional democracy, but it gained broader popular support. Two factors contributed greatly: first, the activities of the Iranian left from socialists to Marxists advocated a mass movement, and second was the mobilization of the people against British imperialism. The latter opposed British oil concession in Iran. Under the leadership of Mohammad Mosaddeq (1890–1967), Iran nationalized its oil and the government insisted on popular sovereignty; however, they again fell victim to an alliance between local modernism and international imperialism.

Changes in the local and global context led to the coming of an all out revolution in 1979 with the promises of "freedom, independence, and Islamic Republic." The system created subsequently was "the Islamic Republic," which simultaneously promised the enhancement of Islam and modernity. This has been the case for the past three decades and will continue to be so into the future. Many of the areas that appear to be Islamicized have indirectly led to modernization from below. For example, the policy of sex segregation necessitates the opening of opportunities for women in all areas of health, education, commerce, and politics. This parallel struggle for establishing modern and Islamic ideas continues.

On the other hand, the assimilators have had their days. They include: 1) the age of concessions and mortgaging Iran in the name of progress, 1850–1890; 2) Westernization in the form of an army-state, 1921–1941; 3) Americanization and the creation of the police state, 1953–1979; and 4) finally Islamization and traditionalism, 1979 to the present. In each case the ruling elite reduces the complex historical development of Iran into a political project of social engineering from above. It is not surprising that in each epoch the state has relied more and more on the army, security forces, intelligence apparatus, and foreign powers for its survival, as was the case for the Pahlavis. The 1979 revolution proves significant in the last phase since it was the first classic revolution in a non-Western society, shaking Iranians to the core. The Pahlavis were committed to modernizing their polity and society, and many Islam-minded Iranians recognize the necessity for a proper dialogue regarding Iranian local and traditional ways and the demands of modernity. As an example, note the dynamic dialogue coming from Islam-minded elites who see a convergence between Islam and democracy. The most eloquent voices are those of Abdolkarim Soroush and Mohsen Kadivar.

Hossein Hajfaraj Dabagh (known as Abdolkarim Soroush, b. 1924) is possibly the biggest name in Islamic discourse in Iran. Soroush undertakes a multidisciplinary approach towards understanding Islam and its place in the public sphere. According to Soroush, a multidisciplinary approach makes it possible for Islam and Muslims to live within the parameters of pluralism. In his opinion, where secularism is dominant, all emphasis would inevitably be on rights, scientific management, rationality, human progress, and worldly gain. To avoid this, Soroush suggests his controversial theory of "contraction and expansion of religious knowledge." He claims that religion is complete and absolute, while its understanding contracts and expands in time and in various places. Combined with this is his idea of a "selective" approach, namely that Muslims should dare to select the truth wherever it is found, in the West, among Muslims, or in any other traditions. This approach requires a critical mind that avoids any kind of generality, positive or negative, about any particular tradition. This runs contrary to a powerful conservative trend that propagates the idea of "the evil essence of the West" that threatens the sacred and pure world of the Muslims. Soroush discussed such complexities both in the West and among Muslims. Both regions are composed of a collection of discord and collaboration, interactions between political actors, religious groupings, scholars, and professionals, and so on.

Public intellectual Mohsen Kadivar (b. 1959) believes one can combine Islam and democracy because both demand that public life be ethical and in the service of the people. He claims a government that fulfills this criteria is a religious democracy or theodemocracy. It is democracy in that it is by the people, or their representatives, and for the people. The criteria for the workings of such a government are not some abstract legal or theological principles, but rather practical principles such as fairness (*edalat*), reasonability (*oqalaaei*) in terms of common sense, and efficiency (*karamadi*). It is at this level that religion and modern democracy converge and can work together. What makes Kadivar's view significant is that he comes from within the clerical rank, thus functioning as a questioning voice from within. While Soroush argues his point from a philosophical and rational standpoint, Kadivar grounds his theory in the history of political thinking in Shi'ism. For example, he is reviving the views of one of the most prominent jurists in the early twentieth century and a supporter of the Constitutional Revolution, Mullah Mohammad Kazem, better known as Akhond Khorasani (d. 1911). In Kadivar's reading, Khorassani thinks there are two types of regimes: *shari`a*-based and non-*shari`a*-based, and the latter can potentially be either just or tyrannical. It is impossible to have a *shari`a*-based regime because it requires the presence of an infallible Imam. But since the state must operate even in the absence of an infallible Imam, the people should rule. The jurists cannot have any special claim and should remain in the field of legal studies and affairs.

Suggested Reading

Adamiyat, F. 1961. *Fekre Azadi va Moqadameye Nehzate Mashrutiyate dar Iran* [The idea of freedom and the beginning of the constitutional movement in Iran]. Tehran: Sokhan.

Hairi, A. H. 1988. *Nakhostin Ruyarueihaye Andishegaran Irani ba Doruyeye Tamadon-e burzhuvazie Gharb* [The early encounter of the Iranian thinkers with the two-sided civilization of Western bourgeoisie]. Tehran: Amir Kabir.Katousian.

Katouzian, H. 1981. *The political economy of Iran, 1926–1979*. London: Macmillan.

Kermani, M. N. a.-I. 1978. *Tarikhe Beidariye Iranian* [A history of Iranian awakening], 2 volumes. Tehran: Agah.

Mahbubi-Ardakani, H. 1989. *Tarikh-e Mo'assessat-e Tamadoni-ye Jadid dar Iran* [A history of the institutions of modern civilization in Iran], 3 volumes. Tehran: Tehran University Press.

FARHANG RAJAEE

✦ MUJAHEDIN-E KHALQ ORGANIZATION

The Mujahedin-e Khalq Organization (MEK) is the largest armed opposition group fighting to overthrow the government of the Islamic Republic of Iran. The MEK is led by Massoud and Maryam Rajavi, a husband and wife team often accused of instilling their followers with a cult of personality. The organization's ideology is inspired by a mixture of Marxism–Leninism and Islamism, and its methods are characterized by armed attacks on regime targets. In recent years, the organization has had little success in its military struggle against the Iranian government. This is despite—or perhaps because of—its extensive military and political cooperation with Saddam Hussein in the 1980s and the 1990s, lasting up until the U.S. invasion of Iraq in March 2003 and the subsequent collapse of Saddam's regime.

MEK is also known as the People's Mojahedin Organization of Iran (PMOI), founded in 1965 by Mohammad Hanifnezhad and students the University of Tehran in opposition to the political regime of Mohammad Reza Shah Pahlavi. In 1979 the Mujahedin participated in the Iranian Islamic Revolution, but soon opposed the regime of Ayatollah Ruhollah Khomeini, which executed the organization's leadership. Since the 1970s, the MEK has mounted a number of attacks against Iranian government officials and institutions in Iran and abroad, as well as against American and European institutions and companies operating in Iran and high-ranking American military officials. Its activities have declined since late 2001. It is not clear how many attacks the Mujahedin has carried out in total, as the group often exaggerates its claims for attacks, while at the same time the Iranian government blames the organization for other attacks.

The Mujahedin is believed to have some 10,000 members. Up until 2003, the organization received most of its military and financial support from the Iraqi regime of Saddam Hussein. It also uses other organizations abroad to get contributions from expatriate Iranian communities. The Mujahedin is composed of the National Council of Resistance of Iran, its political wing, the National Liberation Army of Iran, its militant wing, and the Muslim Iranian Students Society, used to gather financial support. The Mujahedin has sympathizers in Europe, the United States, and Canada. The National Council of Resistance has offices in several capitals, and used to have a branch in Washington, D.C., which was closed down in August 2003 by U.S. officials.

In 1981, during the Iran–Iraq War, the Mujahedin was driven from its bases on the border between Iran and Iraq and resettled in Paris. From there, it supported Iraq in the war with Iran. In 1986, the Mujahedin moved its headquarters to Iraq where it has been operating from camps close to the border with Iran. During the 2003 Iraq War U.S. forces closed the Mujahedin's bases in Iraq, and in June 2003 the French government raided the Mujahedin compound in Paris and arrested 165 people, including Maryam Rajavi, but they were released shortly thereafter. Massoud Rajavi was last known to be living in Iraq, but it is not clear where he is now or whether he is still alive.

Originally, the Mujahedin emerged in 1965 out of the Liberation Movement of Mehdi Bazargan. The Liberation Movement was founded in the early 1960s to support Prime Minister Mohammad Mosaddeq's political regime. In 1963 Mohammad Reza Shah launched the White Revolution as a reaction to the economic crisis in Iran, aiming to modernize Iran and to integrate the country into the world economy. At that time, Ayatollah Ruhollah Khomeini first appeared on the scene criticizing the Shah for his repressive politics. This marked the beginning of a rift between the Shah and both the clergy and the merchants of the bazaar who felt threatened by the White Revolution. In the eyes of some of its members, Bazargan's Liberation Movement and other organizations did not react sufficiently to the Shah's policies, thus they broke away and founded the MEK. The organization admired Khomeini as a "national symbol." It was inspired by Marxism–Leninism and radical social and revolutionary ideas as previously developed by Che Guevara and Guy Debray.

The Mujahedin based their armed struggle on the guerilla movements in Cuba, Algeria, and Vietnam. Its ideology was based on Islamic themes such as *shahadat* (martyrdom), the classical Marxist theory of class struggle and historical determinism, as well as neo-Marxist concepts of armed struggle,

guerilla warfare, and revolutionary heroism. The Mujahedin started its guerilla activities in 1971. In the mid-1970s the Mujahedin and other oppositional organizations were heavily suppressed by the Iranian state. In 1975 the
Mujahedin split into two groups that identified themselves as the Islamic
Mujahedin and the Marxist Mujahedin. After the revolution the Marxist
group came to be known as the Organization of the Struggle for Liberation of
the Working Class or *Paykar*. Ideologically, it rejected the idea that Shi'a
Islam could be a potentially progressive force and relied more on the traditional Marxist concept of class struggle. Despite state suppression and split-
ting, the Mujahedin survived.

When the Islamic Revolution reached its height, the number of members and sympathizers of the Mujahedin had reached 100,000. On February
12, 1979, the Mujahedin and the People's Fedayan-e Khalq Guerilla Organization participated in a revolt which brought down the government of
Shapour Bakhtiar. During the revolution the competition between Ayatollah Khomeini and the Mujahedin grew. The Mujahedin were not unified
in their view of what kind of regime Iran should have after the revolution.
The Mujahedin's leaders officially supported Khomeini and his aim to establish a theocracy, but many members strove for a secular democratic government. Nevertheless, the organization was not willing to risk its coalition
with Khomeini and his followers. In January 1979, the Mujahedin issued
its revolutionary program calling for more freedom for ethnic minorities in
Iran, welfare-state legislation, expropriation of the bourgeoisie, the nationalization of oil and gas resources, equal rights for women, and the establishment of a people's army. The Khomeini regime felt threatened by these
demands. In the first parliamentary elections of the Islamic Republic of Iran
in March and April 1980, the Mujahedin received the second greatest number of votes behind Khomeini's Islamic Republican Party. Massoud Rajavi
received 500,000 votes, and his wife Maryam earned more than 250,000.
Khomeini prevented both from entering the Majles (parliament). The organization then allied with the new president of the Islamic Republic, Abol-
hassan Banisadr.

Banisadr supported the Mujahedin and provided the organization with
weapons from the Iranian regular army. When the war with Iraq started in
September 1980, the regime responded with open terror. It closed the Mujahedin's daily newspaper Mujahed, which, with a circulation of 500,000, had
the largest readership in Iran at the time. The government also persecuted
the Mujahedin's leaders, and arrested its supporters and members, along with
other left-wing organizations. Thousands of people were executed. During a
demonstration with 500,000 participants on June 20, 1981, government

forces killed 50 demonstrators and arrested hundreds more. Having lost to the increasingly more powerful hardliners within the revolutionary establishment, Banisadr had to abdicate his position as president the day after the demonstration. In 1981, Massoud Rajavi fled to Paris where he founded the National Council of Resistance of Iran. The Council's goal was to establish a Democratic Islamic Republic of Iran. Banisadr became its president and Rajavi head of its provisional government. At that time the Mujahedin had substantial support both from secular groups, such as the National Democratic Front, Stalinist groups, and some of the ethnic minorities, including the Democratic Party of Kurdistan-Iran, and Turkish speaking Azeris in the northwestern part of the country.

As the Iranian regime continued its attacks on the Mujahedin, those supporting the organization gradually lost their hopes that the Mujahedin would be capable of overthrowing the Islamic Republic and replace it with another political regime. Most of the organizations that had supported the Mujahedin had left the Resistance Council by 1984. At that time, Massoud Rajavi began organizational restructuring and ideological reform of the Mujahedin, which resulted in a strong hierarchical structure with Massoud Rajavi and his wife Maryam at the top. Maryam Rajavi moved to Paris in 1982. She was elected as the Mujahedin's joint leader in 1985 and in 1989 became the Secretary General of the organization.

When the National Liberation Army was founded in 1987, into which the organization integrated several thousand of its members, Maryam Rajavi was appointed the army's Deputy Commander in Chief. In August 1993, the National Council of Resistance elected Maryam Rajavi as Iran's future President of the transitional government after the overthrow of the political regime of the Islamic Republic of Iran. Under the leadership of Maryam Rajavi, women have attained key positions in the National Council of Resistance. They comprise half of the members of the National Council of Resistance and one third of the combatants of the National Liberation Army. Many of the latter's commanders are also women.

In 1985, the Mujahedin was officially declared a terrorist organization by the U.S. government, and its members were expelled from Europe. The organization then moved its headquarters to Iraq. Its facilities in Iraq include Camp Ashraf, the Mujahedin's military headquarters, which is 100 km west of the Iranian border and 100 km north of Baghdad; Camp Anzali near the town of Jalawla; Camp Faezeh in Kut; Camp Habib in Basra; Camp Homayoun in Al-Amarah; and Camp Bonyad Alavi, close to the city of Miqdadiyah. From Iraq the organization carried out several attacks in Iran. In 1998 it assassinated Asadollah Lajevardi, the director of the Evin Prison, and in 1999 the deputy chief of Iran's armed forces general staff, Ali Sayyad Shirazi. In 2000, the organization launched attacks against the leadership complex in Tehran, housing the offices of the Supreme Leader and the President. The Mujahedin also attacked Iranians outside Iran.

In April 1992, the Mujahedin conducted attacks on Iranian embassies in thirteen different countries. In October 1997, after the election of Mohammad Khatami as President in Iran, U.S. President Bill Clinton put the Mujahedin on the U.S State Department's list of foreign terrorist organizations. It has been on this list ever since, despite strong objections in the U.S. Congress. The European Union (EU) added the Mujahedin to its list of terrorist groups in 2000. The National Council of Resistance's spokesman Alireza Jafarzadeh, on August 14, 2002, gained worldwide attention when he claimed that Iran had clandestine nuclear facilities in Natanz and Arak, leading to inspections by the International Atomic Energy Agency and the eventual sanctions imposed on Iran over its nuclear program by the United Nations Security Council on December 23, 2006.

The fall of Saddam Hussein's regime had great effects on the Mujahedin. After the U.S. invasion in Iraq in 2003, some 3,800 members of the Mujahedin were disarmed by U.S. military forces. The Mujahedin did not confront the U.S military forces despite the bombings of its camps. The members of the Mujahedin were merged in Camp Ashraf and granted protected persons status under the Fourth Geneva Convention in July 2004. As a condition, the members of the Mujahedin handed over their weapons, including tanks, armored vehicles, and heavy artillery. They are now treated as noncombatants. The Mujahedin seeks removal from U.S and EU terrorist lists. As of this writing, their status remains unclear.

On June 17, 2003, French police stormed the homes of Mujahedin members in Auvers-sur-Oise, close to Paris, and in five other towns, and police temporarily arrested 165 people. Sympathizers of the Mujahedin demonstrated against the arrests. In Paris, London, Rome, and Bern people went on hunger strike or attempted to burn themselves. On December 15, 2004, Maryam Rajavi spoke to the European Parliament on the invitation of The Friends of a Free Iran Intergroup. Regarding EU policy towards Iran, Rajavi suggested that the EU should neither contain the current regime in Iran nor overthrow the regime by external war. Change should be brought about by the Iranian people and the Iranian Resistance. Her speech was well received by the European Parliament. The Mujahedin remains the largest armed oppositional group to the political regime in Iran. In recent years, some members of the organization have voluntarily returned to Iran.

Suggested Reading

Abrahamian, E. 1982. *Between two revolutions*. Princeton: Princeton University Press.

Cronin, S. 2004. *Reformers and revolutionaries in modern Iran-new perspectives on the Iranian left*. London: Routledge.

EVA PATRICIA RAKEL

N

✦ NAWRUZ CELEBRATION

Iranian festivals and celebrations usually revolve around the natural movement of celestial elements. The most important festival is the New Year celebration or Nawruz. The word in Persian literally means "new day" and it marks the first day of spring, and thus it has come to indicate both the changing of seasons from winter to spring and the beginning of a new cycle of life. Major cultures of the region, i.e., Sumerians, Babylonians, and Akaddians celebrate it in one form or another. Many countries other than Iran celebrate this day, e.g., Afghanistan, Albania, Azerbaijan, Kazakhstan, Kyrgyzstan, Pakistan, Tajikistan, Turkey, Turkmenistan, and Uzbekistan. Minorities such as Baha'is, Ismailies, and the Kurds also mark it as their new year. The origin of Nawruz is unknown, but Persian mythology traces it to the mythical King Jamshid, who supposedly defeated all Iranian real foes and imagined demons (*divs*), established an orderly and prosperous life for his people, and declared the beginning of spring the Iranian New Year.

Historically, most Iranian customs and traditions actually took shape during the civilized era of the Achaemenid Dynasty (550-333 BC). Their rule extended to Macedonia in the West and India to the East, covering the whole region of Central Asia, the Middle East, and North Africa. It was a time of multiculturalism, tolerance, and civility. The original numbering of the solar calendar has changed, and presently it is based on the beginning of the Muslim Calendar, which is the Prophet's migration from Mecca to Medina in 621.

The Nawruz celebration formally and practically begins at the exact moment of equinox, falling sometimes on the 20th or 21st of March, and lasts for two weeks. It ends with a day of picnic on the 13th day of the New Year. However, there are two events prior to the change of seasons that Iranians take seriously and perform every year. One is a thorough spring cleaning before the New Year, and the second is the celebration of Wednesday (Charshanbe-suri). The main attraction of this celebration is the jumping over of flaming firs on the last Tuesday evening of the existing year chanting, "Take away my paleness give me your red color." The spirit of Halloween is present, as it is believed that the spirits of ones' ancestors will visit on the last day of the year. To symbolically reenact the visit, many people wrap themselves in shrouds and run through the streets banging on pots and pans to scare the spirits away and clear the day before the unlucky Wednesday of the year. There are also fireworks that can be heard throughout the night. The other celebration involves the growing of green in a plate. This begins a few days before the New Year and continues until the 13th day, when the grown greenery is thrown into a flowing river.

On the first day of the New Year, Iranians wear new clothes and join together as a family around *"Sofreye Haft Seen,"* which is a table decorated with seven items that have names beginning with the Persian letter "Seen" ("S" in the Latin alphabet).

The Most Popular Items Beginning with "S" to Decorate the New Year's Table

✦

Sabzeh (green dish): Freshly sprouted wheat or lentils grown in a dish or tray, which is also the symbol of rebirth and rejuvenation of life.

Samanoo: A sweet pudding made from wheat germ as a symbol of food and grain.

Seeb (apple): A symbol of healthy food and fruits.

Seer (garlic): A symbol of natural medicine.

Seke (coin): A symbol of wealth and prosperity.

Senjed (Russian olive): A dried fruit symbolizing love.

Serkeh (vinegar): A symbol of age, patience, cleanliness, and hygiene.

Somaq (sumac): A symbol of spices.

Sonbol (hyacinth): A symbol of nature, fragrance, good scent, and the heralding the coming of spring.

There are other ornaments on the table, including candles (representing enlightenment and happiness), colored eggs (diversity of fertility), and goldfish in a bowl (influx of life and unpredictability). There is also the Zodiac sign of Pisces (which ends the astrological cycle), a mirror (reflection of creation), and for some, an orange in a bowl of water (the earth floating in space).

During the holiday, it is customary for Iranians to exchange visits between relatives and friends, wishing one another health and prosperity. Although no gifts are exchanged, children and younger adults are given a brand new bill (not enormous in value) as a way of marking the New Year. The celebration and the exchange of visits continue for the whole two weeks. Public offices open after the first week, but all educational establishments, including universities, remain closed during the celebration. On the 13th day, people mark the end of the festivities by going on a picnic and throwing the Sabzeh into flowing water and asking it to take away sorrow and sickness from the family. Although the level of intensity may differ in various parts of the country, the celebration happens in all groups, regardless of cultural, religious, and linguistic ethnicity, and it has been occurring for millennia.

The exception to Nawruz may be the introduction of the Islamic Republic that occurred with the revolution of 1979. Since then, certain segments of the Islamic-minded elite have tried to downplay the significance of this festival and have done their utmost to undermine and even eliminate the holiday altogether, but Iran is among the few Muslim societies where people are resilient in preserving the mores and norms that originated in an era before Islam. The Iranian narrative of Islam has always been particular and filled with elements stemming from Iranian culture, which has enabled this timelessness. One indicator of this is that fundamentalist Muslims, including the chief religious officer in Saudi Arabia, the country that considers itself the official guardian of the main shrine of Islam in Mecca, consider Islam in Iran as peculiarly Persian, or as the French philosopher Henry Corbin put it "Iranian Islam." Indeed, when the Safavid ruled Iran (1501–1736), they managed to declare Iranian New Year's day as a sacred religious day. Their policy paid off and they managed to make Iran a powerful civilization for almost two centuries. Despite the official cold reception of the celebration, Iranians have kept it alive both within and outside Iran, and it remains the most important celebration in Iran to date.

Suggested Reading
Olmstead, A.T. 1948. *History of the Persian Empire: Achaemenid period.* Chicago: University of Chicago Press.
Razi, H. 2001. *Gahshomari va Jashnha-ye Iran-e Bastan* [Chronology and ceremonies of ancient Iran]. Tehran: Entesharat-e Behjat.

Shari'ati, A. 2006. Nawruz, in *Majmue-ye Assar* [Collection of Works], Volume 13:543–553. Tehran: Bonyad-e Farhangi Ali Shari'ati.

FARHANG RAJAEE

✦ NOMADS

In late 1979, the Islamic Republic of Iran established the Center for Services to Nomads (*markaz-e khadamat-e ashayer*). It modeled the center after Mohammad Reza Shah's Organization for Mobile Pastoralists (*sazman-e damdaran-e sayyar*), which the new government had situated in the Ministry of Agriculture soon after the revolution. Under the prime minister's authority, the center was responsible for emergency funds for nomads. At about the same time, the Islamic government placed another new organization, the Supreme Council for Nomads (*shura-ye ali-ye ashayer*), under the prime minister's jurisdiction (and later the president's). Aiming to centralize issues relating to nomads, the supreme council contained representatives of ministries and agencies as well as a few formally educated men of nomadic backgrounds who displayed solid revolutionary credentials.

Qashqa'i migratory Iranian nomads arrive in southern Shiraz, some 1000 km from Tehran, 2007. (AP Photo/Hasan Sarbakhshian)

In 1982 the prime minister and the supreme council created the Organization for Nomads' Affairs (ONA; *sazman-e amur-e ashayer*) based on the Center for Services to Nomads. Initially ONA fell under the prime minister's control, and then it became an independent agency within the new Ministry of Rural Reconstruction (*jihad-e sazandegi*) in 1983. (The Ministries of Agriculture and Rural Reconstruction merged in 2000.) The ONA was the primary state agency for delivering services to Iran's nomads, a function it performed effectively through 2008.

The Organization for Nomads' Affairs defined "nomads" (*ashayer*) as "those who travel between winter pastures and summer pastures" and "those who do not stay in one place." The 1986 national census indicates that of Iran's total population of 49.5 million, 251,000 were nomads, which the census defines as those having a tribal social organization (*qabileh'i*), a primary reliance on animal husbandry (*damdari*), and a pastoral (*shabani*) or nomadic (*kuch*) lifestyle. The 1996 national census lists 211,000 nomads in Iran out of a total population of 60 million. The 2006 census lists 105,000 nomads out of a total population of 70.5 million. The three figures for nomads are low because of political and other factors. The census takers used varying definitions of "nomads" and "unsettled" people. They did not count mobile people if they lacked access to them, and many nomads were mobile for only part of the year and spent the rest of the time in villages and towns. The 1996 census, which lists only thirteen nomads in the district of Semirom, reflects these problems. A more accurate figure might be in the tens of thousands during the spring and summer.

Officials sometimes used the phrase "tent dwellers" (*chador neshin*) but understood that it did not necessarily apply to nomads who lived in other kinds of dwellings. They held implicit and sometimes explicit notions about livestock production being the nomads' primary livelihood, which complicated matters. When nomads also engaged in agriculture, especially if they did so extensively, officials sometimes reclassified them as "agriculturalists" or "villagers." In this case, people could lose their official status as "nomads," which might have offered them special benefits from the state. By the 1990s many nomadic pastoralists in Iran also practiced agriculture and possessed permanent dwellings (often for only seasonal residence), and so any limiting definitions became increasingly problematic. Officials deployed these and other often-ambiguous terms differently, according to context. They classified some Qashqa'i schoolteachers in towns, for example, as "nomads" if they traveled seasonally between winter and summer pastures (which many of them did) and if their close paternal kin were still nomadic pastoralists. Officials and the people themselves sometimes used the term "*ashayer*" to refer to a person's descent, meaning an individual who descended from nomads regardless of his or her current occupation, place of residence, or lifestyle. They sometimes termed still-migratory people as *ashayer-e sayyar* (mobile nomads) as compared to those who were not mobile (*ashayer-e sabet*).

Tribal, ethnic, and linguistic terms and identities related to these other terms and posed additional complications. Officials and others sometimes used the phrase "*ilat va ashayer*" (tribes and nomads) to indicate that tribal people were often mobile. Many officials during the 1980s considered the term "tribe" (*il, tayefeh*) to be a political reference and avoided it in their formal duties. They viewed tribes as polities that had opposed the central government in the past and might do so again. Terms such as Turk, Kurd, Baluch, and Arab—usually referring to ethnic and ethnolinguistic traits—also meant "nomad" in different parts of Iran. Names of languages such as Turkish, Kurdish, Baluchi, and Arabic also conveyed sociocultural and sometimes political information about the speakers. Many of Iran's nomads were parts of ethnic and national minority groups, and officials used their labels (such as Kurd and Baluch) for them. (Half of Iran's population in the twentieth century consisted of Persians; the other half comprised Turks, Kurds, Lurs, Arabs, Baluch, and others.)

During and after the insurgency (more accurately, the "defensive resistance") of the paramount Qashqa'i khans in 1980–1982, state officials were especially cautious about the term "tribe." They worried that this and other tribal groups would pose further military and political threats to the new state. Also wanting to avoid the label "Qashqa'i" for the same kinds of political reasons, officials of Mohammad Reza Shah as well as the Islamic Republic instead deployed the nonspecific phrases "*ashayer-e Fars*" (the province), "*ashayer-e junub*" (the south), and "*ashayer-e Bushire*" (the area near the Persian Gulf port of this name). Noting these euphemisms, the Qashqa'i created their own joking, self-mocking ones in response (such as "*ashayer-e biaban*," nomads of the wilderness).

Officials who categorized tribal people without explicitly referring to their tribes (their named sociopolitical groups) created confusing distinctions, such as "nomadic nomads" (*ashayer-e kuchandeh*) and "settled nomads" (*ashayer-e sakin*). They often used the Persian word "nomad" as a misleading substitution for "tribe." Some officials deployed the phrase "livestock farmers" (*dam keshavarzi*) to attempt to bypass these semantic obfuscations and to veer away from any implied association between nomads and tribes.

Especially in the 1980s, some governmental officials did occasionally apply the term "nomad" approvingly, as part of a different kind of political reference. *Ashayer-e mahrum* and *ashayer-e mazlum* were nomads who had suffered under Mohammad Reza Shah's socioeconomic and political oppressions (respectively). Officials of the new regime aimed to bring restorative state services to these "deprived" people, and many nomads benefited from this form of political labeling. The Ayatollah Khomeini had characterized the tribes of Iran as the "treasures of the revolution" (*zakha'er-e enqelab*) and included them as one of four essential military forces that defended the country against external and internal threats. He ordinarily used the term "*ashayer*" to praise these political entities; his English translators often rendered the word as "tribe." Nomads were mobile for ecological and economic reasons and were not military forces per se, in the way that tribally organized men could be.

By the early 1990s, when further "tribal revolt" seemed unlikely in many parts of Iran, officials worried less about employing the terms "tribe" and "tribal." They had not yet devised more accurate ways of categorizing the people to whom these terms applied. By the mid-1990s, many officials routinely referred to the nomads' tribal organizations and deployed these named sociopolitical entities (such as Sanjabi and Afshar) in their administrative tasks. By doing so, they reaffirmed these structures for the people and the state and facilitated their survival. (These names also conveyed information about the groups' cultural systems.) Through 2007, some authorities still remained cautious about using certain labels (such as Kurd and Arab) because of their still-current political connotations (especially regarding periodic outbreaks of "ethnic" unrest in Kurdistan and Khuzistan since 1979), and they avoided them when possible. Others tried to restrict the meaning of all these terms to what they perceived as nonpolitical cultural traits, such as goat-hair tents and colorful weavings, especially if these objects attracted positive international attention and softened the harsh, forbidding image that Iran held globally.

The scholarly literature on Iran is replete with confusion regarding terminology, despite decades of clarifications by anthropologists. References therein to "nomads," "tribes," and "pastoralists" especially (but also to "ethnic groups," "minority groups," and "nationalities") may not accurately depict the people under discussion. Some of these words depict political processes while others refer only to livelihoods or patterns of movement. Scholars and others frequently err when they equate nomads with tribal people and with pastoralists. Nomads are not necessarily tribally organized or practitioners of pastoralism, and tribally affiliated people are not necessarily mobile.

After the revolution, local and regional offices of the ONA determined people's status as "nomads" and their rights to obtain beneficial state services because of this classification. Such services included state-subsidized commodities (such as wheat flour and cooking oil), economic cooperatives, roads, wells, water reservoirs, mobile tankers, irrigation works, pastoral and agricultural aid, veterinary assistance, bathhouses, and low-interest bank loans for improvements in livelihoods and lifestyles. The new Ministry of Rural Reconstruction also provided similar, sometimes overlapping, services to nomads (and other rural people). The ONA assisted individuals in building houses and helped small nomadic groups to establish new settlements (which the agency labeled *shahrak*s).

The director of the ONA office in Semirom argued in 1991 with a Qashqa'i man whose official documents displayed stamps from ONA indicating that he was a nomad and stamps from the Ministry of Rural Reconstruction indicating that he was a settled villager. The petitioner was apparently trying to register at both offices in order to obtain duplicate coupons (used for government-subsidized goods) for a newborn child. Skeptical about the man's nomad status, the official queried him, "Are you *ashayer*? Where are your winter pastures? Do you migrate?" In the end, unhappy about the man's equivocal responses, he nevertheless stamped the man's papers. When a Qashqa'i woman visited Shiraz's ONA office in 1999 to register as a nomad, she told the clerk there that she needed to cancel her legal status as a "town dweller" (*shahri*). Laughing, the man noted that he had never encountered such a request. Rather, he said, people always sought to change from "*ashayer*" to "*shahri*" or "*rusta*" (villager), in part because of the elevated status these latter two terms conveyed.

The ONA established national headquarters in Tehran. In 1991 twenty-two regional headquarters operated efficiently (according to many local sources) throughout Iran wherever nomads were concentrated. Shiraz's ONA office, for example, was the operational center for many dispersed ONA facilities in Fars province and the periphery. Directors of all these offices were tribally affiliated men of nomadic pastoral backgrounds. Many of them originated from the same nomadic groups they now served.

The new Ministry of Islamic Guidance (*ershad Islami*) assigned young clergymen, often current students in theological seminaries, to each of the national and provincial-capital offices of the ONA. In most if not all cases, these men too originated from and identified with the nomads, pastoralists, tribes, and ethnic groups that their facilities served. The cleric assigned to the Tehran headquarters in 1991 was the son of nomadic pastoralists and a member of the Darrehshuri tribe. He was also one of the first Qashqa'i to study theology in a seminary after the revolution, and he was a wounded war veteran (thereby fulfilling crucial criteria for obtaining an influential governmental job).

Since 1979 the nomads of Iran have undergone many changes. Many men and some women of nomadic, pastoral, tribal, and ethnic-minority backgrounds have become officials and employees of governmental agencies. This shift was perhaps the most significant one in the links between the nomads and the state after the revolution. Many employees were members of the same subtribes, tribes, and confederacies of the people under their jurisdiction or were parts of comparable entities. They were more compatible with the individuals they served than Mohammad Reza Shah's agents had been and were less likely to be corrupt.

Before the revolution, the state agents with whom nomads had interacted were almost always urban Persian men who were hostile toward and discriminated against "backward" nomadic and other rural, tribal, and ethnic-minority peoples, especially if they perceived them as potential threats to themselves and the state they served. In contrast, most state agents visiting nomadic and some other rural communities from 1979 through 2007 were tribally affiliated men and women. They conducted their business professionally, avoided situations that provoked exaggerated ritual politeness (ta'arof), and departed at the conclusion of their tasks without waiting for or demanding personal payments. Bribery of state officials and other agents had been rampant during the shah's regime. After the revolution, bribery decreased dramatically, at least for many nomads. New notions about the government's obligations, especially to those parts of Iranian society that the shah and his regime had oppressed and impoverished, inspired some agents. Some held idealistic sentiments about revolutionary Islam, whose faithful could improve the lives of the people they served. Bribery did increase in other sectors of Iranian society, especially cities. Bureaucratic confusion, rapid inflation, economic instability, and the fixed salaries of agents (as well as the hostility of some of them toward the new government) led to rising corruption.

In the early 1980s, ONA encouraged local communities of nomads to establish Islamic councils (shuras), which would operate in the place of tribal headmen (kadkhudas; an office the Islamic Republic had essentially ended). Territorially based communities elected three or five members to each council, which helped people to secure official documents, settle local disputes, and contact governmental agencies. Most council electees were young men and women; some older men were the former tribal headmen.

As during the decades of the Pahlavi shahs, many nomads experienced a dilemma after the revolution. If they sought beneficial governmental services, they would fall under increasing state surveillance and control. If they maintained some political autonomy, they might have to forfeit some of the state's economic and social services. Many individuals strategized to strike a balance while also coping with an unstable, unpredictable political environment. During the troubled times of the revolution, its disruptive aftermath, and the Iraq–Iran war (1980–1988), many nomads were particularly uncertain about their responses to the choices confronting them. By 1991 the government stabilized to some degree, and people grew more confident in their decisions. Moderating state policies in the mid-1990s, followed by Mohammad Khatami's election as president in 1997 and reelection in 2001, furthered people's trust until they saw that the political, economic, and social reforms they desired were unlikely to occur. The election of the conservative, Mahmud Ahmedinejod, as president in 2005 dashed their hopes. His pursuit of nuclear proliferation, combined with his provocation of Western powers, directed his attention and that of his supporters away from Iran's serious internal problems.

Although Iran's nomads demonstrated different economic and social patterns since the revolution, in part because of their varying habitats, they also showed some marked similarities. They were more integrated in the nation-state than they had been in the past, and their livelihoods and lifestyles represented the many accommodations they had made. Their feelings of loyalty to their local communities and their tribal and ethnic groups grew, in part because of the low level of their assimilation in the Iranian state and society. Still suffering economic and social discrimination at the hands of the settled Persian-speaking majority, they found solace and support in their own kinship, tribal, and ethnic groups.

Many nomads no longer relied as heavily on livestock production as before. Their economies diversified as they adopted or expanded agricultural production and relied increasingly on sources of cash income. Many nomadic families chose similar strategies, such as dividing customary and new responsibilities among their members. A man in one family, for example, tended the livestock and migrated with them according to the season and the availability of vegetation and water. His brother performed agricultural tasks in winter and summer zones, thereby furthering the family's patterns of mobility. A third brother secured a job as a wage or salaried worker, perhaps in construction or a state office, while a fourth one handled governmental bureaucracy, market transactions, and intratribal ties. The family increasingly directed its children toward formal education and the new economic opportunities it promised. Ties to the land on which the family depended for seasonal pastoralism and agriculture provided the incentive to maintain control over it, repel encroachers, and secure the government's legal deeds. These territories also held social and symbolic importance, and the family's interest in remaining there enhanced the strength of its kinship, tribal, and ethnic bonds.

New patterns of residence and mobility emerged when nomads diversified their economies. Many nomads built permanent dwellings (however rudimentary) in one or more of their seasonal zones and were less likely to move from place to place within each zone, as they had done while residing in tents or other non-permanent structures. The herders continued these customary patterns of movement for the livestock's benefit, while the home base remained more fixed in location than before. Nomads also sought residences in villages, towns, and cities, depending on their interests there, but often for only part of the year. The importance of formal education, especially beyond the elementary level, meant that families needed to live where schools were located. They maintained their economic and social interests in their tribal and ethnic territories and frequently visited there, despite the distance they would need to travel from their new places of residence.

For centuries, the nomadic women of Iran had earned a reputation for being independent and assertive, a situation facilitated by their mobility, their small kin-based communities in remote and isolated locales, and their vital participation in household and other economic tasks. Toward the end of the twentieth century, women in some nomadic groups expanded their educational and economic opportunities (such as producing textiles and other handicrafts for market sale) and enhanced their personal freedoms. In other groups they felt obligated to adopt the more restrictive patterns of social movement and interaction that they experienced in their new communities of residence.

See also Qashqa'i; and Tribes.

Suggested Reading

Beck, L. 1991. *Nomad: a year in the life of a Qashqa'i tribesman in Iran*. Berkeley: University of California Press.

Huang, J. 2008. *Tribeswomen of Iran: weaving memories among Qashqa'i nomads*. London: I. B. Tauris.

Salzman, P. C. 2000. *Black tents of Baluchistan*. Washington D.C.: Smithsonian Institution Press.

Tapper, R. 1979. *Pasture and politics: economics, conflict and ritual among Shahsevan nomads of northwestern Iran*. London: Academic Press.

Tapper, R., and J. Thompson, eds. 2002. *The nomadic peoples of Iran*. London: Azimuth.

Towfiq, F. 1987. Ashayer. *Encyclopaedia Iranica*, London: Routledge & Kegan Paul. 2:707–724.

LOIS BECK and JULIA HUANG

✦ NUCLEAR PROGRAM

Iran's nuclear program was launched in 1957 when the United States and Iran signed a civil nuclear cooperation accord as part of the U.S. Atoms for Peace Program Under President Eisenhower. In 1960, Iran established a 5-megawatt (MW) research center at Tehran University. In his visit to the United States in 1964, the Shah laid out Iran's ambitious plan for nuclear power. Tehran's Nuclear Research Center became operational in 1967, when the United States supplied limited enriched uranium to Iran for fuel in a research reactor. In the following year, Iran signed the Nuclear Non-Proliferation Treaty (NPT) and ratified it in 1970.

In 1974, Iran signed several agreements to purchase two 1200-MW pressurized water reactors from the German firm Kraftwerk Union to be installed at Bushehr and two 900-MW reactors from Framatome of France to be installed at Bandar-e Abbas. At the same time, the United States under President Gerald Ford pledged to assist Iran in operating a U.S.-built reprocessing facility for extracting plutonium from nuclear reactor fuel, a process that entailed a complete nuclear fuel cycle. Under such conditions, Iran benefited from the competition between U.S. and European nuclear energy companies—especially German and French firms—to assist it in launching its nuclear program.

After the 1979 Islamic Revolution, Iran and the International Atomic Energy Agency (IAEA) agreed to cooperate in the fields of nuclear reactor technology and fuel cycle technology. The IAEA, however, was forced to terminate the

Golamreza Aghazadeh, head of the Atomic Energy Organization of Iran, during a press conference in Tehran, 2003. (AP Photo/Hasan Sarbakhshian)

program under U.S. pressure. Before the revolution, Iran had contracts with Germany, France, and the United States, for a total of six nuclear power reactors and agreements to receive low-enriched uranium and nuclear training. After the revolution, Western countries cancelled these nuclear agreements. The Bushehr reactors, which were not fully operative, were damaged by several Iraqi air strikes during the 1980–1988 war with Iraq. At the end of the war with Iraq, Iran turned to Russia to finish up the Bushehr projects. In 1995, Iran and Russia signed a contract to that end. Similarly, the U.S. sanctions on Iran failed to prevent China from providing Tehran with a conversion plan and gas needed to test the uranium enrichment process.

By 2000, Iranian officials revealed the existence of two nuclear sites under construction in Natanz and Arak. Under the IAEA rules, Iran had no obligation to report the existence of these sites while they were still under construction. Iran's nuclear facilities are located in Anarak, Arak, Ardekan, Bushehr, Chalus, Darkhovin, Esfahan, Karaj/Karai/Hashtgerd, Kolahdouz, Lashkar Abad, Lavizan, Meysami, Natanz, Parchin, Sagend, Qatran, Tabas, and Tehran.

The IAEA reported in late 2003 that it had found no evidence that Iran had engaged in diverting of fissile material for military use. The IAEA deferred a final decision on Iranian nuclear status pending further European diplomatic negotiations with Iran. With Iranians insisting on their right to enrich uranium and Europeans convinced that Iran should forgo this process, diplomatic contacts produced no mutually-agreed results. With the failure of the EU-3 (Great Britain, Germany, and France) diplomatic initiatives, the United Nations Security Council demanded Iran suspend its enrichment and reprocessing-related activities. Having secured no concessions from Iran, the United Nations threatened to put further sanctions on Iran. Two rounds of U.N. sanctions were subsequently imposed on Iran during 2006–2007, with increasing unwillingness on the part of China, Russia, and the EU to push Iran beyond these sanctions by imposing more intrusive sanctions. Russia's reluctance to impose further sanctions on Iran served to underline Moscow's independence from the United States. Meanwhile, the IAEA's head, Mohamed El Baradei, stated on numerous occasions that he had seen "no evidence" of Iran developing nuclear weapons.

Finally, the prospects for a military confrontation with Iran and placing further sanctions on the country receded with the release of the National Intelligence Estimate (NIE) report in the United States in December 2007. The report, which was composed by sixteen U.S. intelligence agencies, emphatically concluded that Iran had stopped the military component of its nuclear program in 2003. This revelation exposed the extent to which Iranian threat had been exaggerated. It has since become evident that the U.S. diplomatic attempts to isolate Iran have also failed. The EU, Russia, and

China resumed trade and commercial ties with Iran. Russia, for example, continued its efforts to help construct the Bushehr nuclear facility and, after the release of NIE report, transferred nuclear fuel to this plant. Likewise, many Persian Gulf countries, such as Saudi Arabia, moved away from the U.S. policy of isolating Iran and have attempted to forge a more cordial relation with their neighbor. Since the NIE report on Iran, U.S. policymakers have found it difficult to convince all regional players (with the noticeable exception of Israel) that Iran still constitutes a nuclear threat. The NIE revelations are likely to have some ramifications for the U.S. containment policy toward Iran, as the political situation appears to have never been more propitious for a diplomatic breakthrough of sorts between the two nations.

The Nuclear Dispute

Looking back at the nuclear dispute, several questions appeared to have shaped the political debate over Iran's nuclear program: were Iran's nuclear ambitions economic/energy related, or were they strategic and security related? What were the possibilities, and what were the likelihoods? With conservative forces in control of the Iranian parliament (*Majles*) and presidency, Iran's leaders seemed to have equated promoting nuclear program with the country's national security. After a long period of negotiation with the EU-3, Iran chose to resume enriching uranium in 2005 when president Ahmadinejad ascended to power. Since then, for all practical purposes and intents, the EU-3 negotiations were forestalled.

The Iranian government claimed that it had suspended its activities on a voluntary basis and that it had a legal right to develop its nuclear program for peaceful purposes according to Article 4 of the NPT. This article stipulates that member states pledge not to seek a weapons capability and that they are entitled to acquire the means of generating nuclear power for civilian purposes. The NPT contains ambiguous language, however. It, for example, does not guarantee signatories the "right" to enrich uranium. It only supports "the benefit of nuclear technology" for peaceful purposes.

In addition to justifying Iran's nuclear program on legal grounds, Iranian officials pointed to pure and simple economics, arguing that while Iran's GDP was likely to grow by 6% in the following year, its young population's demand for energy consumption was projected to grow at 7% annually. Iran's capacity, experts note, must nearly triple over the next 15 years to meet projected demand. At the same time, Iran's daily consumption of 1.5 million barrels of oil per day means the country loses $75 million a day. More to the point, Iran had argued that with diminishing water resources, the use of hydroelectric technology as means to generate power had become less viable. Nuclear energy, Iranian officials have insisted—and continue to emphasize today—seems to be the most economically viable method of energy production, hence Iran's plan to generate 7,000 MW of nuclear power by 2020 through the construction of 20 nuclear power plants.

Many observers argued that Iran had lost its flexibility to negotiate a way out of its nuclear ambitions simply because conservatives at the time controlled the three branches of government and presented a coherent position never seen during the factionalism of the Khatami era. Others argued that the issue of the fuel cycle was not an absolute position but that it was open to bargaining. Iranians were bargaining to get a better deal and in the end they would turn out to be flexible and accommodating. Still others argued that, according to a major U.S. intelligence review, Iran was about a decade away from manufacturing the key ingredient for a nuclear weapon. Thus, the threat of Iran's nuclear program was overstated.

Compounding the picture was the fact that the IAEA had been caught in the middle of this controversy, unable either to issue Tehran a clean bill of health or to confirm the suspicions of the United States and the EU. With the rise of oil prices and its implications for the European economies, Europeans were reluctant—their rhetoric notwithstanding—to press for further UN sanctions against Iran and potentially deprive the international market of the 3.5 million barrels of oil a day produced by the Iranian oil industry, thus further escalating the price of oil.

Regional and global political considerations had compelled the Europeans to resolve this matter peacefully and avoid further diplomatic tension with the United States over Iran, and possibly another U.S. military incursion in the region. Unlike the situation before the war in Iraq, the Europeans had placed their multilateral diplomacy in high gear by going to Tehran and keeping matters from reaching the U.N. Security Council. Meanwhile, the U.S. occupation of Iraq and its policy blunders had, at least on the surface, emboldened Iranian intransigence. The George W. Bush administration's core message that it would not tolerate Iran's growing ability to develop a nuclear weapon fell by the wayside, given that U.S. troops were heavily engaged in Iraq and Afghanistan. Meanwhile, U.S. and Israeli claims that Iran was assembling an atomic bomb remained unproven. For its part, Iran had signed an additional protocol on December 18, 2003, which gave IAEA inspectors access to suspected nuclear research sites.

"REGIME CHANGE" OR SANCTIONS

The talk of "regime change" via the military option was seen as counterproductive in Tehran, even as a genuine political settlement was not in sight.

In the first place, the threat of regime change was not practical given the country's vast terrain and Iranians' nationalistic sentiments. An Osiraq-style attack, which happened in 1981 against Iraq, stood little chance of success in a huge country like Iran that had dispersed its nuclear power plants across the country. If utilized, this option would have undermined any confidence-building measure in the process of securing an eventual compromise. The fact remained that national policy regarding the nuclear program rested with Iran's Supreme leader, whose decision reflected a view shared by many different players—military and otherwise. Ironically, the U.S. presence in the region had enhanced Iran's sense of urgency for acquiring some form of strategic deterrence.

Second, Iran became the target of the U.S. mainstream media who refused to provide compelling reasons as to why Iran posed a real menace. The George W. Bush administration supported a media propaganda campaign aimed at vilifying Iran under the assumption that Iran was trying to become a nuclear power. The option of imposing economic sanctions on Iran was also risky, in part because not everyone was willing to participate in enforcing them and partly because they would have deprived international markets of less than 4 million barrels of oil per day. Moreover, sanctions, as some experts rightly observed, would only hold back in the short run a nuclear assembly line, should Iran's clerical rulers decide to proceed with their presumed desire to obtain nuclear capability. Iranian officials had raised the question all along concerning why other nuclear equipped countries are not subject to such sanction threats. They have said that they would withdraw from the NPT if faced with military and economic threats.

Withdrawal from the NPT remains, however, unlikely, and such withdrawal would prove to be too costly for a country where industrial infrastructure continues to be heavily dependent on production machinery and spare parts from EU countries. Sanctions would hurt Iran's booming trade with the United Arab Emirates (UAE) totaling $8 billion a year. There were nearly 4500 Iranian companies that had invested in the UAE. Thus, the possibility of trade sanctions can arguably be a strong deterrent—more than a reasonable risk for the Iranian government to take.

IRAN'S FUTURE POLICY CHOICES

At a time when almost 30% of the Iranian population lives below the poverty line, the inflation rate is exceeding 16%, and there are more than 7 million unemployed, Iran needs trade and development more than ever before. Mishandling this challenge could have colossal risks and consequences. Some Iranians may embrace the notion that nuclear weapons will afford Iran a modicum of security cover in a neighborhood where it is hard to play and predict political games and dangerous outcomes. But it is important to bear in mind that signing the Additional Protocol to the NPT has led to an international assurance on the part of the majority in the global community that Iran's nuclear program is peaceful.

The failure to reach an agreement with the Europeans placed Iran's European allies in a very awkward position, making it extremely difficult for them to support its security and economic needs. The proliferation of nuclear arms in the region will widen and deepen U.S. involvement there as a step toward efforts to contain the further spread of such weapons. Europeans will certainly regard this development as a scary forecast. France, for example, has made it abundantly clear to Iranian officials: it will not stand up to the United States if Iran–U.S. disagreements were to reach a confrontational stage.

While Europeans had reassured Iran that sanctions on technical assistance on matters relating to Iran's peaceful nuclear program would be lifted in due course, the George W. Bush administration faced a fundamental dilemma: how to deal with a country that it has labeled as part of an "axis of evil"—and driven by domestic concerns that see it as the major threat to Israel—and how to justify Iran's civilian nuclear programs and subsequently find a way to open a dialogue with Iran. The EU diplomatic proposals did not resolve the current squabble between Iran and the United States, but they have defused the tension between the two for a while. Meanwhile, the Europeans continued to argue that trade deals and technical assistance could have a moderating influence on Iran. Economic necessities and pressures for rebuilding the country, as experts say, will eventually compel Iran to engage with the West rather than pursuing confrontation. According to Europeans, multilateral diplomacy and dialogue are the most reasonable way of resolving such tensions.

The U.S. military debacle in Iraq at the same time had awakened some policymakers in the George W. Bush administration to the fact that a military confrontation with Iran would induce questionable and unintended negative consequences at best and a perilous outcome at worst, especially at a time when the United States was largely preoccupied with reconstructing Iraq and Afghanistan. The assassination of Benazir Bhutto in the late December of 2007 fueled the speculation that further instability awaited the region at large. Pakistan—a nuclear power with an army that had close ties with the Taliban regime in Afghanistan—took the center stage. Hence, unlike the prevailing assumption, U.S. military involvement in Pakistan could not be entirely ruled out in the coming years.

Under such circumstances, Iran's part in playing a positive role in stabilizing U.S. efforts in war-torn Iraq, Afghanistan, and Pakistan would dramatically increase. If Iran's true intentions are attaining energy security for the long term, then the standoff with the United States and the EU would be subject to negotiations. Iran will most likely reach a mutual accommodation that will allow it to develop nuclear energy locally in a way that satisfies all parties. If, however, Iranian ambitions truly *are* also military in nature, the nuclear dispute bodes ill for a reasonable accommodation with the West over the long haul.

Suggested Reading
Ansari, A. M. 2006. *Confronting Iran: the failure of American foreign policy and the next great crisis in the Middle East*. New York: Basic Books.
Chubin, S. 2006. *Iran's nuclear ambitions*. Washington, D.C.: Carnegie Endowment for International Peace.
Cordesman, A. H. 2006. *Iran's developing military capabilities*, Washington, D.C.: Center for Strategic and International Studies.
De Bellaigue, C. 2005. Iran. *Foreign Policy*. 148:18–24.
Diehl, S. J., and J. C. Moltz. 2002. *Nuclear weapons and nonproliferation: a reference handbook*. Santa Barbara, Calif: ABC-CLIO.
Ehsani, K., and C. Toensing 2004. Neo-conservatives, hard line clerics and the bomb. *Middle East Report*. 233:10–15.
Javedanfar, M. 2005. Difficult customers. *Iranian.com*.
Kinzer, S. 2006. Diplomacy is the best option for American–Iranian relations. In *Is Iran a threat to global security?*, ed. J. Bauder. New York: Green Haven Press: 46–57.
Linzer, D. 2005. Iran is judged 19 years from nuclear bomb. *Washington Post*. August 2.
Lynch, M. 2008. Why U.S. strategy on Iran is crumbling. *The Christian Science Monitor*. p 9.
Monshipouri, M. 2006. Iran's nuclear program: what does the current impasse mean? *Muslim Public Affairs Journal*. pp 9–13.

MAHMOOD MONSHIPOURI

O

✦ OPPOSITION GROUPS

Opposition groups to the Islamic Republic may be divided into six categories: (1) democratic republicans; (2) monarchists; (3) the People's Mojahedin Organization of Iran; (4) communists; (5) ethnic parties; and (6) loyal opposition.

DEMOCRATIC REPUBLICANS

The democratic republican groups want to replace the system of clerical rule (*Nezam Velayat Faqih*) with sovereignty of the people, i.e., democracy. They advocate civil liberties, pluralist democracy, rule of law, separation of religion and the state, a republican form of government, and free and fair elections. They are divided into the following subcategories: established democrats; young democrats; former Marxists; former fundamentalists; individual democrats; and civil society organizations.

The established democrats trace their roots to the 1905 Constitutional Revolution and the 1950s oil nationalization movement under Mossadeq. The most prominent include the Iran National Front (Jebhe Melli Iran) and the Iran Nation Party (Hezb Mellat Iran). The oldest, and arguably the largest, pro-democracy group operating inside Iran is the Iran National Front (INF), which also operates abroad. The INF was founded in 1949 and led by Dr. Mossadeq as Prime Minister between April 1951 and August 1953, when a CIA-engineered coup overthrew his cabinet. After the 1979 revolution, about one-third of cabinet posts, including Foreign Minister, Defense Minister, Labor Minister, and Minister of Treasury, were held by the INF members.

In July 1981, INF was declared apostate by Khomeini and consequently was severely repressed. Between 1997 and 2005, the regime reduced repression against the activities of the INF, although officially the INF remained illegal and under constant surveillance, harassment, and intimidation. The INF advocates a gradual step-by-step transition from the incumbent clerical dictatorship to democracy. Issuing communiques and pronouncements have become the hallmark of the INF. Members of the INF are secular liberal democrats and secular social democrats. They also tend to be nationalist.

The Iran Nation Party (INP) was one of the founding organizations of the INF in 1949. The INP split from the INF in 1979 and was led by Dariush Forouhar until he was murdered by agents of the Ministry of Intelligence in November 1998. Since the murder of Forouhar, Khosrow Seif has been the leader of INP. The INP is a nationalist party. Initially, INP was not a democratic party, but under the influence of Mossadeq's ideas it embraced democracy.

The second subcategory encompasses young democrats who are in their twenties and thirties. Among the more well-known individuals in this category are Manuchehr Mohammadi, the late Akbar Mohammadi (who died in prison in July 2006 after enduring a combination of severe torture, hunger strike, and lack of medical attention), and Ahmad Batebi. Impatient with the gradualism and cautiousness of the INF leadership, the young democrats tend to support actions such as civil disobedience and rallies instead of merely issuing endless communiques. Compared with the established democrats, the young democrats tend to be more action-oriented, more hostile to the regime, less hostile to monarchists, and friendlier toward the United States.

The pro-democracy student uprising of July 1999 was organized by this group. They have embraced Mossadeq as the symbol of their desire for a secular democratic republic. Several student organizations have grown inside Iran, but by and large, due to repression, they have not been able to arrange themselves into strong organizations.

The third subcategory includes former Marxists living in exile who have embraced democracy in the past few years. Many former Marxists have helped establish coalitions such as the United Republicans of Iran (Ettehad Jomhurikhahan Iran) and the Democratic and Secular Republicans of Iran (Jomhurikhahan Democrat va Laic). Although these two organizations are not exclusively made up of former Marxists, substantial numbers of them are.

The fourth subcategory includes former fundamentalists who have embraced democracy in the past few years. The most famous and articulate include Akbar Ganji, Mohsen Sazegara, and Ali Afshari. They have not formed any organization yet. Some in the opposition believe that the conversion to democracy by many in this category may not be genuine.

There are a large number of individuals and intellectuals, both inside Iran and abroad, who are not members of any organization but are democratic republicans. They usually sign open letters and petitions on various issues such as human rights violations.

There are also civil society organizations, both inside and outside Iran, such as human rights organizations, labor syndicates, and women's groups that may be classified as democratic republicans.

MONARCHISTS

Iranian monarchists support the Pahlavi dynasty and want to restore Reza Pahlavi, the son of Mohammad Reza Shah Pahlavi, to the throne. Monarchists are divided into constitutional monarchists and absolute monarchists. Both subcategories condemn the 1979 revolution. The constitutional monarchists state that they want to have freely elected parliamentary democracy with Reza Pahlavi as a constitutional monarch. The Constitutional Party of Iran, the Constitutional Party of Iran-Front Line, and Derafsh Kaviani are the main proponents of this position. Reza Pahlavi himself has repeatedly stated that he embraces this position. The absolutist monarchists support the reestablishment of dictatorship. This group includes the Rastakhiz Party.

Many in the opposition do not believe the claims of Reza Pahlavi and other constitutionalist monarchists that they respect democracy and civil liberties. They point to the fact that the two Pahlavi kings and Khomeini made similar claims when they were out of power, whereas they established dictatorships and brutally crushed opposition groups as soon as they could.

PEOPLE'S MOJAHEDIN ORGANIZATION OF IRAN

The People's Mojahedin Organization of Iran (PMOI), also known as the MKO (Mojahedin Khalq Organization) or MEK (Mojahedin e Khalq), or NCRI (National Council of Resistance of Iran), is led by Masoud Rajavi and his wife, Maryam Azadanlou-Rajavi. The PMOI was established in 1965, as the result of a split from Liberation Movement of Iran, which itself had split from the INF in 1961. The PMOI's ideology, "Classless Divine Society," combined a Maoist socioeconomic and political system with an egalitarian interpretation of Islam. In 1972, Masoud Rajavi described the PMOI's notion of freedom as that existing at that time in the USSR and China. According to the U.S. State Department and many other sources, the PMOI assassinated several Americans in Iran in the early 1970s, although in the 1980s, the PMOI denied this, to gain U.S. support for its struggle against the fundamentalist regime.

The PMOI has been, and remains, highly disciplined and incredibly well-organized. From 1979 to 1982, the PMOI grew into a large mass-based movement. In June 1981, the PMOI called for an armed struggle against the regime after Khomeini's removal of President Bani Sadr. The armed uprising failed to topple the regime, and Rajavi and Bani Sadr went into exile in France. In 1986, the PMOI's headquarters moved to Iraq. Thereafter, the organization became closely allied with Saddam Hussein. The PMOI has carried out successful assassinations of the regime's military, intelligence, and political officials, as well as numerous mortar attacks on the regime's military targets.

Since the mid-1990s, the U.S. State Department, the British government, and the EU have labeled the PMOI a terrorist organization. The PMOI has been lobbying and litigating to have the terrorism label removed. About 4,000 PMOI fighters in Iraq were disarmed by American forces after the invasion of Iraq and remain under American protection in their camp.

COMMUNIST GROUPS

Iranian communists are dispersed among more than two dozen organizations. The largest communist organization from 1980 to 1991, the Organization of Iranian People's Fedaian (Majority), has since ceased to be communist. Smaller groups remain committed to Marxism–Leninism. Today the most active communist groups are the Workers Communist Party and the Union of People's Fedaian of Iran.

ETHNIC PARTIES

Many ethnic communities in Iran feel oppressed by the regime. They include Azerbaijanis, Kurds, Balochis, Arabs, and Turkomen. The regime's *de jure* and *de facto* discriminations against Sunnis (i.e., all Balochis and Turkomen, and about half of Kurds and Arabs), which have gone so far as to destroy Sunni mosques in Mashhad and prevent the construction of even a single Sunni mosque in Tehran, have made these minorities especially enraged with the regime. Recent years have witnessed increased violence in Balochistan, Khuzestan, Kurdistan, Kermanshahan, and in Azerbaijan provinces.

The oldest and most powerful ethnic party in Iran is the Democratic Party of Iranian Kurdistan (DPIK). The DPIK was a typical pro-Moscow communist party before the 1979 revolution. However, under the able leadership of Dr. Abdo-Rahman Qassemlou, the DPIK established its independence from Moscow, embraced democratic socialism, and became affiliated with the social democratic organization "Socialist International." It also moved away from separatist demands and called for autonomy within a federal Iran. The agents of the Iranian government assassinated Dr. Qassemlou and two of his lieutenants in Vienna on July 13, 1989. His successor, Dr. Sadeq Sharafkandi, his two lieutenants, and another democratic socialist Iranian were assassinated in

Berlin on September 17, 1992 by agents of the Iranian government (and three members of the Lebanese Hezbollah). The leadership and cadres of DPIK operate both inside Iran as well as in the Iraqi Kurdistan.

The second most powerful ethnic party is the Komala. This party used to be a radical Marxist–Leninist party, but it moved away from communism several years ago. It engages in armed conflict with the regime's coercive apparatuses the in Iranian Kurdish region.

In 2006, a small Kurdish group, PJAK, surfaced, which has been allied with the PKK, the radical militant Kurdish party in Turkey. The regime's elite Islamic Revolutionary Guards Corps has exchanged fire with PJAK on numerous occasions.

Several Baloch groups compete both amongst themselves and the central government. The Balochistan United Front of Iran (Republican Federal), Balochistan Peoples Party, and Balochistan National Movement-Iran support a republican federal system. One group, led by Amanoullah Khan Riggi, has been accused by other Baloch groups of being monarchist. The Jondollah Organization of Iran has carried out numerous military operations against the regime in recent times. The regime accused it of being allied with al Qaeda, but the group immediately denied and condemned the accusation and stated that it supports a democratic, federal, and secular system in Iran.

LOYAL OPPOSITION

The Iran Liberation Movement (Nehzat Azadi Iran) and the Nationalist-Religious Alliance (Melli-Mazhabi) have been hoping to be accepted as the loyal opposition to the regime. Both have supported the constitution. Their ideology is an attempt to wed liberalism with Islam. In December 2006, both groups joined a coalition of reformist factions of the regime.

Suggested Reading
Abrahamian, E. 1989. *The Iranian Mojahedin*. New Haven, Conn: Yale University Press.
Bradley, J. R. 2006–2007. Iran's ethnic tinderbox. *The Washington Quarterly*. Vol. 30, No. 1.
Ganji, A. 2002 and 2005. *Manifest Jomhurikhahi* [Republican Manifesto], Two volumes. Tehran: no publisher.
Kazemzadeh, M. 2002. *Islamic fundamentalism, feminism, and gender inequality in Iran under Khomeini*. Lanham, Md.: University Press of America.

MASOUD KAZEMZADEH

P

✦ PERSIAN GULF

Geographically, the Persian Gulf represents an extension of the Arabian Sea, linked to this body of water by the Strait of Hormuz and the Gulf of Oman. Belying its strategic and political significance in the Middle East, the Strait of Hormuz represents the narrowest portion of the Persian Gulf, measuring only 55 to 60 kilometers (approximately 34 miles) in length. The gulf measures approximately 989 kilometers (615 miles) long and an average of 240 kilometers (150 miles) wide, with a maximum width of 370 kilometers (230 miles). With an average depth of 50 meters (55 yards), the Persian Gulf reaches about 90 meters (less than 100 yards) at its greatest depth. The Persian Gulf, with an area of approximately 237,000 kilometers (92,250 square miles) and an estimated capacity of 11,850 cubic meters (4,575 cubic miles), represents a highly contested territory among the surrounding countries and islands. This body of water, along with the Red Sea, is a prolongation of the Indian Ocean, and both give access to Europe.

In terms of political geography, the Persian Gulf refers to a body of water along the southwest border of Iran (Persia until 1935) that separates the country from its neighbors to the southwest. The topography of Iran on its border with the Persian Gulf is predominantly mountainous, containing the Zagros mountain range to the southeast, whereas the southern border of the Persian Gulf near Oman and Saudi Arabia is generally flat. The gulf particularly serves as a border between Iran and the nations of Kuwait, Saudi Arabia, Qatar, Oman, and the United Arab Emirates. Additionally, a small

369

portion of the southeastern border of Iraq falls along the Persian Gulf. Finally, the Persian Gulf contains several islands of critical importance in political and economic arenas including Bahrain, a country located on an island northwest of the Qatar peninsula, between Qatar and Saudi Arabia. The countries that surround the gulf are collectively known as the Persian Gulf states.

To the North, the Tigris and Euphrates rivers flow from Iraq into the Persian Gulf via the Shatt-al Arab. The Karun and Karkheh rivers likewise feed into the gulf from the north. Together, these rivers provide the greatest source of fresh water to the Persian Gulf. Nonetheless, the gulf has a notably high concentration of salt, reaching 40% of the composition of the gulf waters due to the hot climate and a high rate of evaporation. Though certain theories regarding the geography of the marshy northern border of the gulf and the continuously decreasing total area of the Persian Gulf over the past 6,000 years have suggested that deposits from these northern rivers accumulated and formed a large delta along the northern and western coastline of the Persian Gulf, other research findings have indicated that instead, the physical characteristics of this area are due to the movement of the Arabian Peninsula toward Iran.

The Persian Gulf is extremely rich in natural resources and serves as a vital source of resources for countries throughout the world. In fact, the Persian Gulf contains great amounts of coral reefs, pearl oysters, and highly productive fishing grounds. However, production in the Persian Gulf is predominantly centered upon natural gas and oil. The single greatest source of crude oil in the world, the Persian Gulf region contains the highest percentage of the world's oil resources. (The actual percentage cannot be determined because of new resources that pop up every day, however the range of claimed proven resources in this region varies between 57% to 70% of the world's oil resources.) The importance of oil in the Gulf area became fully realized in 1911 when Winston Churchill passed through parliament a bill to purchase 51% interests in the Anglo–Persian Oil Company (APOC), which was later renamed to Anglo–Iranian Oil Company.

The strategic significance of the region comes at the price of gradual environmental degradation. In recent decades, the ecology of the Persian Gulf has been polluted and threatened by industrialization throughout the region. The environment of the Persian Gulf region has also suffered from numerous oil spills due to the high volume of oil tankers passing through the waters, as well as serious oil spills resulting from attacks on oil tankers that took place during the Iran–Iraq War in the 1980s and the Persian Gulf War (or Gulf War) in the 1990s. For instance, on January 23, 1991, Iraq was accused of spilling one million tons of crude oil into the Persian Gulf, constituting the largest oil spill ever to befall the region. Additionally, destruction of water treatment plants during the Persian Gulf War caused the leakage of sewage into the Tigris River. This pollution contaminated the water supply for many Iraqi civilians and caused the spread of disease throughout the region.

The strategic significance and value of the natural resources located in the Persian Gulf as well as the strategic location of the Strait of Hornuz have kindled numerous disputes among the littoral countries of Iran, Iraq, Saudi Arabia, and their smaller neighbors. Strategic, political, and economic interests have also incited territorial disputes over the islands located in the Strait of Hornuz and in the Persian Gulf waters. The greater and lesser Tunb Islands, for instance, have been part of four different states during the recent Islamic era and have changed hands or definition as a village, city, or part of a city some eight times in recent centuries. Though these island are not centrally located in or near the Strait of Hornuz, they are considered strategically important as a geographic link between Iran and the strait. Not too far from the Tunbs, the fate of Abou Mousa Island is also interesting. On this issue a shared administrative Memorandum of Understanding was reached between Iran and the Sheikh of Sharjah in 1971 under the auspices of the British diplomats. This MOU, signed only seventy-two hours before the declaration of the United Arab Emirates, in fact divides the island into two administrative zones. Three days after the signing of the MOU, the United Arab Emirates, as a new political unit to which Sharjah is a member, objected to the MOU and condemned the Iranian occupation of the Islands. In the process, the Shah of Iran had recognized the independence of Bahrain on which previously Iran had a claim. Ever since, the issue has become a highly sensitive one in the region and has shaped the political relation of the Arab States of the gulf and Iran.

The conflict over the disputed islands served as one of the catalysts for some Arab states to question the historic name of the Persian Gulf. The history of the Persian Gulf, known in ancient times as the Sea of Pars or Sea of Fars, extends several millenniums into the past. "Bitter Waters," the first known name for the Persian Gulf, was given to the salty waters of the gulf by the Assyrians prior to the arrival of the Aryan Iranians on the land now known as Iran. For centuries, the gulf has been used by the llamites and ancient civilizations throughout the Asian continent as a vital trade route between what is now known as the Middle East and the West Indies or Nile Valley. Beginning in the early twentieth century, an international consensus began to arise dubbing the body of water the Persian Gulf, due in part to the efforts of the British diplomat Sir Charles Bellgrave. In the 1960s, however, Gamal Abdel Nasser initiated a movement to rename the waters by the fake title of "Arabian Gulf." Abdel Nasser had a simple reason: He believed that calling it the "Persian Gulf," while there are more Arab States around the gulf than Persian states, would be misleading. Ultimately, the United Nations refused to recognize the fake name. Moreover, when the countries of Iraq and Kuwait reached an agreement with Iran to support the current title, the body became generally recognized in the region, as well as internationally, as the Persian Gulf. However, Nasser's politically motivated and emotional reasoning has not been totally abandoned by some Arab states, especially after the Iranian revolution of 1979 when the "export of revolution" became a major concern for many Arab states. The Arabian Gulf had formerly been used to identify the Red Sea.

The political climate of the Persian Gulf has historically varied due to numerous invasions, wars, and shifts in political paradigms and the predominant political discourse. The area reaching from the Qatar peninsula to the borders of Oman used to be referred to as the "Pirate Coast." Evidence from archaeological findings indicates that interest in the Persian Gulf was demonstrated by powerful rulers and states as early as the second millennium BC, when the Assyrians Empire is believed to have stabilized the region along the Tigris and Euphrates rivers. Moreover, in the seventh century BC, the Assyrian king Ashurbanipal aimed to extend the Mesopotamian Empire as far as the Persian Gulf. Among a vast number of subsequent explorations and conquests of the area, Alexander the Great explored the Persian Gulf and surrounding area as early as 325 BC.

A treaty in 1820 between the British and Sheikhs of the Coastal States renamed that area the "Trucial Coast." This was an ideal place for robbers due to its small islands that were indented with narrow and slanting creeks. Navigation in this area is still dangerous today. Until the past century, the Gulf had not been thoroughly surveyed and still necessitated that travelers of the Gulf move cautiously. The British colonial power extended into the Persian Gulf region between 1763 and 1971, with the United Kingdom bearing political power and ruling several of the Persian Gulf states. Most notably during this time the United Kingdom controlled the Trucial Coast States, which are now known as the United Arab Emirates. Additionally, British power was exercised to various degrees over Bahrain, Oman, Qatar, and Kuwait throughout this era. Underscoring the significance of the Persian Gulf as a trade route through the Middle East, during the early 1800s the British were consistently forced to enter into conflict with pirates in the waters of the Persian Gulf in order to protect the ships and trade routes used by the East India Company. In 1853, a Maritime Truce was settled between the littoral Sheikhdoms of the Persian Gulf region and was agreed to by Great Britain. Thus, Great Britain became responsible for the policing and protection of the Persian Gulf waters and surrounding lands.

Two major conflicts that have dramatically changed the history and political atmosphere of the Persian Gulf region in our times are the Iran–Iraq War in the 1980s and the Gulf War (term used to describe the U.S.-led coalition war against Iraq after the occupation of Kuwait, also known as Operation Desert Storm) in the early 1990s. Prior to these wars, the political relations between Iran and Iraq were considered stable by foreign observers such as the United States. Practically there was a regional balance of power regulating the relations between Iran and Iraq until the Iranian revolution in 1979, when Iran was considered a stable U.S. ally and Iraq was recognized as the ally of the Soviet Union. With the outbreak of the Iran–Iraq War, fueled by Cold War tensions on the one hand and the animosity arising from the hostage crisis between Iran and the United States, the latter changed its politically neutral stance in the conflict by removing Iraq from a list of recognized sponsors of terrorism, to which it had been assigned in 1979. Gradually, the United States came to support Iraq in the war, and Iran turned toward the Soviet Union for support.

Essentially, the United States responded to the threats posed by Iran's alliance with its Cold War opponent and the fear that Iran would extend its Islamic Revolution throughout the strategically crucial Persian Gulf region. In doing so, the United States provided military and economic aid to Iraq from 1983 to 1989. Among the aid provided to Iraq, the United States supplied more than $200 million in supplies and weaponry, including arms, helicopters, and biological weapons such as anthrax. Additionally, the United States provided Iraq with more than $5 billion in economic relief through the Department of Agriculture and nearly $700 million through the U.S. Export–Import Bank. The latter funding served as aid for an initiative to construct an oil pipeline through the neighboring country of Jordan.

The Iran–Iraq War, which lasted from 1980 to 1988, represented a manifestation of the continuing tensions between these two nations beyond the persistent conflicts over territorial claims to the area's petroleum resources. Throughout this war, nonetheless, a series of attacks and counterattacks on each country's oil tankers emphasized the value of these resources to the economic vitality of the world in general and the Persian Gulf region in particular.

By contrast, the Gulf War was fought by a coalition mandated by the United Nations for the liberation of Kuwait from Iraqi control from August 2, 1990 through February 28, 1991. On August 2, 1990, Iraq invaded Kuwait under the leadership of Saddam Hussein, accusing Kuwait of illegally withdrawing resources from Iraq by engaging in slant-drilling for petroleum across the Iraqi border. U.S. foreign policy toward Iraq—at least until the occupation of Kuwait by the latter—continued to indicate support for that country. The United States government began to display disagreement with Iraq's human rights violations, its military buildup, and its hostile policy toward Israel. In fact, several motions were presented in the United States Congress advocating the imposition of sanctions on Iraq as punishment for these infringements, but only when Iraqi troops invaded Kuwait did the United States finally take action against Iraq. In response to the initiation of hostilities by Iraq in January of 1991, the U.S.-led force of 34 nations managed to drive the Iraqi forces out of Kuwait with minimal casualties for the coalition forces.

Strategic geopolitical interests in the Middle East, particularly in the protection of the oil fields of the crucial Persian Gulf states of Kuwait and Saudi Arabia, lay behind the actions of the United States and its Western allies in curtailing the Iraqi invasion. The countries of the U.N. coalition feared that Iraq, after gaining control of Kuwait's oil resources, would attempt to seize control over the vital Hama oil fields in Saudi Arabia which were within easy striking distance by the Iraqi troops, thus establishing a monopoly over a great portion of the oil resources in the Persian Gulf area.

On August 7, 1990, the United States sent troops into its historically important Middle East ally, Saudi Arabia, to launch the defensive military action known as Operation Desert Storm, designed to free Kuwait, and protect United States and Western interests in Saudi Arabia and its resources. The United States assembled a force of approximately 660,000 troops from a total of 34 countries to invade Iraq and counter the advance of its troops into Kuwait and Saudi Arabia.

The U.S. invasion of the Persian Gulf met with both opposition and support from Americans. Opponents rallied against the use of force and participation in the war for the underlying interest in the Persian Gulf oil supply. In addition to geopolitical interests in protecting the sovereignty of Kuwait and control of its oil supply, advocates of U.S. involvement in the conflict cited the human rights violations and other political wrongdoings of Iraq under Saddam Hussein, as well as suspicions of Iraq's possession of biochemical weapons and development of atomic weapons, as justification for becoming involved in the Persian Gulf War. By a very narrow margin, the United States Congress finally voted to approve the use of military force to drive Iraqi troops from Kuwait on January 12, 1991. Shortly thereafter, the other countries in the U.N. coalition followed suit, authorizing the use of force and supporting United States troops in pushing Iraqi forces out of Kuwait. Obviously Syria and Egypt entered into this coalition to follow their own agenda of regional influence and Arab world leadership as well as securing further U.S. support.

The immense air campaign known as Operation Desert Storm was launched by the coalition forces on January 17, 1991. This operation underscored the significance of the Persian Gulf for the West and for the Middle

East conflicts in general, as the majority of air raids by the coalition forces originated from strategic locations in Saudi Arabia and the Persian Gulf.

In February of 1991, the coalition forces launched surprise ground attacks on Iraqi troops, overpowering the Iraqi forces and succeeding in discouraging Iraq's advance toward the oil fields of eastern Saudi Arabia. Following this victory, the Iraqi strategy began to display shortcomings and Iraqi troops finally began to withdraw from Kuwait, followed into Iraq by coalition forces from the United States, France, and the United Kingdom. When the Iraqis had retreated to within 150 miles of Baghdad, the United States under President George H.W. Bush officially declared a ceasefire on February 27, 1991, marking the victory of the coalition forces and the end of the Persian Gulf War. Ultimately, the U.N. coalition had succeeded in protecting the sovereignty of Iraq's neighbors and the Western strategic geopolitical interests in the Persian Gulf.

The Persian Gulf region houses a variety of religious and ethnic cultures that simultaneously contribute to the social environment and compete for regional and international power and political influence. Religious diversity, particularly the increasing prevalence of religious extremism in recent decades, is among the central societal concerns that characterize the Persian Gulf region. Tensions constantly arise between Islamic fundamentalists and secular citizens within several countries of the Persian Gulf region, including Iran, Saudi Arabia, Kuwait, and Iraq. For instance, the Iranian revolution occurred in part because of disputing secular and Islamic fundamentalist factions in that country who disagreed over the proper role of Islam in the government of Iran. In 1979, the government of the Shah of Iran was overthrown, and a new government was established under Ayatollah Khomeini and at least initially led by several influential advocates of democratic government in the newly created Islamic Republic of Iran.

Today, the Persian Gulf region is home to a variety of religious extremist groups. Islamic fundamentalism and Islamic extremism are among the more extensive forms of religious extremism in the Persian Gulf area and across the Arab states. Following the Persian Gulf War, Islamic extremism gained momentum in the region, largely because of the American presence in the Middle East, invasion of Iraq during the Gulf War, and disciplinary actions taken in the region, particularly through sanctions and blockades. Political motivations have also led to alliances between Persian Gulf or Arab countries and local religious groups. For instance, the government of Saudi Arabia has historically been associated with supporting the Taliban in Afghanistan, in return for that group's support of the Saudi Arabian regime. During the Persian Gulf War, Saddam Hussein attempted to win the favor and support of nationalist and religious groups such as the late Palestinan leader Yasir Arafat by incorporating Arab symbols and discourse into his campaign. By appealing to these forces, Saddam Hussein hoped to rally Arab and Islamic factions against the invading forces of the Western coalition. Most recently, a similar phenomenon has emerged around the so called Al-Qaeda and like minded groups during Washington's War on Terror, as evidenced by the resistance of both Shi'a and Sunni Muslim factions to the US invasion and occupation of Iraq since March 2003.

Suggested Reading
Belgrave, C. 1966. *The pirate coast*. New York: Roy Publishers, Inc.
Long, D. E. 1978. *The Persian Gulf*. Boulder, Co: Westview Press.

JALIL ROSHANDEL

✦ PETROLEUM INDUSTRY

The socioeconomic transformation and history of oil in Iran can be divided into three stages of development: (1) the era of colonial oil concessions, (2) the 1950–1972 period of transition, and (3) the globalization (and decartelization) of oil from 1974 onward. Iran's oil concessions had a distinct peculiarity of being interrupted by constitutional revolution and then being secured by a pair of coup d'états, first by Britain to empower Reza Khan in 1921 and second by the United States, to return his son, Mohammad Reza Shah, in 1953.

Two parallel phenomena fused the destiny of Iran's economy with oil: (1) an accident of geology and (2) the emergence of the twentieth-century hydrocarbon capitalism. The first oil concession in Iran (known as Persia prior to 1935) was made between Mozaffar al-Din Shah (Qājār) and William Knox D'Arcy in 1901. The oil was struck on May 26, 1908 in Masjed-e Suleiman, a tiny village within the Bakhtiari tribal area in southwestern Persia. This concession had the entire country, except for northern provinces of Āzerbāijān, Gilān, Māzandarān, Astarābād, and Khorāsān, under D'Arcy's control for exploration, production, gathering and storage, and transportation of oil exclusively for the period of sixty years. The term included £20,000 advanced cash; and upon the exploration, £20,000 shares of the company to be formed and 16% of annual net profits as royalty. On April 19, 1909, APOC was formed. But it took the company a few more years (until 1913) to produce oil in commercial quantities, and to build pipelines, storage facilities, and a refinery in Ābādān. In the meantime, the British Navy, which was switching from coal to oil, had an eye on the Persian oil and was unremittingly seeking Parliament's approval to infuse the company with public funds and to control its board of directors for both economic and political gains.

In 1914, the British government eventually obtained more than 50% of APOC's stock and installed two representatives on the company's board of directors. This was a preamble to secretly supplying the British Admiralty with heavily discounted oil, which in turn led to substantial reduction in the company's net profits, at the expense of the Persian government. Thus, in World War I (as acknowledged by Lord Curzon) Britain "floated to victory on a sea of [Persian] oil." The APOC evaded the payments of royalty to the Persian government in a variety of ways, including, but not limited to, "maximizing" stockholder's return (British government being the majority), paying "excess profit tax" to the same government, and secretly granting deep discounts to Brit-

Iranian police officers patrol part of the Caspian Sea in front of an oil facility outside the city of Neka some 190 miles northeast of Tehran. (AP Photo/Vahid Salemi)

ish Navy (an incredible triple-dipping in the profits); plus engaging in illicit accounting practices through vertical integration, special marketing arrangements, and simply fictitious bookkeeping to hide profits and to reduce the magnitude of oil royalties. APOC consistently refused to allow the Persian government to participate in management in accordance with its equity stipulated in the concession. From 1915 onward, APOC refused to pay royalties outright either partially (offsetting the presumed bribes given to the Bakhtiari tribesmen) or completely; and by doing so the company in effect not only suspended the payment of royalty to the Persian government but also refused to accede to the latter's request to arbitrate the dispute according to the expressed provision of concession's Article 17—an egregious breach of contract. Similarly, with the British government's backing, APOC also refused to calculate the royalties based upon the net profit of its consolidated (worldwide) operations, including upstream and downstream activities—implicit in D'Arcy's original (1901) concession. APOC was a party to the *Armitage-Smith* "interpretive" agreement that was a *de facto* dialogue between the company and Britain's emissary, and which was never ratified by the Persian Majles. In 1920, this so-called agreement had "justified" *ex post* the non-payment of royalties based upon the calculation of net profits of APOC's consolidated (worldwide) operations. In Winston Churchill's own words, "Fortune [i.e., Persian oil] brought us [i.e., Britain] a prize from fairyland far beyond our brightest hopes." For the decade of 1914–1924, the non-consolidated net profits of the company were £28.5 million, of which £9.5 million (33%) were distributed as dividends and £3.9 million (13.7%) were paid to the Persian government. Thus, aside from the aforementioned incongruities, the dividend reported on the APOC's non-consolidated books alone amounted to nearly 244% of the royalties.

The royalties, being at the mercy of deliberate APOC booking, on the one hand, and fluctuating oil price and thus net profits, on the other hand, did not remain stable. On September 17, 1928, APOC (a crude-long company) joined with two remaining major oil companies, namely the Standard Oil of New Jersey (Exxon) and the Royal Dutch Shell, at the Achnacarry Castle (Scotland). This led to an agreement that formalized the total control of oil within a worldwide vertically integrated network of companies that was belatedly identified as the International Petroleum Cartel. This agreement is also known as "As Is," having to do with maintenance of the status quo in respect to exploration and development and production activities in respect to transportation, refining, marketing, and retailing of oil and its derivatives worldwide. This further exacerbated the situation between the government and APOC late in the 1920s. The oil royalties then fell from £1.288 million in 1930 to £307,000 in 1931 (for 5.7 million tons of crude)—a drop of more than 75%. However, the corresponding net profits of the company dropped less than 37% for the same period. To make matters worse, on September 21, 1931, Britain went off the gold standard, thus causing the depreciation of Persia's sterling balances in London.

To be sure, D'Arcy's contract had already been breeched by APOC many times since the 1913 commercialization of Persian oil, but the company (and British government) did not wish to see its outright cancellation for fear of losing the concession altogether to its rivals. Therefore, APOC's dilemma was *to have the concession and breech it too*. The dilemma of the Iranians, however, was the reverse, namely, that D'Arcy's original concession had already given them the advantage of owning substantial company shares and 16% of consolidated net profits (upstream and downstream) worldwide. It is true that the continuous lack of payment of royalties by the company amounted to *de facto* unilateral cancellation of the concession; but it *prima facie* needed the expressed consent of the other party to be effectively cancelled *de jure*; hence the dilemma of the Persian government.

In the meantime, the APOC's intransigence in addressing the issues surrounding the payment of royalty deteriorated further until November 27, 1932, when the government of Persia informed the company of the cancellation of the concession. This alone brought the British warships to the Persian Gulf, and, in a deliberate action, the British government also brought the dispute before the Council of the League of Nations and submitted the case to the Permanent Court of International Justice at The Hague. This, of course, resembles the spectacle that was displayed 20 years later during the 1951–1953 nationalization of oil by Mossadegh. Yet aside from unsavory tactics by Britain, hasty cancellation of D'Arcy's concession (and the subsequent acceptance of a much inferior concession) by Reza Shah himself was neither far-sighted nor beneficial to Persia. Article 10 of the 1933 oil concession settled on 4 shillings (gold) per tone of oil as royalty, and minor financial provisions which in due course proved to be either insignificant or practically inapplicable. However, the size of the concession was reduced to 100,000 square miles. Yet given more than three decades of exploration in nearly 80% of the country, APOC had an accurate picture of where oil deposits were at the time. The major gains of APOC were extension of the concession by some 30 years (until 1993) and divesting the government of its stock ownership in the producing subsidiary of APOC.

During the years between 1931 and 1950, the AIOC (following the change of Persia to Iran in 1935) continued to increase its dividend, from 5% in the depth of the Great Depression to 20% in 1936–1938. Dividends rose to 30% in the period of 1946–1950—a maximum rate allowed by Britain's new policy at this time. Despite the nationalization of Iranian oil in March 1951 and significant deterioration of its revenue, AIOC kept on rewarding its stockholders (British government being the majority holder) to the tune of 30% in 1951, 35% in 1952, more than 42% in 1953, and 15% plus 400% scrip bonus in 1954. This generous practice is but to reflect the existence of huge financial reserves hitherto accumulated by AIOC from its extraordinary profits of past operations that also additionally allowed it to finance its massive internal expansion. Indeed, an AIOC spokesman boasted that "the whole of the capital investment during the years between 1930 and 1952 was financed by retained profits and without recourse to outside borrowing of any importance." Between 1935 and 1950, Iran's official (under-) estimate of crude oil reserves by AIOC increased from 2.2 billion barrels to 7.0 billion barrels (an increase of more than 300%), with a negligible fraction of retained earnings as investment.

In 1947, Majles (the Iranian parliament) passed a law that expressed dissatisfaction about the 1933 concession and its unremitting violation by AIOC, and, in the subsequent year, a memorandum (containing a 25-point disputation) was duly sent to the company for negotiation. The gist of this memorandum reflected the longstanding evasion of royalties by a variety of means, including the triple-dipping of discounting oil to British Navy, paying taxes on Iran's oil to British government, and distributing handsome dividends to shareholders (British government being the majority) and the arbitrary calculation of financial reserves. Additionally, this memorandum *inter alia* focused on the deplorable conditions of Iranian workers in the oilfields and in Abādān. This prompted the company to present a very superficial rejoinder, known as the Gass-Golshaian Supplemental Agreement, which was rejected by the Majles outright on March 20, 1951 in favor of nationalization.

Nationalization of oil in Iran is a significant event within the transitional period of 1950–1972 toward decartelization and globalization of oil. It had roots in the two entwined objectives of Iran's Constitutional Revolution (1906–1911), namely, opposition autocracy and foreign domination. Hence, democracy and independence was the twin motivating force behind the nationalization of oil in Iran. The special oil committee of the Majles chaired by Dr. Mossadegh recommended to the Majles that nationalization of oil was but the only choice. At the time, Iranians knew that the AIOC had *de facto* control over scores of politicians in the Majles, in the executive branch, and tucked away in the imperial court. Following the nationalization of oil, Mossadegh was elected as Prime Minister and quickly set himself the twin task of: (1) completing the nationalization of oil and (2) introducing new laws for free and fair elections.

The reactions by AIOC and concerted efforts by Britain were predictable if somewhat anachronistic. It was a *déjà vu* of nearly two decades earlier. The British warships were dispatched to the Persian Gulf, the case was taken to the International Court of Justice at The Hague, and a complaint was filed at the UN Security Council, all in sequence. But, in this time around, the world was much more observant. However, the 1928 Achnacarry Agreement that led to the International Petroleum Cartel was also in its peak. That is why any attempt to purchase Iran's oil by independent oil companies has been labeled as purchasing "stolen property," and any export of oil by Iran was blockaded and embargoed without impunity. Despite all economic hardships at home and political pressures abroad, Prime Minister Mossadegh not only survived but also, in the view of world public opinion, thrived. This time, neither British Navy, nor the International Court of Justice (ICJ), nor even the U.N. Security Council (UNSC) could legitimately and lawfully reverse the nationalization of oil in Iran. The ICJ found no jurisdiction to rule, the UNSC no real cause to act, and the British Navy matched with the formidable mass mobilization in Abādān. Even the agitation of corrupt politicians, duplicity of the imperial court, and deception of clerics like Kashani could not move Mossadegh to the margin.

In the meantime, five different contracts (including a plan under supervision of the World Bank) were proposed to Mossadegh, all of which were utterly evasive of the reality of nationalization and hence deemed unacceptable. The irreconcilable differences between a democratically elected, forward-looking head of the state and a declining colonial power interested in "primitive accumulation," on the one hand, and the contradiction of nationalization of one's oil against the International Petroleum Cartel are indeed a double confrontation of first order. On August 19, 1953, Prime Minister Mossadegh was overthrown by the CIA. The coup d'état restored the Shah (Mohammad Reza Pahlavi), and its official cause was contextualized within the familiar rhetoric of Cold War for posterity and public consumption. The real cause, however, was signing a new (denationalized) concession by the beneficiaries of the coup d'état through a *consortium* or a front for major oil companies, including the AIOC (now BP) with 40% share. The Royal Dutch Shell was given 14% and Jersey, Texas, Socal, Gulf, and Socony acquired 7% each, while French CFP obtained 6% before the remaining 5% went to several U.S. independents. Thus, Iran's oil for all intents and purposes was denationalized once again. The so-called Iranian Consortium, like all the remaining (semi-colonial) concessions, calculated Iran's share based on 50–50 profit-sharing, which lasted only until the restructuring of the industry through the 1973–1974 oil crisis.

Toward the end of the 1950s there was a shared concern over the continuous cutting of the "posted price" of oil from the Persian Gulf. The Cartel was worried that oil from the bountiful (and much cheaper) Persian Gulf reservoirs had already reached the U.S. eastern seaboard, and that the balance of production according to the Achnacarry Agreement of 1928 would have to be disturbed. In a concerted effort, citing "national security" and the rhetoric of dependence on foreign oil, the U.S. government imposed a quota on imports from the Persian Gulf in 1959. In reality, however, this was to discourage the flow of oil from the Persian Gulf region and to defuse competition from the independents. This led the cartel to cut the Persian Gulf "posted prices" further—and, in turn, cut the oil royalties further. This bone of contention led to the formation of the Organization of Petroleum

Exporting Countries (OPEC) by Iran, Iraq, Kuwait, Saudi Arabia, and Venezuela on September 14, 1960. OPEC's primary task was to counter the cuts and to prevent further erosion of the royalties.

The stage theory of oil indicated at the outset provides both historical and conceptual context for analysis of the continuity and change in the worldwide evolution of petroleum, from the colonial concessions to its decartelization and eventual globalization. Iran's oil is no exception. The early 1970s was a moment of grand disruption that transformed the industry worldwide. The 1973–1974 crisis was an equivalent of the "Big Bang" in the modern political economy of oil. The quadrupling of the (nominal) "posted prices" in the Persian Gulf, North Africa, and Venezuela was the consequence of formidable forces that gathered strength during the 1950–1972 transitional period and moved the tectonic plates of change. OPEC had played as a catalyst in all this and, as the events of the late 1970s and 1980s have shown, was reflective of the objective changes between the rentier and the capitalist investor in production of oil globally. The oil crisis had multiple global effects, namely, (1) one global price for both high- and low-cost oil, (2) *de facto* nationalization of oil in the concessionary regions and parallel transnationalization of oil production, (3) universal decartelization of oil, (4) competitive formation of differential oil rents within OPEC and across the globe, and (5) abolition of "posted prices" in favor of spot markets and spot oil prices.

The opposition to the International Petroleum Cartel (IPC) was initiated by Algeria and Libya early in 1970 as independent oil companies entered into the foray. These two OPEC members opted for a united front in negotiation with IPC and displayed a willingness to challenge IPC and uphold nationalization. The Shah of Iran, on the other hand, showed no opposition to IPC and insisted on separate negotiation, while Saudi Arabia and Kuwait *inter alia* stood somewhere in the middle, which ultimately led to separate negotiation for the Persian Gulf producers. Yet, in due time, the Shah and all other oil-producing client states of the Persian Gulf reaped the benefits of what the two North African producers accomplished. In the interim, the 1973 Arab–Israeli war, and the decidedly limited Arab oil embargo that followed it, played as a side show but nevertheless masked the reality of this historic restructuring. When the dust finally settled, the "posted price" for benchmark crude (Arabian light 34°) had increased from $3.01 (July 1973, with $1.88 royalty) to $11.65 (January 1974, with royalty and differential rent of $7.00), as the "uncontrolled" U.S. oil price had also reached a double digit figure—before the "posted prices" were to be abolished in favor of spot prices for all oil. A flashback from 1954 through the early 1970s reveals that the oil consortium controlled 99.9% of Iran's crude oil production and exports, and—despite an eventual number of joint ventures with independent oil producers—the cartel's share was shrunk a little only toward the very end. By 1973, in the face of global oil realities, the control of production (and by implication oil exports) was revoked *de jure*, but the capitulation to the 20-year preferential oil-purchase rights by Mohammad Reza Shah created endless disputes between government and the defunct cartel until 1979.

Finally, decartelization and global restructuring of oil led to manifold oil revenues for all oil-exporting countries. Iran's oil export revenue increased from $3.6 billion in 1972 to nearly $21 billion in 1974. Oil revenues declined slightly in 1975, and then increased to $22.9 billion and $23.6 billion, respectively, in 1976 and 1977, before declining again to $21.7 billion and $19.2 billion, in 1978 and 1979, when the Iranian revolution was in full swing. The impact of the labor strikes in the oilfields and disruption of production, however, was revealed belatedly in 1980 and 1981, as oil revenues declined precipitously to $11.7 billion and $10 billion, respectively. The level of Iran's oil production nearly mimicked the pattern of oil revenues. In the Shah's era, the production peak in 1974 was reached just above 6 million b/d. Such a level, however, could not be sustained for long (notwithstanding secondary and tertiary recovery costs) without long-term investment for additional capacity. Hence, the steady decline in production, combined with the disruptive impact of revolutionary upheaval (which forced the removal of the Shah early in 1979), diminished the production level just below 1.3 million b/d in 1981. The 1981 oil exports were even substantially less—at 55% of production. In 1981, the proven oil reserves in Iran were estimated at 57 billion barrels (13% and 8% of respective estimations for OPEC and the world). The proven natural gas reserves at this time were estimated at 14.1 trillion cubic meters, second only to Russia's—standing at 44% and 16% of respective estimations for OPEC and the world.

The Shah's post-oil crisis (ostentatious) programs and the Nixon Doctrine (in the Persian Gulf) obtained their organic unity in the oil revenue. So, the crisis was a boon to programs that went much further than the ambition for development and modernization of Iran. Massive military expenditures, on the one hand, and limitless imports necessitated by conspicuous consumption, on the other hand, soon led to an inflationary spiral that fittingly fed the rising oil revenues. In addition, the oil boom of the 1970s led to further class polarization and income inequality. The Shah's rentier state was in deep trouble and, as history proved inescapable, the economic and social crisis led to political upheaval that soon engulfed the entire country. Unlike the summer of 1953, Iranians tried not to be taken by the conundrum of

American duplicity once again; and—at long last, in a widespread, spontaneous, and powerful revolutionary insurrection, the monarchy was overthrown.

Suggested Reading

Abrahamian, E. 1982. *Iran: between two revolutions*. Princeton, NJ: Princeton University Press.

Alfonso, P. 1966. The Organization of Petroleum Exporting Countries. *Monthly Bulletin of Ministry of Mines and Hydrocarbons*. Caracas 1, nos. 1–4.

Becker, P. J. 1974. The Anglo-Persian oil dispute of 1932–33. *Journal of Contemporary History*. 9: 123–53.

Bina, C. 1985. *The Economics of the Oil Crisis*. New York: St. Martin's, 1985.

Bina, C. 1989. Some controversies in the development of rent theory: the nature of oil rent. *Capital & Class*. 39: 82–112.

Bina, C. 1990. Limits to OPEC pricing: OPEC profits and nature of the global oil accumulation. *OPEC Review*. 14: 55–73.

Bina, C. 1992. The laws of economic rent and property: applied to the oil industry. *The American Journal of Economics and Sociology*. 51: 187–203.

Bina, C. 2005. Mossadegh, oil crisis, and the price of independence, in Keshavarz-Sadr, H., and H. Akbari, eds., *Mossadegh and the Future of Iran*. Bethesda, Md.: Ibex Publishers; 71–138 (in Persian).

Bina, C. 2006. The globalization of oil: a prelude to a critical political economy. *International Journal of Political Economy*. 35: 4–34.

Blair, J. M. 1976. *The control of oil*. New York: Pantheon.

Elm, M. 1992. *Oil, power, and principle: Iran's oil nationalization and aftermath*. Syracuse, NY: Syracuse University Press.

Elwell-Sutton, L. P. 1955. *Persian Oil: a study of power politics*. London: Lawrence & Wishart.

Fesharaki, F. 1976. *Development of the Iranian oil industry*. New York: Praeger.

International Court of Justice. 1952. *Pleadings, oral arguments, documents: Anglo-Iranian Oil Co. Case*. The Hague.

Lenczowski, G. 1949. *Russia and the West in Iran, 1918–1948*. Ithaca, NY: Cornell University Press.

Mikdashi, Z. 1966. *A financial analysis of Middle Eastern oil concessions: 1901–65*. New York: Praeger.

National Security Archive, Electronic Briefing No. 28, *The Secret CIA History of Iran 1953 Coup*. Washington, DC: George Washington University: (accessed 3/9/2007). http://www.gwu.edu/nsarchiv/NSAEBB/NSAEBB28/index.html#documents.

OPEC. 2005. *Annual statistical bulletin*. Vienna, Austria: OPEC Secretariat.

Tariki, A. 1963. Towards better cooperation between oil producing and oil consuming countries. *Petroleum Intelligence Weekly*. November 11 (Special Supplement).

United States Congress. Senate. Select Committee on Monopoly. 1952. *The international petroleum cartel: staff report to the Federal Trade Commission*. 82nd Congress, 2nd session. Washington, DC: U.S. Government Printing Office.

Walden, J. L. 1962. The international petroleum in Iran—private power and the public interest. *Journal of Public Law*. 11: 64–121.

CYRUS BINA

✦ POLITICAL PARTICIPATION

The Islamic Republic has unified the divine right of sovereignty, which is derived from God's laws, with the people's rights of sovereignty, which originates from the people's will. The state labels itself as an Islamic Republic whose official nationalism is an Islamic–Iranian nationalism, which classifies "the people" into a faithful Muslim community (*umma*) with political rights and obligations or unfaithful others with no rights but obligations.

As an Islamic state, Iran claims to have the divine right sovereignty embodied in the supreme leader. Based on the *Shi'i* school of thought, after the passing of twelve *Shi'i* Immams, who the *Shi'ites* consider to be infallible and thus the most qualified men to interpret God's laws, *mara-je taqlid* (sources of emulation) are considered to be the most qualified people to interpret Islamic laws according to exigency of the time. Becoming a *marja-e taqlid* (a source of emulation) is a long peer-review process, which is regulated by the norms, rules, and traditions of the Shi'i clerical institution. The process of becoming a *marja-e taqlid* also requires the people's participation. Traditionally, faithful Shi'ites freely selected their choice of *marja-e taqlid,* and the power, wealth, and prestige of a *marja-e taqlid* was (and is) directly proportional to his following among the community of the faithful. As such, the relationship between a *marja* and his followers was a faith-based voluntary relation between a religious leader and his followers, not a relationship between the ruled and rulers. In fact, *mara-je taqlid* shun politics in most cases and for centuries considered the divine right of sovereignty belonging to kings who had the power to provide security and peace for the people.

Since the establishment of the Islamic Republic of Iran, *mara-je taqlid* have become religious as well as political leaders. The people elect "qualified" and well-known *mara-je taqlid* to the Council of Experts (*Majlis Khubregan*). The Council of Experts then selects the supreme leader as the embodiment of the divine rights of sovereignty. The state considers the people's faithful submission and commitment to the leadership as the most virtuous political-religious obligation necessary to perpetuate the unity of the Islamic community. The state contends that the faithful obligation of the Islamic community maintains national Islamic unity, enhances Iran's independence, and provides peace, the reign of morality and virtue, and makes progress for the nation possible.

As a republic, the state represents the 1979 Islamic Revolution, which led to the establishment of the Islamic Republic, as a covenant among the faithful Iranian citizens and their government. The covenant confers a mandatory obligation on the citizens to follow the laws of the Islamic Republic, but also gives the people the right to express their collective will, only if it is to serve the "imagined community" of Muslims. In competitive electoral processes, the state represents the will of the people embodied in the parliament (*Majlis*) and presidency as the sovereignty of the people (*mardum salari*). Since 1979, at least twenty-eight national elections have been held, and each election has had the stated purpose of enforcing the Islamic–Iranian nationalism headed by the supreme leader.

The most important criterion for candidates to public office is one's submission and commitment (*ta'a-hud* and *ta'qa-yud*) to the divine right of the supreme leader (*Valayat-e Faqih*). The measure of one's submission to the leader is assessed in terms of one's commitment to willingly sacrifice self for perpetuating the divine rule of the sovereign. In other words, submission and commitment to the supreme leader are deemed as virtuous political and religious obligations necessary to promote independence, peace, morality, and progress for the nation, as well as securing one's eternal salvation.

By fusing these two seemingly opposing ideals of sovereignty, the Islamic Republic obliterates the distinctions between political and religious obligations, secular and religious rights, and personal and private domains. The Islamic Republic contends that the unity between politics and religion promotes good and forbids evil (*amr-e beh ma'ruf va nahy-e az munker*) on earth as it simultaneously secures eternal salvation of the faithful. The state calls the unity between politics and religion as *Tohid* (monotheism). The state claims that separating politics from religious ethics is a Western form of polytheism, which has spread injustice in the world. According to the Islamic Republic, colonialism, two world wars, moral decadence, alienation of man from God, and poverty for many and wealth for the few are manifestations of polytheism in the name of "liberal secularism." In contrast, the Islamic Republic offers the theory of *Tohid*, which could bring independence, peace, virtue, and progress not only for Iran but also for the entire world. In short, by imagining Iran as a nation of Islamic–Iranians, the theory of *Tohid* unifies political concepts that have been historically divided in Western context— political from religious rights—and obligations, private from public, personal from political.

THE UNITY OF POLITICAL AND RELIGIOUS RIGHTS

In the Islamic Republic, political and religious rights and obligations are inseparable in theory and practice. The 1979 Islamic Revolution institutionalized the unity between political and religious rights and obligations. For instance, the mobilization of the Revolutionary Guard, now one of the most potent, modern, and well-equipped military forces in the Middle East, began as a grassroots organization bound by civic, political, and religious obligation in the service of the nation. In some important ways, the Islamic Revolutionary

Guard continues to operate as a grassroots organization. For many years, volunteers in local defense committees patrolled neighborhoods. They provided security and enforced strict compliance with Islamic codes of conduct. In recent years, police departments have assumed the role of providing physical and "moral" security for neighborhoods, but Revolutionary Guards continue to recruit and operate out of neighborhood mosques and Islamic centers. Neighborhood Revolutionary Guards organize political, educational, and religious campaigns. In doing so, the Islamic Revolutionary Guard considers itself a military force mandated to protect the Islamic Republic, a political organization committed to the supreme leader, a civil association empowered by the people and for the people, and an association of faithful believers committed to teaching Islam. Today, military training accompanies religious studies.

Similarly, during the war between Iran and Iraq (1980–1988), mobilization of masses (*basij*) was framed in terms of protecting not only the territorial integrity of Iran, but also the integrity of Islam. Hence, the political was inseparably religious. The Islamic Republic represented Saddam Hussein as a brutal dictator attacking Iran and Islam.

Saving Iran and Islam was the main theme of the political campaign for the Islamic Republic to defeat Saddam Hussein. It is also the main theme of the official state nationalism.

Since the 1979 Islamic Revolution, the Islamic Republic has represented the United States as the Great Satan (*shayta-ne buzurg*) or the world's most arrogant power (*estekba-re Jahani*). Believing in such labels invokes religious and political obligations upon the faithful followers. For example, every year, millions of people flood the streets of Tehran and other major Iranian cities on February 11 to celebrate the anniversary of the establishment of the Islamic Republic. The common theme in these protests is to demonize the United States as a threat to the Islamic Republic, but more importantly, to demonstrate that the state can still mobilize millions of people. Regardless of the state's motivation or themes, the very act of participating in these demonstrations is an expression of political support for the regime. This participation is considered a political-religious obligation on the part of faithful citizens.

Attending prayers and other traditionally religious rituals has become a form of political participation. For example, traditionally, Friday prayers were considered religious obligation on the part of faithful Muslims, not a political act. Since the establishment of the Islamic Republic, Friday prayers have become weekly political events under the institutional control of the supreme leader. Depending on the political events of a given week, the talking points for speeches delivered before and after the prayer are centrally coordinated. More interestingly, attendees of Friday prayers are active political participants and are among the most influential political actors in Iranian society. In fact, attending Friday prayers is one of the metrics by which faithful submission and commitment to the state is measured; therefore, all political actors in Iran regularly attend Friday prayers.

Friday prayers and other state-promoted and subsidized ceremonies, gatherings, and pilgrimages produce and reproduce a particular Islamic–Iranian nationalism—an imagined community in which the "Iranian-ness" of a citizen is measured in terms of a particular submission and commitment to Islam. A central theme in these traditionally ritualistic and currently political events is the representation of the Islamic community counterpoised by an abstract foreigner who aims to break the unity of Islamic community and, therefore, to dominate it by first corrupting its Islamic soul and then by using its demonic military force. In other words, maintaining the Islamic unity of the country is more than a religious obligation. Islamic unity is a political strategy that requires faithful submission and commitment to the community led by the supreme leader.

Other religious rituals are as political as they are religious. For example, during *Ashura,* the state sponsors processions, sermons, and gatherings. *Ashura* is the period of commemorating Immam Hussein's martyrdom in the 7th century. By representing Immam Hussein as a role model in the struggle of good versus evil, the ten-day commemoration becomes a highly charged arena in which political participation meets religious faith. As expected, not participating in this type of ritual is understood as the silent expression of disapproval of the regime, at worst, or the lack of commitment to the state official nationalism, at best.

Similarly, political differences within the state correspond to differences in the interpretation of religious rituals. For example, principlists (*usul grayaan*) prioritize the Islamic character of the state and reformists (*eslah talabaan*) privilege its republican spirit. This tension pervades the interpretation of rituals. For instance, in the 2007 commemoration of Immam Hussein held in Husseini-ya-he Ershah north of Tehran, attendees belonged to the reformist minority faction in the state. They interpreted Immam Hussein as a reformist, nationalist, and Iranian role model who established an Islamic Republic. The reformists argued that the Islamic Republic would have been more democratic than Islamic had they been allowed to remain in power. In other words, the government considers a particular way of demonstrating religious submission as political commitment. But the state regards refraining or deviating from the official version of submission as a lack of commitment and loyalty. In short, differences in how the people perform religious obligations and take part in rituals permeate all aspects of governance, including bureaucracy.

Accordingly, the state bureaucracy runs on two different modes of behavior. On the one hand, the parliament (*Majlis*) sets layers of codes, norms, and regulations for bureaucracy. On the other hand, religious obligations set the tone for the operation of a particular office. As the theory of *Tohid* obliterates the distinction between political and religious obligation, it also determines the distinction between private and public, or personal and political.

Today, the state vision of an Islamic–Iranian nationalism is attached to a particular social morality, which the state politicizes by rewarding conformity and disciplining non-conformity. Accordingly, the public display of personal or private preferences becomes public and political signs of conformity or non-conformity with the state's official nationalism. For example, conformity to the Islamic dress code for women is the sign of submission and commitment to the state rather than an expression of religious beliefs. In spite of the standard for Islamic dress codes shifting in recent years, the personal appearance of a woman in public is the subject of a political debate at the national level. Women's dress codes are also a form of political participation and expression, which demonstrates one's level of submission and commitment to the state's official nationalism. To show their submission and political commitment to the state, men conform, among other behaviors, by having facial hair, wearing long sleeves, and not putting on neckties. Other aspects of personal and private life that reflect submission to the state's public and political ideology include: music preferences, shaking or not shaking hands with the opposite sex, and ways of greetings, salutations, and acknowledgments. Other political and public signs of an individual's private and personal commitment to the state's official nationalism include the way one ends letters or conversations. In short, the public display of personal preference is a non-verbal form of political communication and commitment to the official state nationalism.

Suggested Reading

Anderson, B. R. 1983. *Imagined communities: reflections on the origin and spread of nationalism*. London: Verso.

Bazargan, M. 1344 [1965]. *Musalman: Ejtema-I and Johan-I* [*Muslim: social and global*]. Tehran: Ershad, 1965.

Dahl, R. 1971. *Polyarchy participation and opposition*. New Haven: Yale University Press.

Kashi, A. R. 1383 [2006]. *The order and trend of the discourse of democracy in Iran*. Tehran: Gam-e No.

Khomeini, R. 1980. *Islam and revolution: writings and declarations of Imam Khomeini*. Berkeley, Calif.: Mizan Press.

Shariati, A. 1379 [2000]. *Johan Beeni and Ideology* [*Ontology and Ideology*], 5th ed. Tehran: Enteshar.

Sharifi, M. 2007. *Imagining Iran: contending discourses in Iranian modern history.* Gainesville: University of Florida Press.

Vahdat, F. 2003. "Post-revolutionary Islamic discourses on modernity in Iran: expansion and contraction of human subjectivity." *International Journal of Middle Eastern Studies.* 35: 599–631.

MAJID SHARIFI

✦ POLITICAL PARTIES

Political groups that participate in elections and are capable of electing candidates for public office have existed in Iran since the establishment of the Islamic Republic of Iran in 1979. Although the Political Parties Activities Law of 1981 remained unimplemented until after the opening of the Third Parliament and the concomitant end of the eight-year war with Iraq in 1988, the laws governing multi-party electoral contestation within the newly defined confines of the Islamic Republic system had been enacted and put into effect in time for the second parliamentary election held in 1984. The 1984 procedural compact (the new Parliamentary Elections Law) excluded outright the regime opponents and the secular leftists from electoral politics and drove one tolerated opposition group, the Freedom Movement of Iran (*Nehzat-e Azadi-ye Iran*), into boycotting the election in protest. Nevertheless, during the 1984 parliamentary elections, four politically distinct groups—two conservative and two radical/pro-government organizations—in addition to the pro-system umbrella body Islamic Republic Party (*Hezb-e Jomhuri-ye Eslami*), formally competed for the thirty-seat capital district of Tehran. The June 1987 dissolution of the factionalism-stricken Islamic Republic Party did not alter the nature of the electoral politics, as the constituent groups of its two rival wings had already entered into open competition. During the first decade after the 1979 revolution, however, two factors inhibited the institutionalization of party-based electoral politics on a nationwide scale: the ban imposed by the then Leader Ayatollah Ruhollah Musavi-Khomeini on extra-district interferences in candidate selection, and the fact that 84% of the nation's then 193 electoral districts were single-seat ones in which candidates' personal traits, much more than their factional affiliations, seemed to have had impact on their electoral outcomes.

Under the 1981 law, political parties had been required to register with and obtain licenses for activities from the five-person committee called the Article 10 Commission of the Parties Law, composed of the representatives from the Judiciary, the Parliament, and the Interior Ministry, and established within the Ministry. After the demand by some deputies of the Third Parliament, the Interior Ministry activated the Article 10 Commission for the first time in late 1988, and began accepting the applications from political parties and other groups and organizations. It granted its first licenses in July 1989. Certain prominent groups that regularly compete in elections—such as clerical establishments like the Tehran Combatant Clergy Association (*Jame'eh-e Rouhaniyyat-e Mobarez-e Tehran*), the Qom Seminary Teachers Association (*Jame'eh-ye Modarresin-e Houzeh-ye 'Elmiyyeh-ye Qom*), and the student group the Unity Consolidation Office (*Daftar-e Tahkim-e Vahdat*)—had never registered as political parties. A number of others, however, including the Tehran Combatant Clerics Assembly (*Majma'-e Rouhaniyun-e Mobarez-e Tehran*, established in 1988), the Executives of Construction of Iran Party (*Hezb-e Kargozaran-e Sazandegi-ye Iran*, established in 1996), and the Islamic Iran Participation Front Party (*Hezb-e Jebheh-ye Mosharekat-e Iran-e Eslami*, established in 1998) went on to do so under the framework of the 1981 law. The Freedom Movement had, by 1989, antagonized the dominant political factions so much so that it has never been allowed to register under the 1981 law. The number of the licensed parties grew slowly during the presidency of Akbar Hashemi-Rafsajani (1989–1997), reaching 10 in 1992 and 36 in 1996, then quickly expanded under Mohammad Khatami (1997–2005), reaching 130 in 2001 and close to 200 by 2005.

In February 2001, the Sixth Parliament approved, for the first time, as part of the Budget Bill for Year 1381 (March 2001–March 2002) the provisions to political parties of funds to be distributed by the House of Parties (*Khaneh-ye Ahzab*), an umbrella organization newly created under the auspices of the Interior Ministry. In a rare legislative achievement for the pro-Khatami reformists, the Expediency Council approved the provision of funds, overriding the opposition by the Guardian Council. In year 1381, some 8 billion Rials were distributed among 80 parties; in the following year, as the membership of the House of Parties increased, some 6 billion Rials were distributed among 114 parties.

In addition to the parliamentary elections, multi-party electoral competitions also take place in the presidential, the Leadership Experts Assembly, and the city and rural councils elections, as political parties and groups similarly publish the name or the list of their nominated candidate(s). The nomination of a candidate by a political party, however, does not usually mean that he or she is a member of that particular party. As a result, it so happens that certain prominent candidates receive simultaneous nominations from rival political parties and/or *ad hoc* electoral coalitions, a characteristic that often confounds not only outside observers but also many local voters. Nonetheless, certain enduring politico-ideological differences do separate those political parties and groups operating within the Islamic Republic system into several semi-permanent political currents, often called factions (*jenah-ha*), a fact that helps keen voters and observers identify the candidate's political orientations. To a certain degree, the existence of such overarching factions has also filled the gap created by the lack of established political parties active on a nationwide scale, a tendency that continued to be a norm even after the ban imposed by Ayatollah Khomeini apparently expired with his death in 1989.

During the first decade, the conservative faction comprising the powerful clerical establishments such as the Tehran Combatant Clergy Association and their lay allies such as the Islamic Coalition Society/Party (*Jam'iyyat/Hezb-e Mo'talefeh-ye Eslami*) and the Islamic Society of Engineers (*Jame'eh-ye Eslami-ye Mohandesin*) stood against the oft-called radical faction comprising the left-leaning supporters of the Mir-Hossein Musavi Cabinet, such as the Islamic Associations of Students of the Universities of Tehran (the Unity Consolidation Office), the Labor House (*Khaneh-ye Kargar*), and those clerics who later formed the Tehran Combatant Clerics Assembly. Into the second decades of Hashemi-Rafsanjani's presidency, a centrist, pro-government faction comprising the newly formed Executives of Construction Party and the Labor House took shape after having quarreled for some time with the dominant conservatives. During the same period, the revitalized Islamic Revolution Mojahedin Organization (*Sazman-e Mojahedin-e Enqelab-e Eslami*, reestablished in 1991) led the Islamic left faction while the Combatant Clerics Assembly suspended its political activities after its defeat in the 1992 parliamentary elections. Despite the formation of a third faction, two consolidated lists of candidates each nominated by a rival ad hoc electoral coalition have, from time to time, appeared in several multi-seat districts, in both the parliamentary and the city and rural councils elections (first held in 1999), with the centrists joining either the conservative or the Islamic left faction.

Unlike the parliamentary elections in which electoral contestation has led to a radically different factional composition among the elected deputies almost every four years, the first several presidential elections (except for the very first held in 1980) were unaffected by the uncertainty that, in part, defines democratic election. The winners of these presidential elections were largely pre-determined due to the lack of serious competition among the candidates. Only in the seventh election, in 1997, and the ninth, in 2005, (especially during the second round of voting) did the two rival factions fight against each other, offering real choices to the voters. By contrast, the successive elections of the Leadership Experts Assembly (held every eight years since 1982) have been void of multi-party contestation in part because the potential candidates of the Islamic left faction either lacked sufficient credentials (in 1982) or were excluded as the result of approbatory supervision exercised by the Guardian Council (in 1990, 1998, and 2006).

Despite their status as permanent fixtures during various elections and their apparent proliferation during Khatami's presidency, political parties remain nothing but loose coalitions among a relatively small number of like-minded politically active individuals and are still crucially disconnected from the body politic. The elitist tendencies of most of the parties, as well as the cadre mentality of their members, are inferable from the fact that no prominent post-revolutionary political party or group sought to seriously expand their membership on the general voter level. Even the Islamic Iran Participation Front Party, the most successful in terms of both organizational structure building and electoral achievements among the so-called Second of Khordad Front reformist parties, had no more than 500 party members nationwide before its fall from power in 2004. The relatively fragile and highly volatile voter-level support for the pro-Khatami reformist parties that became apparent after 2001 was attributable, at least partially, to the lack of focused efforts on their part to expand membership and/or build support structures on the general voter level when their popularity remained high.

If, as some argued, the dissipation of voter-level support for the elected reformist elite—not the well-expected resistance by the arch-conservatives power-holders *per se*—was *the* precipitating causal factor behind the political downfall of the pro-Khatami reformists and the resultant lack of promised democratic consolidation during the presidency of Mohammad Khatami, the underdevelopment of political parties may well have been among the key factors that separated some of the successful consolidation episodes elsewhere from the case of Khatami-era Iran. Furthermore, the disconnected nature of political parties from the general voters under the Islamic Republic system is a reminder also of the fact that despite the far-reaching changes in the composition of political elite, the nature of dominant political discourse, and the significant expansion in voter participation in the elections, the institutionalization of political parties and a party system has remained highly elusive in the Iranian context throughout the century-long period from the Constitutional Revolution (1905–1909).

Suggested Reading

Akhavi, S. 1994. Iran. In *Political parties of the Middle East and North Africa*, ed. F. Tachau. Westport: Greenwood Press; 133–173.

Baktiari, B. 1996. *Parliamentary politics in revolutionary Iran: the institutionalization of factional politics.* Gainesville: University Press of Florida.

Matsunaga, Y. 2007. *Struggles for democratic consolidation in the Islamic Republic of Iran, 1979–2004.* Ann Arbor, Mich: UMI. Moslem, M. 2002. *Factional politics in post-Khomeini Iran.* Syracuse: Syracuse University Press.

Qavanin-e, A. Iran. http://www.ir-ph.org/irph11.aspx.

Sartori, G. *Parties and party systems.* New York: Cambridge University Press.

Zarifinia, H. R. 1999. *Kalbod-shekafi-ye Jenah-ha-ye Siyasi-ye Iran, 1358 ta 1378.* Tehran: Azadi-ye Andisheh.

YASUYUKI MATSUNAGA

✦ PRINT MEDIA

The history of print media in Iran dates back to the 1660s, when a version of the Gutenberg printing press was introduced. The first published book was a 570-page religious volume by an Armenian church in Isfahan printed in Armenian. The first book in Persian was published in 1818.

Kaghaze Akhbar (News Sheet), claiming to "educate and inform" people, was the first newspaper published during the Qajar dynasty in 1837. A few years after the first newspaper was discontinued, *Vaqaye'a Etefaqiyeh* (News and Current Events) was published in 1851. This weekly paper was spearheaded by Mirza Taqi-Khan Amir-Kabir, a famous prime minister, during the reign of Nasser-al-din Shah Qajar (1848–1896).

Reading the last issue of the Farsi-language *Nowruz* in Tehran, 2002. (AP Photo/ Hasan Sarbakhshian)

The first bilingual Persian–French newspaper, *Rooznamaye Vatan* (Nations Newspaper), was published in 1876. However, Nasser-al-din Shah did not support this paper and stopped its distribution on its first day of publication. He claimed that Iran should first establish a viable domestic press before attempting to produce foreign language publications.

From the very beginning, the print media in Iran faced a multitude of governmental restrictions and censorship, and was expected to align itself with the wishes of the rulers. In fact, prior to the 1890s, there was barely any independent or private press in Iran.

After the 1905 Iranian Constitutional Revolution, the long legacy of press censorship and dictatorial control ended, and the Majlis (parliament) introduced and approved the first law—the 21st Amendment to the Constitution—ensuring the freedom of press in Iran. Based on the 18th Amendment of the Belgian Constitution, the law provided broad freedoms and even stipulated that reporters could attend governmental meetings and inform their readers in a factual manner, provided they serve the public interest. It was also stipulated that publishing falsehood or libelous materials would subject one to prosecution through legal channels.

During the Pahlavi dynasty (1925–1979), the Iranian press was generally expected to serve as a platform for government propaganda and was restricted from criticizing the rulers and their policies. Press censorship was particularly intensified after the 1953 CIA-orchestrated and financed coup d'etat which overthrew Dr. Mohammad Mossadeq's democratic government in Iran and reinstated Mohammad Reza Shah Pahlavi who had previously fled the country. In this new political climate, some newspapers were closed while new pro-government papers emerged. In the 1970s, approximately 28 dailies, 88 weeklies, and

Table 4   1975 Estimated Figures for Major Iranian Newspapers and Magazines

Dailies	Circulation	Weekly Magazines	Circulation
Kayhan	300,000	*Zane-Rouz*	150,000
Etella'at	250,000	*Etella'at Banova*	100,000
Iran-e-Novin	50,000	*Tamasha*	60,000
Ayandegan	30,000	*Etella'at Javanan*	30,000
Mardom	20,000	*Khandaniha*	30,000
Tehran Journal	10,000	*Kayhan Varzeshi*	30,000
Paygham-e-Emrouz	6,000		
Journal de Tehran	6,000		
Bourse	6,000		

SOURCE: *Iran Almanac and Book of Facts*, 14th edition, 1975, Echo of Iran, Tehran.

29 weekly and 57 monthly magazines were being published. Of those, two dailies, *Kayhan* and *Etella'at*, were dominant in popularity and circulation.

A feature of developing countries has been the existence of a gap between government and public interests; hence the two sectors are often at odds. Historically, with a few exceptions, the Iranian newspapers have functioned as an extension of government organs and have faced a variety of restrictions. For instance, in Iran, no one is allowed to publish a newspaper without obtaining a legal permit from the government. Furthermore, the line between "private press" and "public press" is blurry due to the fact that even privately owned newspapers are dependent on the government for their vital needs such as paper supplies, printing plates, and advertising income.

Immediately after the 1979 Islamic Revolution in Iran, which ousted the Pahlavi monarchy, the print media experienced a free press and, therefore, did not hesitate to publish reports about an array of issues—particularly political matters. This, however, was shortlived. The next window of opportunity emerged in 1997, when the fifth president of the Islamic Republic of Iran, Mohammad Khatami, was elected by overwhelming public support. Although this period of free speech was shortlived (1997–1998), its positive impact still resonates in the country. Generally speaking, during Khatami's two-term presidency (1997–2005), a liberalization movement began which resulted in the emergence of liberal newspapers and a dynamic period for the print media in general. But, in 2005, with the election of Mahmoud Ahmadinejad, a non-cleric conservative, restrictions on the press and media were intensified.

The Ministry of Culture and Islamic Guidance, which operates the Islamic Republic News Agency (IRNA), is the regulatory body for all media outlets and cultural products, including music, newspapers, videos, movies, books, and the Internet. It should be noted that all broadcast media in Iran are owned and operated by the government, and no private ownership is allowed. All cultural products must be reviewed and approved by the Ministry prior to public distribution; therefore to obtain such approvals, one has to practice "self-censorship." The work of authors, artists, and journalists is scrutinized, and newspaper publishers are constantly on guard in order to avoid being shutdown by the government.

In March 2007, the Association of Iranian Journalists (Ajomane Senfiye Rouznameh Negarane Iran) reported that at least seven journalists were in Iranian jails and more than four newspapers and 20 weekly and monthly magazines were banned from publication. AIOJ is an independent professional body whose aim is to promote freedom of the press, ethical conduct, and to protect the rights of journalists in Iran.

According to UNICEF, in 1975, the estimated literacy rate in Iran was 57% for men and 32% for women, whereas in 2004 it was 84% for men and 70% for women. Interestingly enough, despite this positive development, newspaper readership in Iran remains marginal to the point that none can claim a one-million circulation in a country with over seventy million people—more than 60% of whom are younger than 35 years.

According to official estimates, in 2006, the number of government-licensed newspapers and magazines published reached 3,367, which is the highest in the history of print media in Iran. The number includes all daily, weekly, biweekly, and monthly newspapers, as well as weekly, biweekly, monthly, bimonthly, quarterly, semiannually, and annually published magazines. It also includes cultural, ethnic, corporate, regional, provincial, religious, sports, and organizational publications in domestic languages (Arabic, Azeri, Turkic, Kurdish, Lori, Balouchi) and foreign languages (Arabic, English, French).

In 2007, more than twenty daily newspapers—with varied and unknown circulations—were published in Iran. An interesting aspect of journalism in

Table 5 2007 Major Iranian Daily Newspapers

Paper	Orientation	Circulation	Affiliation
Abrar	Reformist	n/a	Private
Afrab-e Yazd	Reformist	160,000	Private
Entekhab	Pro-conservative	50–100,000	Private
Etella'at	Moderate	50–80,000	Government
Etemaad	Reformist	n/a	Private
Etemaad-e Melli	Reformist	50-80,000	Private
Farhang-e Ashti	Pro-reformist	n/a	Private
Hamshahri	Pro-reformist	150,000+	Tehran governor
Iran	Reformist	100,000+	IRNA (government)
Iran Daily (English)	Conservative	100,000	Government
Jaam-e-Jam	Conservative	450,000	IRIB (government)
Jomhuri-ye Eslami	Conservative	n/a	Government
Kargozaran	Reformist	100,000	Private
Kayhan	Conservative	60–100,000	Government
Khorasan	Conservative	50,000	Private
Mardom Salari	Pro-reformist	n/a	Mardom Salary Party
Quds	Conservative	n/a	Quds Rezavi Foundation
Rasalat	Conservative	30–50,000	Rasalat Foundation
Seyasat-e Rouz	Conservative	n/a	Private
Sharq	Reformist	100,000	Private
Tehran Times (English)	Conservative	15,000	Government

SOURCE: Based on BBC and online Persian and English sites.

Iran is that the majority of reporters are young while the majority of owners and editors are of an older generation. Since the early days, newspapers have been utilized by government and government officials as vital communication channels for public persuasion and dissemination of political and social ideologies and policies.

In general, Kazem Motamed-Nejad, who completed his graduate education at the University of Tehran and the University of Paris, is considered to be the father of new journalism in Iran. Since the early 1960s, he has taught university-level courses and is now a distinguished faculty of the College of Mass Communications at Allameh Tabataba'e University, Tehran. In addition to teaching some of the first journalism courses, he has been instrumental in the growth and development of journalism education and research in Iran. He has also been active in national and international organizations and has contributed to the establishment of the Association for Defending Press Freedom (Anjomane Defa'e Az Aazadiye Matbo'at).

Suggested Reading

Echo of Iran. 1975. *Iran almanac and book of facts*, 14th edition. Tehran, Iran: Echo of Iran.

Inter Press Service News Agency online. http://ipsnews.net/news.asp?idnews=34688.

Iranian Association of Iranian Journalists online. http://www.aoij.org/english/index. htm.

Kamalipour, Yahya, and Hamid Mowlana, eds. 1994. *Mass media in the Middle East: a comprehensive handbook*. Westport, Connecticut: Greenwood Press.

Mohsenian-Rad, Mehdi. 2006. *Iran in four communication galaxies* (3 volumes in Persian). Tehran, Iran: Soroush Press.

YAHYA KAMALIPOUR

✦ PROPAGANDA AND INDOCTRINATION

In the Islamic Republic of Iran, propaganda (*tablighāt*) and indoctrination (*hoqneh kardan, elqā'*) are essentially the primary and most important functions of the Islamic government. Iranian Shi'ite clerics, as the founders and protectors of the Islamic regime, are indoctrinated to be indoctrinators. The main mission of Shīite clerics is to propagate and spread Shi'ite Islam by preaching and persuading believers that Shi'ite Islam is the only religion that carries the truth and salvation and that other faiths are wrong and misleading. The ideology of the Islamic state is based on Shi'ism as understood and introduced by classical canonical reading of Twelver Shi'ism, presented by Sheikh Saduq (306 AH/AD 918–381 AH/AD 991), Mohammad Kolaini (d.328/ 329 AH/AD 939/940) and Mohammad Baqer Majlesi (1056 AH/AD 1646–1131 AH/AD 1719). Khomeini (1900–1989), Motahhari (1920–1979), Shariati (1933–1977), and Bāzaegan (1907–1995) ideologized this faith in their own ways to be used in the fight against the monarchy and for the establishment of an Islamic state, as they had different perspectives on the foundations and missions of this form of governance.

Iranian clerics, in general, are well trained to do an excellent job in advocacy, public relations, and propaganda. Almost all classical Shi'ite didactic texts, like *Lomeh* and *Makāseb*, lack an analytical and interpretive approach but rather are based on apologetic and persuasive approaches. Shi'ite seminaries' curriculum is aimed at influencing the opinions and behaviors of people and has nothing to do with providing religious and spiritual information. The basic section of clerical training in Shi'ite seminaries is internship in Islamic propaganda organizations. The seminary students are sent to small cities and villages to preach and propagate Shiite Islam and prepare for bigger challenges.

The ruling clerics of Iran look at Iranians as minors; this is the underlying idea of the theory of guardianship of the jurist (*velāyat-e faqih*). The guardian decides what the minor needs and which way s/he should be headed in her/his life. This idea is supposed to be indoctrinated in the hearts and minds of Iranians. The constitution of the Islamic Republic of Iran gives priority to propaganda and indoctrination by founding the Islamic regime on the basis of Islamic ideology and putting the Islamic jurist above the law. According to the preamble of the Constitution, "the mass-communication media, radio and television, must serve the diffusion of Islamic culture in pursuit of the evolutionary course of the Islamic Revolution." Article 175 gives the upper hand in this respect to the jurist/leader: "The appointment and dismissal of the head of the Radio and Television of the Islamic Republic of Iran rests with the Leader". Propaganda and indoctrination are pursued as integral parts of the real politics. Radio and TV stations are run by the government, most of the press is controlled by the high-ranking officials, and all news items, analyses, and reports are heading toward satisfying the ruling clerics. The free flow of information has no place in this media system: the regime considers propaganda as the only function of media outlets. Education, entertainment, and their mixtures, i.e. edutainment and infotainment, are also reduced to propaganda and indoctrination.

IRI propaganda and the indoctrination machine date back to the time of the 1979 Islamic Revolution and Iran–Iraq War of 1980–1988. This machine was an effective weapon during the war, and due to its success it has since been used constantly in peacetime. The main aim of indoctrination is to dehumanize and create hatred toward a supposed enemy, either perceived to be internal or external in nature. This external enemy is rooted in a vague perception of the West, and it focuses more on the United States, Israel, and some European countries, especially England; the internal enemy is any entity which does not agree with the pillars of Islam, the Islamic regime and government, and the administration. The propagandistic machine is designed to produce a false and confusing image of the so-called enemies. State run radio and TV usually report the negative events and aspects of the West and completely ignore such events that occur domestically. This is usually done by using and avoiding certain words, or by assigning responsibility to the enemy for certain things in the country, e.g., air accidents are due to sanctions. The textbooks are written in a way that introduces only the clerics as patriots and fighters for independence and justice. All secular groups and individuals, mystic figures who did not agree with the jurists, and dissident religious groups are washed away from the history of the country.

Propaganda and indoctrination exist and are pursued and institutionalized in the Islamic regime because they serve various social and political purposes. They help the regime to mobilize its base, which has been shrinking from the 1980's; they are reactions to the regime's legitimacy crisis and cover up the decreasing popularity and influence of the unelected leaders of the regime. In a post-revolutionary Iranian context, indoctrination is intended to prepare people to enter the group of true believers. The Iranian government does its best to persuade its subjects that the government is right and that the people should not challenge the officials to think it through for themselves. Strategies and methods of Islamic indoctrination, very similar to other religious and political indoctrinations, appeal to one's emotions, information manipulation, making a non-intuitive relationship between concepts and behaviors, and presenting suppositions as facts. The more sophisticated strategies, usually used in universities and in the political sphere, include diversion from critical issues, suppressing critical thinking, limiting the debate spectrum, and exclusion of "outsider" views. Subtle propaganda techniques used by the ruling clerics are involved in disseminating covert propaganda in the form of television programs, movies, songs, and plays.

Flag-waving, glittering generalities, intentional vagueness, oversimplification, rationalization, scapegoating, red herring, excommunication, repetition as verification, accusation of heresy, blasphemy and profanity, slogans, cursing, stereotyping, testimonial, unstated assumption, and labeling are the common techniques used in preachings and Friday prayers. The governmental media are experts in using virtue words and loaded terms, transmitting unstated assumptions, associating the ruling clerics with Shi'ite Imams and symbols, quoting out of context, name-calling, demonizing, and using euphoria. The authorities also appeal to fear to seek popular support. They usually ask the dissidents to join the crowd that is supposedly obedient. Iranian media in general appeal to the same techniques that have been used by totalitarian and authoritarian states. To support a position, idea, argument, or course of action, they resort to political and religious authority and cite prominent religious-political figures.

The Islamic propaganda system of Iran has five pillars; uncritical thinking, censorship by trustees of the ruling class, univocality of the public sphere, monopoly of the media, and window dressing. The propaganda factory of the IRI produces its products in different makes and models. It is used to recruit followers and keep them. Some realities facilitate this recruitment process: about 50% of the population live under the poverty line; about 20% and 60% are illiterate and underliterate, respectively; and the wealth of the country is concentrated in the hands of a few who have access to religious authorities. Transferring the facts of Islam and other religions and providing alternative ideas, explanations, and doctrines does not even have secondary places in almost all Iranian clerics' teachings and lectures. So-called mavericks and disobedient clerics who believe and preach otherwise are not accepted in the mainstream mosques and huseiniehs and are usually defrocked for violating the unwritten code of clerical conduct. The techniques used by the Islamic regime are more negative than affirmative. Propaganda is mainly run not by filling people's minds with approved information, but by preventing people from being confronted with opposing points of view.

The Constitution is absolutely silent on the topics of religious and ideological education, but the government has always tried to Islamicize the educational system, from elementary school to higher education, in terms of curriculum, materials, policies, and conducts. The official governmental policies in the area of education and information are totalitarian, but due to the resistance of the public, these policies have not been fully enforced and implemented. Iran's educational system confuses education with indoctrination and scholarship with scholasticism. According to the perception of the ruling clerics, there is not and also should not be any free flow of information; people need propaganda, not information. The Islamic Republic has systematically replaced reflective conversations with emotionally appealing phrases.

Indoctrination is carried out in three areas of life: education, the workplace, and leisure/entertainment. According to Islamic ideology and IRI style, all educational facilities are factories for making new kinds of humans: true believers of the ruling-class ideology and individuals obedient to the leader of the country. Working in the Islamic republic is not really a right but a privilege that will be easily revoked if a worker, especially a public one, violates the unwritten code of conduct for the second order citizens. Entertainment is considered a vice unless it is provided, manufactured, and controlled by the government. Any resistance against the procedures of indoctrination through education, work, and entertainment will result in excessively harsh punishment, rejection of social and political rights, and the withholding of rewards. In the circle of loyalists, any positive behavior modification is rewarded by compliments, approval, encouragement, and affirmation.

By resorting to identity crisis, the government gives it subjects a false impression of the quality or policies of their own country. The national pride is used to reject certain proposals or certain remarks and ignore the experience of other societies. Islamic propaganda is used to disapprove "others," including other religions (even Sunni Islam) and other ideologies, especially secular ideologies and isms. Among the isms, liberalism is demonized more than any other ideology, whereas communism and socialism were equally demonized in the 1980's. The positive propaganda is used to support enforcement of *shari`a* law and to propagate the ideologized morality of Shi'ite Islam.

Coercive and brutal persuasion is only used for intellectuals, writers, journalists, and political activists through torture, obligatory confessions in front of state-run TV cameras, solitary confinement and deprivation of social and political rights, and even intellectual work. The show trials against "enemies of Islam and Islamic state" are an inseparable feature of the judicial system.

The Islamic Propaganda Organization (*Sāzmān-e Tablighāt-e Eslāmi*), the Qum Office of Islamic Propaganda (*Daftar-e Tablighāt-e Eslāmi-ye Qom*), and the Islamic Culture and Communications Organization (*Sāzmān-e Farhang va Ertebātāt-e Eslāmi*) have a clear and distinct mission of propaganda and indoctrination. Ministries of Education, Islamic Culture, and Guidance, and Justice, the Judiciary, seminaries that now are all funded by the public budgets, Radio, and TV channels, Baseej (militia), IRGC, IRA (military forces), and the Disciplinary Forces (police) work directly as sections of the ministry of propaganda and indoctrination. Other governmental ministries, departments, and offices are indirectly involved in Islamic propaganda and indoctrination through ideological recruitment, training, ombudsman, and ceremonies.

All Iranian media are directly or indirectly funded by the government; the government owns all big media organizations, and its ideology is the basis of mass culture and politics. Almost all media outlets, whether publicly or privately owned, must carry propaganda and indoctrination directly or indirectly to be allowed to continue their work. For transmitting propaganda messages and reenforcing indoctrination, the Iranian government uses almost all media forms and formats, including news reports, government reports, historical revision, fake science, books, leaflets, movies, radio, television, news websites, blogs, murals, and posters. In the case of radio and television, propaganda exists on news, current-affairs and talk-show segments, public-service announcements, and even commercials.

Since few Iranians have access to different media outlets and sources to double-check what they learn at school or hear from governmental media, repetition of such disinformation reinforces the idea that the disinformation item is really a "well-known fact." The disinformation is recycled in the media and in the educational system, without the need for direct governmental intervention on the media. Almost all independent press, even licensed to the loyalists of the regime, has been under constant pressure or has been closed when presented alternative explanations and/or reports. The government has the monopoly over electronic media and does not let any group have a share of the information industry. News agencies are all in the hands of conservative and authoritarian groups.

Suggested Reading
Mohammadi, M. 2003. *Deen va Ertebātāt* [*Religion and Communications*]. Tehran: Kavir.
Mohammadi, M. 2001. *Simā-ye Eqtedārgrāyee* [*Authoritarian Face: Iranian TV, 1990–2000*]. Tehran: Jame'eh ye Iranian.
Mohammadi, M. 1998. *Sar bar Āstān-e Qodsi, Del dar Gero-ve `Orfi* [*Sacred vs. Secular: Islamicization Process in Iran*]. Tehran: Qatreh.

MAJID MOHAMMADI

✦ PUBLIC RELATIONS

Some forms of public relations and persuasion were practiced in Iran during its thousands of years (more than 5,000) of history. In modern times, public relations, media, and persuasion are inherently tied to the political, economic, and social circumstances of nations, and Iran is no exception. One of the most significant events that ushered in a new post-feudalism era in Iran was the Constitutional Revolution of 1905. The revolution, which took place during the reign of Mozzafar-al-Din Shah (1896–1907) of the Qajar dynasty (1781–1925), led to the establishment of new laws and a Majles (*Edalat Khaneh* or House of Justice) in Iran (then called Persia). The revolution, which was intended to change the traditional autocratic political system into a modern democratic system in Iran, was—and still is—regarded as an unprecedented social and political movement in the Middle East. One of the outcomes of the revolution was the appearance of new publications in which public issues were vigorously debated. New social and political institutions emerged and paved the way toward the emergence of a modern form of persuasion and communication, public relations. Most of the Iranian social movements were organized by the literate populace who had access to published materials.

Among the Constitutional laws passed by the Majles was the guarantee of freedom of expression and social rights for Iranians. Shortly after these laws were established, the governmental and nongovernmental institutions sought to establish a mechanism for public persuasion and dissemination of news and information in accordance with those practiced in developed countries. Initially, such efforts were carried out by chief officers and directors of organizations, but soon they realized the need for hiring PR practitioners and establishing PR departments within their organizations. Between 1910 and 1920, a new "office of press and publicity" was added to the organizational charts of a few organizations.

However, World War I (1914–1918) in Europe combined the political and regional ambitions of the British and Soviets, and impacted Iran's domestic and international affairs. On October 26, 1923, an army officer, Reza Khan, seized control of Iran and forced the last king of the Qajar dynasty, Ahmad Shah Qajar, into exile in Europe. Reza Khan adopted the last name "Pahlavi," to impress upon the Iranian people a new era of nationalism and modernity, and established the new Pahlavi dynasty. This dynasty ended with the popular 1979 Iranian revolution and the establishment of the Islamic Republic of Iran. One of Reza Shah's controversial decrees was deeming the wearing of traditional hijab or chador by women illegal. In fact, his policies of introducing Western cultures and industries into Iran were similar to the policies of Kamal Ataturk of Turkey.

Reza Shah Pahlavi, once again, reverted to absolute control and, consequently, ignored the constitutional gains by suppressing political parties and controlling the media and freedoms. Nonetheless, in his attempt to "industrialize and modernize" Iran, he utilized all means of communication and persuasion, including mass media and public relations, to publicize his government's policies and activities and, reportedly, devoted a sizable budget to the press, publicity, and propaganda. Furthermore, during Reza Shah's rule, two amendments were added to the constitution. One focused on the sponsoring of immoral and questionable materials shown in movies, and the other required all owners of radio-receiving sets to obtain a permit—this, apparently, was to combat the spread of communism via the Persian broadcasts of Radio Moscow.

In view of the foregoing and subsequent political events, including World War II, the Mohammad Mossadeq nationalistic movement (early 1950s), the nationalization of the Iranian oil industry (1951), the CIA coup (1953), the reign of Mohammad Reza Shah Pahlavi (Reza Shah's son, 1941–1979), and the Islamic Revolution (1979), one can surmise that the history and development of mass media and public relations in Iran has gone through tumultuous and uncertain periods. During Mossadeq's period, the number of newspapers increased and a relative sense of freedom prevailed.

Reportedly, the Anglo–Iranian Oil Company was the first major company to establish an office of "Press and Publicity" during the nationalization movement in the early 1950s. The goal was to combat the ongoing push for the nationalization of the British-controlled oil industry by the Iranian nationalists and Iranian Communist Party (supported by the Soviet Union). Hamid Notghi, who had completed a law degree at the College of Law, University of Tehran, and a Ph.D. in law, at Istanbul University, was hired by the Anglo–Iranian Oil Company, in 1948, to serve as a publicity expert. Other British-educated employees, with close ties to the British publicity firms, were also hired to work in the newly created office. After Mossadeq's success in nationalizing the Iranian oil industry (1951), the office of "Press and Publicity" was renamed "Ravabet Omoomi" or "Public Relations." Interestingly enough, in accordance with President Harry Truman's "Point Four Program," announced in 1949, Syracuse University began a cooperative project with Iranian governmental ministries. It was intended to produce educational programs and documentaries aimed at educating the Iranian masses about social issues.

In 1942, Notghi was appointed director of the public relations department at the National Iranian Oil Company (NIOC). It is widely acknowledged that Notghi was the first PR practitioner, PR teacher, and author of the first PR book, *Public Relations Management* [*Modiriyate Ravabete Omoomi*], in Iran. In 1969, he was invited by the College of Mass Communication in Tehran to teach courses in his areas of expertise. In 1973, he traveled to the United States and visited a dozen universities to review their public relations degree programs. Upon returning to Iran, he planned and established a public relations degree program within the College of Mass Communication and was appointed as director of the PR program—a position that he held until the 1979 Islamic Revolution. Notghi, also known as the "father of PR in Iran," paved the way for growth and development of Public Relations programs within the universities as well as public and private institutions. In the earlier years, some of the Iranian government ministries, including the Ministry of Foreign Affairs, sent a selected number of their staff to Great Britain and the United States to enroll in short-term programs and seminars in public relations.

During the tenure of Prime Minister Amir-Abbas Hoveida (1965–1977), a number of Iranian intellectuals were recruited, such as Ibrahim Golestan and

Jalal Al-Ahmad, and encouraged to produce cultural products, including significant films and documentaries about social and cultural issues.

In view of the foregoing, it is safe to say that the modern practice of public relations in Iran began in the 1960s. As is the case in the United States, some of the first PR practitioners in Iran were former journalists. The higher education institute of the "Press and Public Relations" started its operation in the fall term of 1967, and the first group of graduates received their degrees in June of 1971. Today, with the establishment of PR courses and programs at colleges and universities, along with an increased level in research and publications, many of the approximately 100,000 Iranian PR practitioners have obtained formal degrees, taken courses in mass communication or public relations, completed PR workshops, or have obtained certificates in the field. On average, 400 graduate and 10,000 undergraduate students are enrolled in public relations programs at fifteen universities throughout the country. For example, Allameh Tabataba'e University, Azad Islamic University, University of Tehran, Imam Sadegh University, and Practical-Scientific University offer B.A., M.A., and Ph.D. degrees in communication studies.

From 1966 to 2006, more than fifty books on public relations have been published in Iran—many of them translated from English into the Persian language. A comprehensive *Public Relations Encyclopedia* was added to this collection in 2004. Several books have been published by Kargozar Public Relations Institute and others by independent publishers and public relations groups. As of 2007, six PR journals and newspapers are published in Iran, including *Kargozar Public Relations Quarterly*, *Public Relations Research*, *The Eighth Art*, *Public Relations Monthly*, *Public Relations Quarterly*, and *Public Relations Skills*. Founded by Mehdi Bagherian, Kargozar initiated an annual International Public Relations conference (http://www.icpr.ir) in 2004, which takes place in Tehran and is attended by experts and scholars from throughout the world.

The first PR digital databank, Internet Institute for Public Relations (http://www.iranpr.org), was established in 2001, and contains more than 3000 pages of information, papers, and research results related to public relations. In addition, the first Electronic Public Relations Software Group (http://www.eprsoft.com) was established in 2005. This group organized its first annual ePublic Relations conference in 2006 to explore the emerging opportunities in communication and persuasion in the digital age. About 20 PR-related weblogs are also available online, including Applied Public Relations, Public Relations Programming, Public Relations Research, Iran Public Relations, Public Relations News, and Electronic Public Relations.

Most Iranian private and public institutions and companies have their own internal public relations departments and web pages. Some of the public relations groups include Public Relations Society of Iran (http://www.prsir. org), which publishes the journal *Public Relations Monthly*; Kargozar Public Relations, which publishes *Kargozar Public Relations Quarterly*; Public Relations Students, which publishes *The Eight Artists*; and the Press and Publicity arm of the Ministry of Education and Culture of the Islamic Republic of Iran, which publishes *The Eight Arts*. Many of the thirty provinces in Iran have established their own regional public relations societies, including Kerman, Isfahan, Mazandaran, Qom, and Yazd.

By 2007, a public relations song (anthem) had been composed and recorded, a public relations day had been designated, and a code of practice and ethics for public relations had been developed—all of which are indicative of the importance of public relations and its significant role in social, political, and economic developments in Iran. Today, even the religious individuals, groups, and organizations are actively involved in public relations and utilize the Internet as a vehicle for communication, information, and persuasion.

Suggested Reading
Kargozar Public Relations website: http://kargozar.eprsoft.com.
National Iranian Oil Company website: http://www.nioc.com.
Public Relations Association of Iran, *Ravabet Omoumi Magazine* [in Persian]. January 1997.
Public Relations Society of Iran website: http://prsir.eprsoft.com.

YAHYA KAMALIPOUR

✦ QASHQA'I

The Qashqa'i are a group of approximately one million people residing in the southern Zagros Mountains of southwestern Iran. The Qashqa'i confederacy consists of five large tribes and many smaller ones, and a hierarchy of leaders unify the polity: an *ilkhani* at the top, tribal *kalantar*s and khans in the middle, and headmen and elders for the subtribal sections. The Qashqa'i are a distinct ethnolinguistic minority in a nation-state whose dominant population is Persian in language and culture. (Half of Iran's population consists of Persians; the other half contains Turks, Kurds, Lurs, Arabs, Baluch, and others, many of whom are tribally affiliated.) The Qashqa'i speak a form of western Oghuz Turkish, a language derived from the time that some of the group's ancestors lived in Central Asia, and they trace their origins to this vast region. The Qashqa'i confederacy rose to prominence in southwestern Iran in the mid-eighteenth century when a ruling elite family consolidated many tribally organized nomadic pastoralists in the area. These tribal peoples descended from Turkic, Lur, Kurd, Arab, and Baluch groups, and over time a distinctive Turkic-based culture and society grew dominant among them. There are presently four major economic sections within the Qashqa'i tribal confederacy.

A Qashqa'i nomadic pastoralist representing one of the economic sectors, Turan tended the newborn lambs and kids near her campsite while her brother herded the sheep and goats on a distant mountain slope. Deploying designs that represented her cultural heritage, Turan's mother wove an intricate knotted carpet on a horizontal loom she had assembled just outside the family's black goat-hair tent. Turan's father was spending the day traveling to the bazaar in the city of Shiraz so that he could purchase rice, tea, and salt. The family spent the winter in its customary lowland pastures near the Persian Gulf, then migrated in the spring to its highland pastures southwest of the city of Isfahan, where the family stayed the summer, before returning to its winter pastures in the autumn. Until the 1970s, Turan's grandparents had traveled by foot during the arduous, two-month seasonal migrations, but her parents had gradually adopted vehicular transport for their household goods. Turan's father and brother continued to migrate with the livestock so that the animals could exploit the vegetation along the route, while she and her mother and young siblings traveled by truck to their seasonal pastures, set up camp, and waited for the rest of the family to arrive.

Typifying the second economic sector of the Qashqa'i confederacy, Mehrdad and his wife and children raised sheep and goats and migrated seasonally between winter and summer pastures, but they also pursued compatible livelihoods. They planted a small apple orchard alongside their summer pastures, and the crop they harvested brought them welcome cash income. They cultivated alfalfa and clover between the trees and cut the crop several times every summer to use as fodder for their livestock. They planned to establish a small citrus orchard near their winter pastures but needed the government's permission before they could begin. When the apple trees matured, they built a one-room stone house near the orchard and appreciated the comfort it provided during the late spring and early autumn. For the period in between, when the weather turned mild, they erected a goat-hair tent as their dwelling. They wanted to construct a small stone house in winter pastures also, especially if their plans for the citrus orchard progressed. They had grown accustomed to a shelter offering them more protection than the airy tent provided, and they appreciated having a secure place for storage. In winter pastures they cultivated wheat for the flatbread they ate as their staple food, and they also grew barley for the pack animals and pregnant ewes.

The Qashqa'i in the third sector often still consider themselves to be "nomads" (*ashayer*), regardless of their current educational and economic endeavors and their new places of residence. Being a "nomad" entails more than just physical mobility; the word also holds cultural connotations, some of which overlap with the term "Qashqa'i." Both labels offered people a way to identify themselves and their distinctive society and culture and to differentiate and unify themselves within the wider Iranian society, where ethnic Persians have dominated.

Iran's Ministry of Education employed Golnar as a teacher in a girls' tribal school in the town of Chenar Shahijan, located near the mountainous winter pastures of her Qashqa'i group. Golnar exemplifies the third economic sector, those Qashqa'i who pursued livelihoods as salaried state employees and as paid workers in the private sphere (where they transported commodities and served as farm laborers, builders, and musicians). Many people in this sector continued their economic interests in pastoralism and agriculture, usually by cooperating with their still-migratory kin. Golnar's parents and brothers were nomadic pastoralists who migrated seasonally between winter and summer pastures, and she often visited them there. Her family had enrolled her in the elementary school established for her tribal group in the two seasonal locales, and later she attended secondary school in the town of Kazerun. A good student who performed well in the nationwide university-qualifying examinations, she entered university and earned a degree in biology. Sought by the government for her academic expertise as well as her tribal affiliation, she began to teach in the tribal middle school for girls. Soon she married a paternal cousin with whom she rented a small house in Chenar Shahijan. There they arranged their few possessions in the same fashion as they had furnished the small space of their tent. After their son was born, her husband stayed at home to care for the child while she performed her teaching duties.

The revolution that had created the Islamic Republic of Iran in 1979 soon sparked conflicts within the country, including efforts by Iran's ethnolinguistic minorities to achieve some political and cultural autonomy. The government's revolutionary guards (*pasdaran*) seized and imprisoned a preeminent Qashqa'i leader (Khosrow Khan Qashqa'i, a newly elected member of the Islamic Republic's first parliament).

Koroush represents the fourth economic sector, the Qashqa'i living outside of Iran as wage laborers, salaried employees (some in the higher professions), university students, and exiled leaders. Koroush joined the
small, armed group that formed in Khosrow Khan's defense. He reluctantly left Iran after the government's defeat in 1982 of the Qashqa'i
tribal insurgency (more accurately, a "defensive resistance"), because he
feared capture and possible execution. Koroush had wanted to attend
university in Iran, but his affiliation with the insurgency ruled out that
possibility, and he lacked economic opportunities within the country. He
was unwilling to join the ranks of the disillusioned, unemployed urban
youth who often engaged in risky, personally destructive behaviors. After
a long sojourn in Turkey while he waited for a visa, he traveled to Paris,
France, where he eventually found temporary unskilled employment.

Some Qashqa'i in the fourth sector—the diaspora—also considered themselves to be "nomads," especially when the difficult conditions they faced
abroad forced them to change jobs, relocate their residences, move to other
cities, and find new countries to host them. By claiming the label, they also
acknowledged their cultural identity, stressed their dissimilarity from the majority population in their new countries (and from other Muslim immigrants
there), and reduced their feelings of alienation. Identifying themselves as
Qashqa'i, nomads, and tribal members, these people in Iran had been fortified
in their efforts to resist the oppressive policies of a succession of central governments. As labels of identity, the terms served in similar ways abroad, especially in Europe, where the majority population often disapproved of arriving
immigrants, especially those who were Muslims coming from a country such
as Iran.

The Qashqa'i are Shi'i Muslims, unlike many of Iran's other tribally
organized ethnic and national minorities, who are Sunni Muslims. As such,
they appear to have escaped some problems experienced by Iran's religious
minorities: Sunni Muslims and members of other faiths (Christians of different sects, Bahais, Zoroastrians, and Jews). The religious faith of the Qashqa'i
centers on their love of God and their respect for ethical conduct. Partly
because their seasonal territories were often remote and distant from religious
centers, the Qashqa'i had not been as familiar historically as many other Iranian Muslims to Islamic law and customs, including attending mosques, performing daily prayers, fasting during Ramadan, making the pilgrimage to
Mecca, and reading the Qur'an.

Since the Islamic Republic's formation in 1979, Iran's ruling clergy and their supporters have attempted to propagate their version of Islamic beliefs and practices among the Qashqa'i. For schoolchildren especially, mandatory modest dress, compulsory prayers and fasting during schooldays, and required instruction in Islam, the Qur'an, and Arabic have influenced their attitudes and practices. State-stipulated modest dress for girls (over the age of nine) and all women limited their choices of attire, especially when they visited towns and cities where vigilantes and the government's mobile moral squads enforced the state's requirements for proper dress, appearance, and behavior.

Since the early 1990s, after an uneasy decade in which many Qashqa'i feared to act in their own interests, women and girls resumed wearing full Qashqa'i dress—including the translucent headscarf that revealed their hair—in their own spaces at home and within their Qashqa'i communities. Most of them avoided state sanctions. In increasing numbers, they also appeared wearing Qashqa'i attire in urban and other public settings. Governmental officials applied one set of standards to urban dwellers (who were primarily Persians) and another set to the ethnic minorities that they perceived to be colorful, exotic, and appealing to the international audiences that otherwise might have viewed Iran negatively.

Some customs found in urban areas concerning death and mourning were not specifically state-mandated, yet some Qashqa'i began to adopt these practices for their own commemorations. They could have retained their own expressions, but many people complained that the non-Qashqa'i urban people on whom they depended economically and politically would criticize and berate them. The Iraq–Iran war (1980–1988) served as a transformative period when many Qashqa'i wanted to acknowledge their own war dead in the same ways they observed in towns and cities. By the middle of the war, most Qashqa'i engaged in the practices they witnessed in urban society, and soon they extended these customs to deaths occurring because of other reasons. Before the war, the Qashqa'i (especially those who did not reside in towns and cities) conducted ceremonies of burial and mourning in customary fashion. These low-key, austere rituals ordinarily drew only immediate and extended families and other close kin. (The rites for tribal leaders and other prominent figures were larger, more elaborate events.) During and especially after the war, these rituals changed to include printed announcements adorned with Qur'anic verses, ornate floral displays festooned with banners, amplified Qur'anic recitations (by mullas from outside their communities), and the physical separation of hundreds of male and female participants. Some people commented that after they had adopted these practices, they could not return to pre-war expressions without incurring the condemnation of outsiders.

The extent to which many Qashqa'i changed their beliefs (as compared with their practices) is difficult for outsiders to determine accurately. Yet most people complained about the version of Islam that the ruling clergy tried to force on them for overtly political reasons. Many of them stressed that their spirituality focused on their personal relationship with God, and they criticized the way Iran's clerics manipulated Islam in order to retain political and economic power for themselves and their supporters.

During the nearly three decades since the revolution, most Qashqa'i have struggled to balance two features in their lives. They benefited from a modernizing, centralizing nation-state (such as formal education and new kinds of jobs), and yet they retained advantages from the political, social, and cultural systems that had sustained and strengthened them as a group in the past. Their tribal structures, organizations, and values offered them ways to protect themselves and their families, especially in unstable, unpredictable political circumstances. Central governments come and go, but their tribal groups always embraced them. They worried about the fate of the youngest generation, which increasingly fell under the influence of urban schools, the state-controlled media, governmental agencies, and the Persian-dominated society with which they had to interact.

To maintain and enhance their sense of "Qashqa'i-ness," the people devised some effective strategies. They emphasized the importance of communal gatherings, such as weddings, funerals, and memorial services, in which people renewed kinship, tribal, and ethnic ties. If their new residences were elsewhere, they frequented the customary winter and summer pastures of their parents and grandparents. They tried whenever possible to separate themselves from non-Qashqa'i society, especially those elements that disrupted their lives (such as the mobile morals police, revolutionary guards, and militia volunteers). They acknowledged the distinctive ways they expressed their culture. Certain forms of music, dance, song, poetry, weaving, attire, dwellings, and technology helped them to assert their heritage, especially when these practices violated the state's restrictive social regulations and set the Qashqa'i apart from those who supported the regime.

Women's customary attire especially displayed the people's values about ethnic identity and gender roles. In addition, it revealed women's resistance to the government's stern edicts about modest dress. Qashqa'i women (along with many of Iran's tribal women) had a reputation for independence and assertiveness, traits they did not hesitate to demonstrate, especially when confronted by female Islamic militants enveloped in black.

Painters, graphic artists, musicians, poets, calligraphers, weavers, and others attuned to the Qashqa'i arts strove to teach their knowledge and skills to others, especially the youth. Young individuals with growing expertise in modern technology, use of the Internet, and new forms of publishing reached people who might not otherwise have been aware of new trends. The publication of many different Qashqa'i magazines, available in cities near tribal territory and increasingly popular among all segments of Qashqa'i society at home and abroad, demonstrated the conjunction of these interests. A typical magazine issue contains essays on Qashqa'i history (often based on newly gathered oral traditions), biographies of eminent Qashqa'i individuals, old and newer forms of poetry, photographs of recent Qashqa'i festivals, demonstrations of Qashqa'i dress (which, for women, violated state standards), illustrations of customary technology (such as different forms of weaving), and reviews of books relevant to the Qashqa'i.

In 2007 Qashqa'i Turkish was not yet a written language possessing its own alphabet or using one derived from other forms of Turkish (such as the Latin-based alphabet found in modern Turkey). The new Qashqa'i magazines deployed the Persian alphabet to render (inaccurately) the sounds of Qashqa'i Turkish, and many Qashqa'i disliked the practice, especially because it proved their continuing subservience within a Persian-dominated Iran. They knew that the Persian alphabet derived from the Arabic one, and they witnessed the growing presence of Arabic words in written and spoken Persian—brought about by the rapid Islamization of the government, educational system, media, and parts of popular culture. They often joked that the Islamic Republic represented the "second Arab invasion," the first one accompanying the insertion of Islam in Iran many centuries ago.

Many Qashqa'i remained uncertain in 2007 about the future. The revival of their distinctive culture and society inspired them, but the unstable political conditions in Iran impeded them from fulfilling their envisioned plans for economic betterment. They shared these uncertainties with most other Iranians; the majority of Iranian citizens also disfavored the current government, a circumstance that fortified the Qashqa'i in their own acts of resistance. Yet as many Qashqa'i lamented, "The years keep passing, and we are still waiting for change."

See also Nomads; and Tribes.

Suggested Reading
Beck, L. 1986. *The Qashqa'i of Iran.* New Haven, Conn.: Yale University Press.
Beck, L. 1991. *Nomad: A Year in the life of a Qashqa'i tribesman in Iran.* Berkeley: University of California Press.
Beck, L. 2004. Qashqa'i women in post-revolutionary Iran. In *Women in Iran from 1800 to the Islamic Republic,* eds. L. Beck and G. Nashat. Urbana: University of Illinois Press.

Huang, J. 2006. Integration, modernization, and resistance: Qashqa'i nomads in Iran since the revolution of 1978–1979. In *Nomadic societies in the Middle East and North Africa: Entering the 21st Century*, ed. D. Chatty. Leiden: Brill.

Huang, J. 2008. *Tribeswomen of Iran: weaving memories among Qashqa'i nomads*. London: I. B. Tauris.

Oberling, P. 1974. *The Qashqa'i nomads of Fars*. The Hague: Mouton.

LOIS BECK AND JULIA HUANG

R

✦ RAFSANJANI, ALI AKBAR HASHEMI

Former Iranian President Akbar Hashemi Rafsanjani was born on August 25, 1934, in southeastern Bahraman in the province of Kerman in central Iran. He was one of nine children (five boys and four girls) born into a pistachio farming family near Rafsanjan. At the age of five, Hashemi began his schooling. At fourteen, his parents sent him to the Qom, Iran's theological center of learning, where Hashemi commenced his religious education. Rafsanjani studied Islamic law, morality, and mysticism, achieving the level of a mojtahed. He studied with Ayatollah al-Ozma Boroujerdi, Ayatollahs Khomeini, Shariatmadari, Haeri Yazdi, Najafi Marashi, Allameh Tabatabai, Zahedi, and Montazeri.

During the period of Rafsanjani's religious education, Ayatollah Khomeini inspired a political atmosphere at the seminary which contrasted with the quietist Shi'a religious tradition. Khomeini called upon the clerical youth to challenge the monarchical status quo. Indeed, Mohammad Reza Shah's ambitious modernization drive, White revolution campaign of land redistribution, and pro-American relations deeply agitated monarchical-clerical relations. Many clerical students, including Rafsanjani, were arrested for anti-monarchical activity.

After the assassination of Prime Minister Hassan Ali Mansour, in 1964, Rafsanjani was jailed for four and a half months. He resumed his clandestine organizational work in Qom and was jailed again in 1967 for publicly opposing the Shah's coronation ceremonies. In 1973, he was sentenced to eight

417

Former Iranian President Hashemi Rafsanjani. (AP Photo/Vahid Salemi)

years in prison on charges of collaboration with the Mojahedin-e Khalq guerrilla organization; he served four years of this sentence.

After the triumph of the Iranian Revolution in February 1979, Rafsanjani was appointed to the Council of Islamic Revolution, and when the government of Mehdi Bazargan resigned in November of that year, he was also appointed acting minister of the interior. He became one of the most powerful figures as co-founder of the Islamic Republican Party (IRP), which had a key role in Iranian politics until it dissolved in 1987 following internal conflicts over policy. He was elected Speaker of the Parliament—the Majles al-Shura—which was dominated by that party and its allies. He held this position from 1980—1989. Through the skillful use of this office, he swiftly became one of the most visible and influential politicians in the country, a process that was accelerated when his senior colleagues in the IRP became victims of assassination.

Also important in the growth of his popular appeal were the nationally televised sermons he frequently delivered for the Friday prayers at Tehran University.

Despite the official foreign policy of independence evidenced through Ayatollah Khomeini's statement "neither east nor west," it was Rafsanjani who began to open the door to moderation towards the United States. In a 1983 sermon, he stated that "Iran was ready to have relations with all countries ready to have relations with us and ready to honor the revolution." A year later he laid the groundwork for what later become known as the Iran–Contra affair by acknowledging that Tehran would be willing to buy spare parts through a third army. Ironically the Reagan Administration transferred those arms to Iran on the condition that Tehran would use its persuasion with Lebanon's Hezbollah to free six American hostages. For Iran and particularly for Rafsanjani who was directly implicated in this scandal, dealing directly with the "Great Satan" in the midst of the Iran–Iraq War proved to be a challenging domestic crisis to overcome. Needless to say, Rafsanjani emerged from the scandal without public criticism or loss of stature. Those who were implicated were among the cadre who disclosed the information to the public. This event foreshadows Rafsanjani's willingness to compromise ideological rigidity for the national interest.

Rafsanjani has been repeatedly described as a "pragmatic conservative" and a political chameleon. He has been astute at reading the popular pulse and often been the driving force of moderation within the Islamic Republic. He has held numerous elected and appointed posts within the Islamic Republic of Iran. He continues to wield political power not only from elected office but also due to his imposing reputation and appointed positions. In 1988, he was appointed by Khomeini as acting commander of the armed forces. He was among those responsible for convincing Ayatollah Khomeini to accept the ceasefire offered by UN Resolution 598, ending the Iran–Iraq War.

After the death of Ayatollah Khomeini on June 3, 1989, President Ali Khamenei was elevated to the position of leader *(rahbar)* of the Islamic Republic. Rafsanjani was twice elected president of the Islamic Republic from 1989–1993 and 1993–1997. On June 11, 1993, he was reelected to a second term with 63.2% turnout, which represented 57.6% of the electorate.

His political mandate as president was directed to rebuilding the country after the devastating economic and political consequences of the eight-year Iran–Iraq War. Often known as Leader of the Reconstruction or "Sardar e Sazandegi," in his first term he applied the First Economic Plan to redistribute wealth among the *mostazafin* or dispossessed and the Second Economic Plan to stabilize the economy. Rafsanjani directed the economic reintegration of Iran into the global economy coupled with the refurbishment of the housing, infrastructure, and oil industries. During his tenure as president, Rafsanjani attempted to introduce privatization and liberalizing economic policies to Iran's statist economic system. During his term, Iran's trade with the European Union almost quadrupled.

However, Rafsanjani's term as president was not met without significant internal factional opposition. Traditional factions within the government opposed his economic and social policy that challenged the fundamental tenets of the ideological basis of the revolution. These internal groups also opposed Rafsanjani's ideas of foreign policy moderation. With Rafsanjani's efforts to encourage foreign investment, stimulate private investment, and renegotiate loans, so too came World Bank and IMF programs that were considered extensions of "hegemonic Western policy."

Rafsanjani's pragmatism extended to his foreign policy agenda as well. He believed that U.S.–Iranian relations would improve if the United States would only release frozen Iranian assets as a gesture of goodwill. Rafsanjani had sent his own signals of Iranian neutrality during the 1991 Gulf War. However, not only did relations with the United States not improve during his presidency, but his term coincided with a series of legislation to ban trade and investment in Iran imposed under the Clinton Administration. The first measure blocked Conoco and other American companies from investing in Iran's energy sector. The second effort in May 1995 banned trade and investment in Iran and was followed in August 1996 by the Iran Libya Sanctions Act (ILSA) which imposed sanctions on any foreign company investing more than $20 million in Iran's energy market. With such forceful opposition emerging from Washington, Rafsanjani's hopes of rapprochement with the United States were obviously dashed.

In the regional policy arena, Rafsanjani struggled to re-ingratiate Iran into the international community. Moderating its ideological predilections in favor of a national interest–oriented policy, Rafsanjani proved more flexible and pragmatic in dealing with Iran's neighbors. After the collapse of the Soviet Union, he was careful not to provoke Moscow. Moreover, after the trying decade of the 1980s, Rafsanjani was determined to renew ties with the Gulf States.

A steadfast policy even for Rafsanjani was Iran's Israel policy. Even Rafsanjani could not extricate Tehran from Ayatollah Khomeini's ideological anti-Israeli legacy. For many in Iran, compromising on this issue would lead to other concessions on the revolutionary ambitions. Hence, Rafsanjani, in responding to popular sentiment in 1989, called upon Palestinians to retaliate against Israel by attacking Westerners and their interests globally suggesting that, "If in retaliation for every Palestinian martyred in Palestine, they kill … five Americans or Britons or Frenchmen … the Israelis would not continue their wrongs." As international sentiment pushed for peacemaking settlements in Madrid in 1991 and Oslo in 1993, Iran only hardened its position towards Israel, calling its own conference and obstructing efforts by calling for concrete action against all parties.

In 1997, the criminal court of Berlin issued an international warrant for Rafsanjani's arrest for ordering the assassinations of Iranian–Kurdish dissidents abroad in the Mykonos restaurant in 1992. These accusations launched against the highest echelons of Iran's leadership lead to a withdrawal of European ambassadors from Iran. Rafsanjani's past is heavily tainted with involvement in international terrorism. During his tenure as president, bombings occurred at the Khobar Towers in Saudi Arabia in 1996, which killed 19 U.S. servicemen, and the bombing of the Jewish community centre in Buenos Aires in 1994, which killed 80 and wounded 300. In October 2006, an Argentine judge called for the arrest of Rafsanjani among others for his collaboration with Hezbollah in organizing the attack.

Rafsanjani is widely seen as the father of Iran's nuclear weapons program. The initial phase of the program was carried out in the 1980s under his supervision as the acting Commander in Chief. As President, Rafsanjani placed enormous resources at the disposal of the country's military-industrial complex to develop the nuclear bomb project. The greatest advancements in the nuclear project, from uranium enrichment technology to plutonium extraction methods, were made under his direction. Rafsanjani traveled to China in 1985, finalizing the parameters for Sino–Iranian nuclear cooperation that would continue for over a decade.

Having promised the people an improved standard of living after the injustices of war, public expectation grew in response to his repeated economic and social pledges. The end of his term saw little success in effecting change. The impact of factional politics and pressure of U.S. embargos and sanctions also complicated Rafsanjani's presidential legacy. While he had sought to amend the constitution to run for a third term, public support for the president had declined significantly.

In 2000, Rafsanjani participated in another election since his presidency seeking a seat in the parliament. The election was a critical battle between the reformist and conservative factions. In the campaigning, Rafsanjani was targeted as responsible for the reformist press crackdown and dissident killings that had taken place during President Khatami's first term. After voting was complete it became clear that Rafsanjani was not among the 30 representatives elected from Tehran. The Council of Guardians nullified numerous ballots in an effort to get him elected as the 30th representative. However, Rafsanjani withdrew to "protect national unity," having suffered one of the worst humiliations of his career.

In April 2005, Rafsanjani yet again announced his candidacy but this time for the ninth presidential elections. Rafsanjani had been regarded as the frontrunner and had positioned himself as a centrist. The election took place in two rounds and led to the victory of former mayor Mahmood Ahmadinejad. The first round of the election was a very close race with minor differences in the number of votes won by each candidate, which led to a runoff a week later between Ahmadinejad and the ex-president. After the first round of the election Mehdi Karroubi, the pragmatic reformist candidate who ranked third in the first round but was the first when partial results were first published, alleged that a network of mosques, the Islamic Revolutionary Guards Corps military forces, and Basij militia forces had been illegally used to generate and mobilize support for Ahmadinejad propelling him into higher position. This election is among the most controversial in Republic's history.

In 1997, Rafsanjani was appointed to head the Expediency Discernment Council which was created in 1988 to mediate disputes between Iran's parliament and the Guardian Council as well as to serve as a consultative council to the Supreme Leader. In 2005, this body was charged with additional oversight of the executive, legislative, and judicial branches through Supreme Leader Ayatollah Khamenei. Rafsanjani also has been elected to the position of deputy Chairman of the Assembly of Experts, the body of 86 mujtahids that appoints Iran's supreme leader, the highest political and religious authority in the country. In the election for the fourth assembly which took place in December 2006, Rafsanjani received the highest number of votes. Despite a career that has ebbed and flowed in popularity, Rafsanjani continues to wield power and influence in the factional political system of the Islamic Republic of Iran.

From a marriage in 1958, Rafsanjani has three sons, Mohsen, Mehdi, and Yasser, and also two daughters, Fatemeh and Faezeh. His younger daughter, Faezeh Hashemi, is a women's right activist whose journal *Zan* (Woman) was closed down by hardliners in 1997. Rafsanjani is one of the richest men in Iran. He owns many properties in the country, around the town of Rafsanjan, and has many connections in Iran's huge oil industry. Little information is available regarding his wealth or his business in Iran and abroad due to the opaque nature of the Islamic government.

Rafsanjani has authored a few books. His most ambitious and popular includes a book on Amir Kabir titled *Amir Kabir: the Hero of Fighting against Colonialism*, which was published in Qom in 1968.

Suggested Reading
Menashri, D. 2001. *Post-revolutionary politics in Iran: religion, society and power*. London: Frank Cass Publishers.

SANAM VAKIL

✦ REFORMISM, ISLAMIC

From its very inception, the Islamic Republic of Iran was divided into various factions based on class, political ideology, economic goals, and diverse interpretations of Shiite Islam, including Ayatollah Khomeini's views and decrees. Since Khomeini's death in 1989, factional politics have grown in both intensity and complexity, revealing the power bloc's dilemmas with policymaking in a rapidly changing society. The reformist faction in the Iranian post-revolutionary power structure, or what is loosely termed as the "reform movement," constitutes one such contending force in the last decade. To fully comprehend the Islamist reformism one needs to historically examine its genealogy based on the three dimensions of religious modernism, economic reformism, and political reformism.

Generally speaking, the historical antecedents of post-revolutionary Islamist reformism can be traced to a trend of thought commonly referred to as "religious modernism," defined as an attempt to free the religion of Islam from the shackles of an excessively rigid orthodoxy, and to accomplish reforms that will render it adaptable to the complex demands of modern life; while "religious reformism" and "religious modernism" strongly overlap, a number of differences separate the two. Most notably, religious reformists come from within the religious establishment, and they also seek their solutions from within the religion. Although the viewpoints of the Iranian reformists cannot be directly traced to the pre-revolutionary generation of religious modernists, it would also be a mistake to totally ignore the overall intellectual and political climate provided by a diverse group of Muslim thinkers and activists. For example, from the late nineteenth century to the 1970s, the contributions of individuals such as al-Afghani, Na'ini, Sangelaji, Kasravi, Taleqani, Bazargan, Motahhari, and Shariati on Iranian society have been considerable.

Religious modernism in the post-revolutionary era is closely identified with the intellectual circle (*rowshanfekran-e deeni*), centered around Abdolkarim Soroush, a scientist and philosopher. In the mid-1980s, Soroush and his colleagues were engaged in a controversial theoretical debate, challenging the traditionalist reading of Shiite jurisprudence (*fegh-e sonnati*) on social, political, and epistemological grounds. Between April 1988 and May 1990, a series of his articles entitled "The Theoretical Contraction and Expansion of Religion" were published in the journal *Keyhan-e Farhangi*. After the journal closed down in 1990, a new bimonthly journal, *Kiyan*, became the new medium for serious religious intellectual debates.

Led by Soroush, lively and critical discussions surfaced in *Kiyan*, involving a number of future Islamist reformists, including Seed Hajjarian, Mohsen Kadivar, Akbar Ganji, Mohsen Sazgara, Mostafa Rokhsefat, and Reza Tehrani. In addition, a number of open-minded clerics, such as Mohammad Mojtahed-Shabestari, and even a few secular intellectuals (not directly associated with the "*Kiyan Circle*"), also made valuable contributions to a modernist reading of Islam, as well as to sociopolitical issues. Targeting totalitarian interpretations of Shiite Islam, the writings of Soroush, Kadivar, and Shabestari, in particular, have effectively led to a new religious discourse termed a "sacral defense of secularism." Whereas Soroush emphasizes the variable nature of religious knowledge and Shabestari underlines the limited nature of it, Kadivar substantiates the multiple nature of religious thesis. As far as Soroush's basic principles are concerned, the following may serve as a summary:

While religion and *shari`a* (due to their divine character) have a permanent nature, religious knowledge (as a part of the domain of human knowledge) is subject to change.

1. Transformations in sciences and fields of knowledge will, in the final analysis, affect human understanding of religion (*ma'refat-e deeni*).
2. Comprehension of religion is imperfect, relative, and evolving, and should not contradict scientific findings.
3. These arguments allow him to de-ideologize Islam and to distance himself from pre-revolutionary ideologues such as Ali Shariati.

All in all, the post-revolutionary religious intellectualism had a liberating effect on the young generation of Islamist activists who had increasingly become disillusioned with the dominant totalitarian readings of Shiite Islam. During the Iran–Iraq War (1980–1988), however, expression of dissent was taboo. They had to wait for political opportunity.

The war finally ended in 1988, and a year later, Ayatollah Khomeini, the revolution's charismatic leader, passed away. In the same year Ali-Akbar Hashemi-Rafsanjani became president. All these events facilitated a period of socioeconomic reform under Rafsanjani. Popular demands, suppressed for a decade under the pretext of war exigencies, were now assuming a more powerful role in dictating public policy. The first term of Rafsanjani's presidency (1989–1993) corresponded with new economic reforms including: reconstruction of war-torn areas, renewal of the economic infrastructure, structural adjustment centered on "marketization" of the economy, privatization, creation of free-trade zones, and promotion of foreign investment. A number of factors had converged to pave the way for the rise of new economic policies: the passing away of Khomeini (the main supporter of the left faction during the war); the disintegration of state socialism in Eastern Europe which accelerated neoliberal globalization; and a major shift in the popular mood toward consumerism, a culture of joy, materialistic values, individualism, and de-politicization of daily life. This was a natural reaction to the adverse economic conditions of the war period: a 26% inflation rate and more than 30% unemployment rate in 1988; rationing of basic economic necessities through "couponism"; growing class inequality along with rising poverty and corruption.

Rafsanjani, sensing this widespread discontent, took the banner of "economic adjustment" (*ta'adil-e eghtesadi*) via economic development and moderation.

The full implementation of such policies necessitated neutralization of the Islamic left faction. The parliamentary elections of March 1992 (the Fourth *Majles*) provided the political opportunity, when a coalition of the Rafsanjani faction (the "modern right") and the conservative right disqualified the majority of the leftist candidates through the Guardian Council. This act deprived the Islamic left from their strongest base, the *Majles*. Consequently, they withdrew from day-to-day politics and retreated into the institutions of higher education or research centers. A period of "redefinition' of their political identity ensued and lasted well into 1997.

In addition to strict economic measures, Rafsanjani's reform package also included foreign policy overtures to the West, particularly to European states, but also to international institutions such as the World Bank. There was also a limited dosage of cultural liberalization, manifested in partial relaxation of strict censorship laws against the press, as well as more tolerance applied to the dress codes, entertainment and the expression of joy in public, dating norms, and issuing invitations to certain wealthy/expert members of the expatriate community to return to Iran. All in all, Rafsanjani made an effort to de-ideologize the Islamic Revolution and establish a new technocratic-pragmatic approach to social problems.

These reforms, however, did not include political liberalization. Rafsanjani was not any more tolerant of political dissent than his authoritarian predecessors in the first decade of the revolution. His "Iranian Perestroika" never even came close to a political opening. Even his partial cultural liberalization policies lost momentum by 1992. This was symbolized by the resignation of his open-minded minister of Culture and Islamic Guidance, Mohammad Khatami, under incessant pressure by the conservatives. They also removed Rafsanjani's ministers of the state and the economy, and in effect crippled his program of "reconstruction."

While Rafsanjani's second term (1993–1997) was still based on an informal partnership with the conservatives, it was increasingly becoming evident that the latter, now enjoying the support of both Ali Khamenei (the new Supreme Leader after Khomeini) as well as the (fourth) *Majles* majority, would not allow Rafsanjani's socioeconomic reforms to proceed. Rafsanjani's poor performance in the sixth presidential elections (1993) also helped the conservatives. He only received about ten million votes in an election that marked voter participation rate at only 51%, whereas in 1989 Rafsanjani had received more than 15 million votes, when 56% of the eligible voters had cast their votes.

The March 1996 (fifth) *Majles* elections provided Rafsanjani with a new opportunity to revive his economic reforms. Approaching the elections in a somewhat more organized fashion, Rafsanjani and his close allies formed *Kargozaran-e Sazandehi* (Functionaries of Reconstruction) in January 1996. They consisted of fifteen members of his cabinets, hastily coming together to prevent the monopolization of power by the conservatives. They even introduced a new publication, *Bahman*, to spread their perspectives among the intellectuals. *Kargozaran*, sensing a latent but growing desire in urban Iran for openness, development, and modern values, presented themselves as the only challenge to political monopolism, cultural obscurantism, and economic traditionalism (rooted in the *bazaar*). Despite heavy rigging of the elections, *Kargozaran* performed fairly well and succeeded in gaining 60 seats.

The 1996 parliamentary elections has been called a "dress rehearsal" for the 1997 presidential election. In fact, *Kargozaran* ended their informal alliance with the conservative right before the *Majles* elections and consequently formed a parliamentary alliance with the Islamic left. Factional politics in *Majles* now had a broader goal: victory in the presidential election of May 1997.

The third dimension of Islamist reformism deals with the discourse of political reform. The latter represents a new moderate approach to sociopolitical change, adopted by a new generation of young and disenchanted Islamist revolutionaries turning away from strict ideology, utopianism, charismatic authority, the culture of martyrdom, violence, and authoritarianism, toward some type of democratic Islamic political culture. This attitude is documented in the words of writer and essayist Alireza Alavitabar: "After the end of the [Iran–Iraq] war, we were not supporting oligarchic rule, and we assumed the role of critics of the oligarchy. From then on, we were transformed from enthusiastic supporters to critics of the system.... The only way ahead was the democratic path." These words, in effect, echoed the growing sentiment among many ex-revolutionaries, now distrustful of the post revolutionary authoritarian leadership.

Two events, in particular, raised serious questions about the revolutionary commitments of the new power elite: the abrupt and unexpected defeat in the war, and the conspiratorial method by which Ayatollah Montazeri, Khomeini's heir, was removed from his position in 1989. This was due to his critical stance on some of the regime's policies, particularly on the mistreatment of political prisoners. Most of these alienated young men were associated with the leftist faction and some of the notable ones came from the ranks of Muslim Students Followers of the Imam's Line, the group that occupied the American Embassy in Tehran in November 1979. Some of them, about two decades later, became indispensable to the reformist camp: Abbas Abdi, Mohsen Aminzadeh, Mohsen Mirdamadi, Mohammad-Reza Khatami, and Ma'soumeh Ebtekar.

The political socialization of other key reformers (during the mid 1990s) took place in other state organizations/institutions such as the ministry of Islamic Guidance headed by Khatami and in the Center for Strategic Studies (associated with the President's Office) headed by Mohammad Mousavi-Khoiniha, a left-leaning cleric. This center performed a vital role in the formation of a new reformist discourse in Iran. Among different research projects conducted in the center, three stand out: "political development," "Islamic thought," and "culture and society," supervised respectively by Saeed Hajjarian, Mohsen Kadivar, and Abbas Abdi. Soon, many democratic-oriented leftists pushed out of the polity joined the center. It is commonly believed that most of the new ideas and concepts (later) associated with the May 23 Front were either formulated here or studied in social science departments (both in Iran and abroad). Exclusion from centers of power, in fact, provided this group of activists with a rare opportunity to critically evaluate their past performance. All of a sudden, liberal democracy, reform, pluralism, political development, rule of law, civil society, and human rights were no longer viewed as "un-Islamic" ideas.

By the mid-1990s a new Islamic political (sub) culture was in the making. During the first half of the 90s, similar politico-cultural developments were also shaping student activism. A new generation of Islamist activists, mainly organized in The Office for Consolidation of Unity (*Daftar-e Tahkim-e Vahdat*), was becoming more alienated from the state's policies and consequently was turning to liberal discourse and Soroush's ideas. In the meantime, the conservative right, already successful in isolating Rafsanjani, having maintained its majority in the *Majles* and strong voice in the judiciary, and pushing the left faction out of the power bloc, was making the necessary preparations for capturing the presidency. Their candidate was Ali-Akbar Nateq-Nuri, a conservative/traditionalist cleric, who started his informal campaign after the 1996 Parliamentary elections, as the new *Majles* speaker.

By the summer of 1996, political and cultural repression was widespread in the country, reminiscent of the war period. Rafsanjani, who was finishing his second term as president, initiated a relentless effort to modify the Constitution, allowing him to run for a third consecutive term. Soon, it became clear that this would fail due to the conservatives' resistance.

The "new left," sensing a life and death situation, started mobilizing for the approaching seventh presidential election. Despite their political marginalization, the leftists still enjoyed significant social support in the universities and among the religious sections of the middle class. In the summer of 1996, they approached Mir-Hossein Mousavi, the wartime prime minister, as their candidate. However, Mousavi refused the offer (possibly due to pressure by the conservatives). At this point, in January 1997, Khatami's name emerged as the candidate of diverse groups and organizations on the left, particularly the Islamic Associations. Khatami was eventually convinced to join the competition, despite his initial reluctance to accept the candidacy. He only hoped to capture a respectable share of the electorate, but the unfolding of events resulted in a very different outcome.

In mid-March 1997, *Kargozaran* and Rafsanjani finally opted to support Khatmai's candidacy. Aside from Rafsanjani's political weight, the role of Gholam-Hossein Karbaschi, the then-mayor of Tehran and the chief officer of the popular newspaper *Hamshahri*, is indisputable, particularly in the financing of Khatami's campaign.

Energized by growing support after March, Khatami issued a 12-point political and economic program, centered on the ideas formed earlier, in what is known as the "*Ayeen Circle.*" The latter refers to a fairly small group of Islamist democrats, such as Hajjarian, Khaaniki, Tajzadeh, Abdi, Kadivar, and Mohammad Reza Khatami (all associated with Mohammad Khatami). Khatami's campaign also included a bus tour of Iran which brought him extraordinary support. By April 1997, a few polls reported that Khatami had, in fact, surpassed Nateq Nuri. The conservative bloc, alarmed by Khatami's rising popularity, engaged in a series of character assassination tactics. These included associating Khatami with "Westoxicated" youths, secularists, and even implying that he was a devout enemy of the *Vali-e faqih*, Ayatollah Khamenei. Such tactics backfired, and, in fact, added to Khatami's popularity among certain modern social groups.

On May 23, 1997, in an election that also included three other candidates, Khatami was victorious by winning more than 20 million votes (almost 70% of the votes cast). This victory demonstrated that Iranian society was yearning for major reforms and the status quo was no longer acceptable to the majority. The press dubbed the May 23 mobilization the "Big no!" against the establishment. After May 23, factional politics in the Islamic Republic assumed a new form: authoritarians versus reformists. Interestingly, for the first few months, Khatami's key intellectual associates did not publicly refer to themselves as "reformists." The term, perhaps, was introduced by the pro-Khatami media. In some of the writings of Saeed Jajjarian, "the mastermind behind reforms," the term "reform" is introduced in the context of political development: Political modernization is a reformist arrangement to regulate relations between the state and the nation, to normalize people's political behavior, and to increase the state's responsiveness for the sake of postponing the revolution. A year into Khatami's presidency, however, "reform" became the very identity of the coalition of forces formed after May 1997.

The reasons for the turn toward reformism can be thus summarized: (1) popular reaction against the Islamic Revolution and its ideological, dogmatic, and harsh approaches to mounting social problems; (2) the collapse of the state socialist bloc and the associated decline of revolutionary values in the Third World (Iran included); (3) the Iranian intellectuals' gravitation toward liberal-democratic discourses, symbolized by the writings of thinkers such as Karl Popper, Imre Lakatos, Immanuel Kant, John Stuart Mill, Isaiah Berlin, and Richard Rorty; and (4) as far as the Islamist reformers are concerned, it should be taken into consideration that it was morally and psychologically impossible for them to radically turn against their "brothers" only a decade and a half into the revolution—they shared with the conservatives a myriad of familial, emotional, economic, politico-cultural, historical, and generational linkages. Thus, "reform" would provide them with the perfect political justification to represent themselves to the power bloc as well as their own supporters alternately as either a pro-system state faction or a change-seeking social movement.

Khatami's landslide victory had made him the *de facto* leader of the May 23 Coalition; his policies would define the collective character of Islamist reformists. From the very outset he made a conscious decision to preserve the boundaries of the system, as defined by the Constitution and observed by the Supreme Leader and the associated institutions. The heterogeneous composition of his first cabinet laid the foundation for Khatami's compromising approach *vis-à-vis* the conservatives and the *vali-e faqih*. To the broader society, however, the impact of the reformists' victory was initially more encouraging. It facilitated the flourishing of a number of civil society forces, and organizations, particularly, among women, students, youths, intellectuals, artists, journalists, workers, and ethnic minorities. This was evident in the proliferation of the NGOs, (Islamist) political organizations, gatherings and demonstrations, journals, magazines and books, art exhibits and concerts, and intellectual speeches, all taking place in a more relaxed social climate.

The intellectual core of the reformists, who never expected to find themselves in charge of the executive power, was slow to react to the new conditions. Most of their cadres had to handle different responsibilities. They had one leg in political organizations and another in cultural-intellectual activities. Among their most successful cultural projects was a series of reformist publications mobilizing public opinion against the conservatives; they included *Jameh'eh, Rah-e No, Neshat, Khordad, Zanan, Sobh-e Emrooz, Hayat-e No*, and *Asr-e Ma*. Some publications, with a secular orientation, also surfaced in this period. This was most evident in book publication, which clearly showed a shift in public interest to non-religious topics: political, historical, psychological, literary (novels), and philosophical themes. The main (non-clerical) reformist political organization, the Islamic Participation Front of Iran (*Jebheh-ye Mosharekat-e Iran-e Eslami*), was formed in December 1998. In addition, there were also seventeen political organizations and associations that collectively formed a somewhat heterogeneous "reformist front" during the elections, involving progressive democratic reformists on one end to fairly conservative clerical groups on the other.

Most noticeable in the reformist camp was the absence of a long term vision or a political strategy. The reformists were mostly unified by their common opposition to the conservatives' policies and outlook. These dogmatic orientations had, accordingly, caused "the Islamic Republic to completely distance itself from the earlier revolutionary ideals and goals." The reformists were thus convinced that in order to correct this deviation they should capture other state institutions such as the parliament and the judiciary, toward the ultimate formation of an Islamic democracy. Beyond this, there were very few concrete roadmaps or well thought tactics. An exception, perhaps, was the theoretical writings of Saeed Hajjarian, who believed that reform, in the concrete case of Iranian factional politics, required the gradual transformation of the dysfunctional dualistic rule to a functional dualistic rule, which he called the essence of political development.

After being in a state of political paralysis during Khatami's first two years in office, the Conservatives slowly regrouped. Their main tactic was to create crisis on a permanent basis. Khatami has, reportedly, complained about "one crisis every nine days" during his first term. Some of these include: the sexual scandal case involving a German citizen; the trial and jailing of Karbaschi (the mayor of Tehran) on corruption charges; physical attacks against two outspoken ministers of Khatami; the jailing of Abdollah Nuri, his Minister of the Interior; periodic closings of reformist journals; serial murders of secular activists and intellectuals; attacking an American tourists' bus; the closing down of *Salaam*, a reformist daily, (which sparked massive student protests in several cities); the brutal attack against a Tehran University student housing complex, which led to the largest student rallies since 1979; the assassination of Saeed Hajjarian; the arrest of several intellectuals for attending a conference in Berlin; disqualification of prominent reformist candidates before the elections; rejection of the reformist bills passed by the sixth *Majles* (by the Guardian Council).

By the year 2000, a combination of aggressive conservatives' tactics as well as the reformists' lack of resolve to confront them changed the momentum and effectively marked the beginning of a new retreatist phase in the life of Islamist reformism, dubbed as the period of "agony." This retreat continued to unfold despite the reformists' effective control over the executive office, the sixth *Majles*, and a landslide victory in the City Councils' elections in March of 1999.

Consequently, the twenty million enthusiasts, frustrated by steady conservatism on the part of Khatami and other reformists, and their failure to organize civil society forces, became more hesitant in their support for the May 23 Front. This uncertainty was evident in the eighth presidential election, when Khatami was running, albeit reluctantly, for a second term. The twenty-one million votes cast in favor of Khatami was, essentially, a last ditch effort on the part of the electorate to prevent the conservative takeover. Even in his victory, there were new worrisome signs for Khatami; his relative support among the electorate was actually smaller than the 1997 election (51% compared to over 55%); more importantly, 14 million eligible voters (out of 42 million total) chose not to vote (about 33% compared to 20% in 1997). Soon it was clear that Khatami was not the man to oppose the conservative strategy. He had consciously decided to be the "system's president" rather than the opposition's leader. Signs of dissent were also emerging within the Reform Front. *Kargozaran* and Rafsanjani had already distanced themselves as a result of sharp criticisms waged by "radical reformists" against Rafsanjani over his possible involvement in the "serial murders" of 1998.

A considerable segment of students were critical of Khatami after the July 1999 Tehran University incident, in which Khatami labeled student protesters "hooligans" and "anarchists." Hardcore reformers were also losing patience in the face of the slow pace of reform initiatives. Abbas Abdi, for example, put forth a radical proposal "to exit the state" to his reformist colleagues. In light of the growing pressures on Khatami to confront the conservatives, he proposed two bills to the *Majles*: one to amend the parliamentary election laws, and the second to enhance the president's prerogatives. Predictably, both were rejected by the Guardian Council, vividly demonstrating to legalists where the real power lies in the Islamic Republic. The public's alienation from the reformists was silently growing in 2001 and 2002. The first electoral shock came in March 2003, during the elections for City and Rural Councils. The voters, by opting not to vote (especially in big metropolitan areas), indirectly helped the conservative coalition to handily capture most council seats, including in Tehran. The same trend continued in the seventh *Majles* election in February 2004, when only 50.0% of eligible voters voted (in contrast to 1996 and 2000 elections when, respectively 71.1% and 67.3% voted). In big cities (more than one million in population), the rate was only about 35%. Once again, low voter turnout helped the neoconservative candidates win the majority seats. Despite the fact that many disqualified *Majles* representatives took part in a sit-in against the Guardian Council's policy of massive disqualifications (about 3,600 of them), there was hardly any mass support backing the protesters. Their "social movement" tactic was too little, too late. The colossal energy generated in 1997 had subsided by this point.

Finally, in June 2005, Mahmoud Ahmadinejad, the neoconservative Tehran mayor, shocked most observers by winning the presidency and by defeating Hashemi-Rafsanjani in the runoff. Mostafa Mo'in, the Islamic Participation Front's candidate, only gained about 4 million votes (13.6%).

Among other shortcomings of the Islamist reformist "movement" include the confusion that emerged regarding whether it was a grassroots movement for structural reforms and democratization or a state faction content with minimal procedural changes. Even Mr. Hajjarian's recommendation of "negotiations from above, pressure from below" was hardly followed in practice, and was a vivid sign of the May 23 Front's bureaucratic elitism. If one is going to evaluate the reformist's contributions by solely relying on the reforms formally institutionalized in Iran, there will only be disappointment. Nevertheless, many moderate critics of the reformists may agree on one or more of the following positive contributions: While religious intellectualism, economic reformism, and political reformism all operated individually, either under the Islamic Republic, or in the course of twentieth-century Iran, the May 23 Front succeeded in integrating these currents into a collective "movement' for change. Its main long-term impact, ironically, may not be as much political, as its practitioners intended, but rather politico-cultural.

A new generation of reformist journalists was particularly instrumental in promoting a new political culture characterized by ideas such as reform, democratization, rule of law, pluralism, the compatibility of religion with democracy, non-violence, and a peaceful approach to diplomacy (Khatami's "dialogue among civilizations"). Also, by placing the Islamic Republic's foreign policy on a less ideological and more realistic foundation, Khatami was fairly successful in reducing tensions between Iran and Europe as well as its Sunni Arab neighbors.

Suggested Reading

Abdo, G., and J. Lyons. 2003. *Answering only to God*. New York: Henry Holt & Company.

Adams, Charles. 1968. *Islam and modernism in Egypt*. New York: Russell and Russell.

Amuzegar, J. 1993. *Iran's economy under the Islamic Republic* New York: I. B. Tauris.

Buchta, W. 2000. *Who rules Iran?* Washington, DC: The Washington Institute for Near East Policy.

Chehabi, H. E. 1990. *Iranian politics and religious modernism*. Ithaca, NY: Cornell University Press.

Hajjarian, S. 1379 [2000]. *Jomhouriyat: Afsson-Zodayi az Ghodrat* [*Republicanism: disenchantment of power*]. Tehran: Tarh-e No.

Jahanbakhsh, F. 2001 *Islam, democracy and religious modernism in Iran (1953–2000)*. Leiden: Koninklyke Brill.

Mahmoud, S. 2001. Sacral defense of secularism. *International Journal of Politics, Culture and Society.* Vol. 15, No. 2.

Mashayekhi, M. 2007. *Behsooy-e Demokracy va Jomhouri dar Iran* [*Toward Democracy and a Secular Republic in Iran*]. Washington, DC.

Moslem, M. 2002. *Factional politics in post-Khomeini Iran.* Syracuse, NY: Syracuse University Press.

Postel, D. 2006. *Reading legitimation crisis in Tehran.* Chicago: Prickly Paradigm Press.

Quchani, M. 2003. *Baradar-e Bozorg-tar Mordeh Ast* [*The Big Brother is Dead*]. Tehran: Entesharat-e Naghsh-o-negar.

Salimi, H. 1384 [2005]. *Kalbod-Shekafi-e Zehniyat-e Eslah garayan* [*An Autopsy of the Reformists' Subjectivity*]. Tehran: Gaam-e No.

Zarifinia, H.-R. 1999. *Kalbodshekafi-e Jenah hay-e Siyasi-e Iran* [*The Autopsy of Iranian Political Factions*]. Tehran: Entesharat-e Azadi-e Andisheh.

MEHRDAD MASHAYEKHI

✦ REGIONALISM AND REGIONAL DEVELOPMENT

Broadly understood, a "region" is a broad geographic area distinguished by similar features, and regionalism is loyalty to or prejudice in favor of a region. On a theoretical level, however, no single definition of regionalism is agreed upon. What constitutes the common features of a region remains disputable. Nevertheless, Iran's historical geography connects East, Central, and Western Asia to the Persian Gulf and to Europe via the Caucuses and Turkey.

Historically, the Silk Road—which in reality consisted not of a single road, but multiple different routes crossing Central Asia—connected the commercial interests of China and Central Asia to Persia. The Silk Road also facilitated trade in other products, such as gold, ivory, exotic animals, and plants. Today, the commercial interests of the region are centered on the vast oil and natural gas reserves of the five Caspian Sea littoral states (Azerbaijan, Iran, Kazakhstan, Russia, Turkmenistan) as well as Uzbekistan, Kirgizstan, Tajikistan, and Afghanistan. There are existing and planned pipelines connecting these countries.

The landlocked Central Asian states of the former Soviet Union also share an Islamic heritage and common historical experiences with Afghanistan, Iran, Azerbaijan, and Turkey; they all are members of the Organization of the Islamic Conference (OIC), which is an assembly of fifty-seven Muslim

The moon shines above the Tower of the Azadi in Tehran, 2001, during a lunar eclipse. (AP Photo/Hasan Sarbakhshian)

countries. The Economic Cooperation Organization (ECO) is yet another organization promoting a preferential trade arrangement among Iran, Turkey, Pakistan, Azerbaijan, Kazakstan, Turkmenistan, Kyrgyzstan, Uzbekistan, Tajikistan, and Afghanistan. The level of regional trade among these states remains modest; for instance, in 1995 the volume of exports among the ECO members accounted for less than 5% of their total export volume.

Iran is the only non-Arab Shi'a dominated Muslim country in the Middle East, and it has a strong stake in the economic and political affairs of the region. Oil and natural gas, trade, Persian Gulf security, and the future of Islam are concerns Iran shares with the rest of the Middle East. Iran is not a member of the Gulf Cooperation Council (GCC) or the twenty-three–member Arab League, but it is a major player in the Organization of Petroleum Exporting Countries (OPEC) and shares a vast shoreline along the Persian Gulf with its Arab neighbors.

The International Monetary Fund (IMF) now has a Middle East and Central Asia Department (MCD) that provides the Regional Economic Outlook for these countries. Among major regional disputes involving Iran are disputes over: the flow of dammed tributaries to the Helmand River in periods of drought; Iraq's territorial reach at the mouth of the Shatt al Arab in the Persian Gulf; possession of the Tunb Islands and Abu Musa Island in the Persian Gulf with the United Arab Emirates (UAE); and a division of the Caspian Sea into five equal sectors with littoral states, instead of the length of shoreline.

Suggested Reading

Baker, J. A. III. 2004. International gas trade in Central Asia: Turkmenistan, Iran, Russia and Afghanistan. Program on Energy and Sustainable Development, Institute for Public Policy Energy Forum, Working Paper #28. http://www.rice.edu/energy/publications/docs/GAS_InternationalGasTradeinCentralAsia.pdf

ALI ABOOTALEBI

✦ RELATIONS WITH THE ARAB WORLD

Iran's relations with the Arab world have always been problematic—even before the establishment of the Islamic Republic. However, Iran's 1979 Islamic Revolution put it on a collision course with much of the Arab world region as Tehran sought to export its anti-Western ideology. For instance, just after the revolution, Iran cut off its diplomatic relations with Egypt because of its peace treaty with, and recognition of, Israel. Iran has also always been a concern for the Gulf Cooperation Council (GCC). The full name of the GCC is the Cooperation Council for the Arab States of the Gulf, a formulation that deliberately excludes the non-Arab Persian Gulf state of Iran. The organization was founded in 1981, shortly after the Iran–Iraq War started and when fears of the spread of Iran's Shi'a Islamic Revolution pervaded the Sunni-dominated Persian Gulf. Saddam Hussein's Iraq won key financing from regional states in his war against Iran in the 1980s.

But relations with much of the Arab world improved under former president Mohammad Khatami, whose presidency saw improvements in ties with key regional countries such as Saudi Arabia. The roots of the rapprochement between Iran and Saudi Arabia, the biggest Arab country in the Persian Gulf, were planted in the early 1990s during the presidency of Hashemi Rafsanjani, who, in 1991, advocated the notion of collective security in the Persian Gulf as part-and-parcel of a new "pragmatic turn" in revolutionary Iran's foreign policy. But it would take several more years of reciprocal confidence-building, punctuated by the Kuwait crisis of 1990–1991, when Iran opposed Iraq's invasion of Kuwait yet remained neutral during the conflict. Only then did Iran and Saudi Arabia actually normalize their relations. Iran and Saudi Arabia—the two "pillars of stability" in the oil-rich region—have much in common. For example, they are both members of the Organization of Petroleum Exporting Countries (OPEC) and the Organization of Islamic Conference, and they both face the threat of al-Qaeda.

In the aftermath of Khatami's victory in the presidential elections on May 23, 1997, Iranian foreign policy featured steadily fewer provocative measures and slogans. The Islamic Republic's new strategy was one of détente in relations with other countries and engagement in confidence-building measures. This was an indication of President Khatami's awareness and understanding of two basic problems in Iran's foreign relations. First, he believed that Iran's interactions with the outside world were overburdened by tensions and that the continuation of this trend would be harmful for Iran. Second, he thought that responsibility for part of this tension was borne by Iran's diplomacy, and this had to be reversed. Iranian foreign policy therefore sought to remove past misunderstandings while making efforts to end various international conflicts and disputes. Under Khatami's direction, Iran undertook several regional and even international mediation roles, seeking, for example, to reduce tensions between India and Pakistan and acting as a mediator in several regional disputes in Africa.

Not surprisingly, relations between Iran and the Persian Gulf countries expanded quickly and dramatically in contrast with the two decades after the Islamic Revolution, when Iranian–Arab relations were marked by tensions, suspicions, and distrust. The improvement of Iran's relations with the regional countries reached its peak with Khatami's visit to a number of the Persian Gulf countries, including Saudi Arabia, Qatar, and Bahrain in late May 1999. His visit to Saudi Arabia was the first by an Iranian head of state since the advent of the Islamic Revolution, and he was therefore given a very warm welcome by Saudi leaders. King Fahd, bound to a wheelchair, personally received Khatami at the airport. This visit paved the way to an agreement on low security cooperation with the Saudis in 2000.

Iranian presidential advisor Mohammad Sadr said in this regard that President Mohammad Khatami's government was determined to bolster relations with the Arab states and ignore the unfavorable Iran–Arab political memories of the past. "Some Arab countries have responded to such a call positively, while others have either shown no reaction or have first welcomed the proposal but changed their approach later on, such as King Hussein of Jordan," he said. Sadr hoped that the Arab states would not follow the efforts of certain Western countries—namely the United States—to isolate and marginalize Iran.

Some analysts hold that despite some improvement in Arab–Iranian relations, especially during Khatami's presidency, several fundamental issues and differences stand out between the two sides. Saudi–Iranian relations, for instance, have begun a new course, but they are still overshadowed by history-bound misperceptions. With the exception of Syria, which is a unique case, Iran lacks in-depth relations with any Arab state. In the post-revolutionary period, Iran has experienced its most troublesome relations with the Arab world. Naturally, it will take time to remove all the misperceptions. Some observers even relate these differences to the nature of the Iranian polity with its multidimensional and ideological aspirations. They suggest that if we look at the pre-revolutionary era, Iranian–Arab relations were influenced by a larger strategy that the United States followed in relation to the Middle East. In certain Arab states—particularly in King Abdullah's Jordan, where there is often talk of the threat of a supposed "Shi'a crescent"—Iran continues to be seen as an adversary regardless of its overtures and its attempts to improve relations.

Notwithstanding these concerns, it is interesting to note that several Arab countries welcomed the election of Iranian president Mahmood Ahmadinejad in June 2005 despite historically cool relations with the Islamic Republic. Ahmadinejad's surprising landslide win in a second-round runoff was seen as a blow to US plans for Middle East democracy and raised fears among some analysts of further instability in the turbulent region. But oil-rich gulf Arab neighbors sent warm messages to the new president, despite longstanding disputes with the Islamic Republic, and Ahmadinejad himself said he would prioritize efforts to improve relations with the Arab and Muslim world. Leaders from Saudi Arabia, including the ailing King Fahd, were among the first to congratulate Ahmadinejad. Similar sentiments were expressed by Kuwait and the United Arab Emirates (UAE), despite the latter's longstanding dispute over three strategic Persian Gulf islands—Greater Tunb, Lesser Tunb, and Abu Musa—controlled by Tehran since 1971. The Gulf Cooperation Council, which comprises Bahrain, Kuwait, Oman, Qatar, Saudi Arabia, and the United Arab Emirates, said it hoped the new president would work toward "turning a new page" in Iran's relations with its neighbors.

But Persian Gulf analysts warned that Ahmadinejad's election would worsen the Islamic Republic's ties with the oil-rich states of the region. "The victory of the new president will lead to a kind of isolation of Iran in the region," said liberal Kuwaiti academic Ahmed al-Rubei, a former government minister and member of parliament. Iran, however, maintained that its "policy of détente" with the Arab and Muslim world would continue under the new government. "Great progress has already been made, and more progress will be made," President Ahmadinejad said in his first press conference after the elections. "We will see a development of relations with the Muslim world and countries of the region."

The postponement of Iranian Foreign Minister Manouchehr Motaki's visit to Saudi Arabia in the early months after the new government came to power in Iran only reinforced the suspicion that the recent anti-Iran pronouncements by key Saudi officials have not been aberrations but are rather ominous signs of a growing rift in what has recently been a pillar of stability in the turbulent Persian Gulf region. In his statements, Saudi Foreign Minister Saud al-Faisal described some of Ahmadinejad's statements as extremist and expressed his wish for Iran to remain faithful to its obligations to avoid military nuclear activities. He also promised that his country would never enter a nuclear arms race, even if Iran were to obtain nuclear weapons.

During the past decade, the dispute between Iran and the United Arab Emirates over the three islands in the Persian Gulf has overshadowed Iran's relations with all GCC countries. Even Khatami's overturns could not succeed in solving the dispute. Rather, his efforts kept the problem under control. But at the first summit of the GCC leaders after Ahmadinejad's government was formed, once again the issue came to the fore. GCC Secretary-General Abd al-Rahman al-Attiyah said in Abu Dhabi on December 18, 2005, that Iran continues to occupy the islands despite many UAE calls for "direct, peaceful negotiations" or the matter's referral to the International Court of Justice.

On December 19, 2005, in Tehran, Iran's Foreign Ministry spokesman Hamid Reza Asefi described the views of the Gulf Cooperation Council on the three disputed islands in the Persian Gulf as "baseless and unacceptable." Asefi said Iran and the UAE should pursue bilateral talks to reach an agreement on the fate of Abu Musa. This dispute continues while a recent report by an Iranian cultural publication estimated that up to 400,000 Iranians control some $200 billion in assets in Dubai; other estimates put the number far lower, at $20 billion—still quite a significant sum. Iranian businesses constitute about a tenth of the companies operating in the so-called "Dubai Free," helping to boost trade between the United Arab Emirates and Iran to an expected $7 billion in 2005 from $4 billion in 2003. That does not include the illicit trade that can never be documented or recorded.

Dubai and Iran have long had a special relationship, unusual even in the Arab world. A quarter of the citizens of the UAE trace their roots to Iran.

During the Iran–Iraq War in the 1980s, Dubai became a crucial transshipment point for goods and supplies, and the late president of the United Arab Emirates, Sheikh Zayed bin Sultan al-Nahyan, argued for a more balanced relationship with Iran's leaders compared with the policies pushed by the United States. In a visit by President Ahmadinejad to the United Arab Emirates in May 2007, the first visit paid by an Iranian president to the country after the Islamic Revolution, there were hopes that the two sides would find a mutually acceptable solution to the dispute, but nothing was achieved publicly.

In October 2005, President Ahmadinejad called for Israel to be "wiped off the map," and later on a trip to Mecca, he called the Holocaust a "myth" used to create a Jewish state in the Middle East. Almost all Arab leaders declined to express their viewpoints about the statements made by Ahmadinejad on Israel. That is because they prefer to pursue a more pragmatic policy toward Israel. Furthermore, the Arab leaders do not want to threaten their firm ties with the United States by taking a position against Israel. At the same time, most Arab people agree with what Ahmadinejad said about Israel. The Iranian president's sharp rhetoric may appeal to the Arab street, but it certainly does not please the conservative Arab leaders.

Persian Gulf countries have frequently expressed their concerns about Iran's intentions, especially in the first decade after the Islamic Revolution. They thought that Iran sought to politicize and provoke the Shi'a minorities that are spread throughout the region. For instance, most of Bahrain's estimated population of 700,000 is Shi'a. The rise of the Shi'a to political prominence in Iraq is also seen as a source of rising influence for Iran.

Iran's controversial nuclear program is also fuelling regional fears that it is seeking to develop weapons, which Tehran denies. But President Ahmadinejad's verbal salvos at Israel—in which he called for the Jewish state to be wiped off the map—are stoking fears about its nuclear activities and making Persian Gulf states even more anxious. Interestingly enough, the Arab countries, including the Persian Gulf nations, have remained silent toward Iran's nuclear program since the early 1990s, when Iran resumed its nuclear program once the Iran–Iraq War had ended. Even during the last two years of Khatami's government, when Iran's nuclear crisis was at its peak, Arab states kept a silent policy toward the issue.

Shortly after Ahmadinejad took office, however, Arab states began voicing deep concern over Iran's nuclear program and its intentions in the Persian Gulf region. They think that these new elements in Iran's power structure might cause the United States or Israel to ignite a new war in the region, which will have considerable adverse effects on the entire region. Many Arab states even think that if Israel decides to attack Iran's nuclear facilities in Bushehr because of Ahmadinejad's harsh anti-Israeli rhetoric, their countries will also be adversely affected. Indeed, the Arab states will be profoundly affected by all the possible outcomes, but their previous silence had suggested that they believed involvement entailed only greater risks.

GCC Secretary General al-Attiyah observed that GCC states do not fear Iran's program if it is peaceful, though if it is not, "the issue will not be neglected." He suggested "we do not want to see" the Bushehr reactor, "which is closer to our coast than ... Tehran," posing "perils and damages to us." In response, Iranian Foreign Minister Mottaki observed that "Bushehr is still in Iran" and that any attack on the nuclear facility would harm Iranians more than anyone else.

With the fall of Saddam's regime in Iraq in 2003, the Persian Gulf region entered a new stage in terms of balance of power. Although Saudi Arabia and Kuwait, and to a lesser degree, all the other Arab states of the Persian Gulf, welcomed the US attack on Iraq and the overthrow of Saddam Hussein, the subsequent course of events did not proceed in the a direction that they would have liked. With the Iraqi Shi'a filling the country's ensuing power vacuum, the Arab countries became increasingly worried about the prospect of an Iraq entirely allied with Iran. It led to the talk about an emerging "Shi'a crescent" and a Shi'a-Sunni divide running across the region. Even Saudi Arabia has bluntly accused Iran of meddling in Iraqi affairs. There is no doubt that there are increasing levels of political consciousness among the politically marginalized Shi'a communities across the region, which could potentially lead to a new type of Shi'a identity politics.

This has led once again to increased tensions between Iran and Saudi Arabia, tensions that have been exacerbated by increasing concerns about a U.S.–Iranian or Iranian–Israeli military confrontation. Interestingly enough, both Iran and Saudi Arabia think that they are duty-bound to protect the respective Shi'a and Sunni people across the region. The Saudis in particular are worried about the prospects of a different regional balance of power in the post-9/11 era; the U.S.'s historical commitment to them has at times appeared less firm than has been the case in the past.

It seems that in the event of any possible military confrontation between Iran and the United States, the Arab countries of the Persian Gulf will remain silent to protect themselves from possible retaliatory measures launched by Iran and will not cooperate with the United States, even though they will become extremely happy if their archrival is weakened. Preservation of the status quo, with U.S. sanctions against Iran in place, has been a big economic and diplomatic advantage for the Arab countries, especially the United Arab Emirates. A weakened Iran serves the interests of the Persian Gulf states, whereas severe crisis in the region will benefit neither their economies nor their longer-term political stability.

Suggested Reading
Assadi, B. 2001. Iran and the Persian Gulf security. *Discourse: An Iranian Quarterly*. 3:1.
Haseeb, K. E. (ed.) 1998. *Arab-Iranian Relations*. London: I. B. Tauris.
Henderson, S. 2005. The elephant in the gulf: Arab states and Iran's nuclear program, in *Policy Watch No. 1065*. Washington DC: Washington Institute for Near East Policy.
Sariolghalam, M. 2002. "The foreign policy of the Islamic Republic of Iran: A theoretical renewal and a paradigm for coalition." *Discourse: An Iranian Quarterly*. 3:4.

MOHAMMAD HOSSEIN HAFEZIAN

✦ RELIGIONS AND RELIGIOUS IDENTIFICATIONS

It is believed that nearly 98% of Iranian population is Muslim—9% of which belongs to Sunni sector of Islam. Yet other religious groups such as Ahl-e Haq, Armenians, Assyrians and Bahai'is, Jews, and Zoroastrians need to be mentioned duly. There are no reliable statistics about these religious groups since their population has declined because of mass migrations after the Islamic Revolution in Iran.

Ahl-e Haqq is believed to be the largest religious group after Shi'a and Sunni Muslims in Iran. The exact number of its members is not known because of the faith's secretive policies, yet Ahl-e Haqq followers are estimated to reach two million living in Kurdistan and Azerbaijan of Iran as well as Iraq and Turkey. Due to Ahl-e Haqq's belief in the transmigration of the soul, there have been attempts to relate it to pre-Islamic religions of the region. However, most scholars believe that it strongly bears Islamic marks of mysticism and Christian manifestation of the divine essence in human form. Also known as Ali-allahis (deifiers of Ali), Ahl-e Haqq have lived among Shi'as, the glorifiers of Ali, at a relative peace in Iran.

Armenians have lived in the region since the ancient times. They have inhabited and moved over the vast territory encompassing from west of the Caspian Sea, Caucasus, Iranian Azerbaijan, east of modern Turkey, parts of Mesopotamia, and modern Syria—the land that has been claimed by Persians, Romans, Turks, and Arabs. It is believed that the Urartuan Kingdom established in the territories between Urmye Lake and the Mesopotamian plains from the ninth to sixth centuries BC can be regarded as the institutional predecessor of the later Armenian kingdoms. The disappearance of Urartuans, mentioned in Assyrian inscriptions as their enemies, paved the way to Armenian rule. Despite persecutions and other difficulties elsewhere, Armenians in Iran prospered and lived in relative peace beginning with the reign of Shah Abbas Safavid (r. 1588–1629). During his reign many Armenians settled in Isfahan, the Iranian capital—the district called New Julfa. They built many churches and schools and became a unique force building stately churches and monuments. The constitution that was drafted after the 1906 revolution recognized the rights of the country's religious minorities and gave them constitutional guarantees of civil liberties and the right to practice their religious rituals. The present population of Armenians is estimated to be close to 200,000.

Assyrian is the term used for the modern East Syrian Christian families in Iran. The confusion with the ancient name "Assyrian" attributed to the Semitic kingdom of north Mesopotamia is not recent (Iranica II P. 817). It is believed that Iranian Assyrians have lived under better conditions than their brethren under the Turkish Empire. Urmye being their spiritual capital during the Qajar era, they defended Iranian territories against Turkey and Kurdish invaders (Iranica II P. 817). Assyrians of Iran are affiliated to two main churches of Nestorians and the Catholic Chaldean. Their population in Iran at present is estimated to be 35,000.

The Bahai'i faith, a new religion born from Islamic culture, has never been given any space in the orthodox Shi'a environment of Iran since its birth in mid 19th Century. As with many other new religions, the Bahai'i faith has given recognition to its preceding religions, yet assuming a complementary role, it has to abrogate them since every religion claims to the righteous one and the final revelation of God's order. No wonder, according to the followers of an older religion, a succeeding religion is a heresy and its neophyte followers are punishable heretics. It is believed that there are around 300,000 Bahai'is still living in Iran despite their mass exodus after the Islamic Revolution.

The Jews' habitation in Iran has been traced back to biblical times and Babylonian exile. Like in other places, Jews have lived in their communities in many cities of modern Iran, yet over time most of them became indistinguishable linguistically from other Iranians. Like the followers of other religions who hold Holy Scripture, Jews are recognized as *ahl-e ketab* from the Islamic point of view. By the same token, according to the Iranian constitution of 1906, Jews had their representative in parliament before the Islamic Revolution, a privilege that they still hold, like other religious groups of *ahl-e ketab* in the Parliament of the Islamic Republic.

Zoroastrianism, the oldest religion in Iran, was taught by Zoroaster, also known as Zarathustra. Neither the time nor the birth place of Zoroaster has been confirmed. Avestan texts compiled and written during the early centuries after the Islamic conquest of Iran are thought to have been transmitted orally through generations. It is unknown when Zoroastrianism became widely accepted by the populace or by the Persian rulers. However, king Darius (549–485 BC) mentions the great God of Zoroastrianism, Ahuramazd's name, in one of his inscriptions. Zoroastrianism became a state religion during Sassanid rule of Persia (AD 224–651). Because of the Arab Conquest of Persia and gradual Islamization of Iran, Zoroastrianism was confined to the communities which could resist the rapid dissemination of Islam. Many Zoroastrian families left their homeland and settled in India where they could practice their religion freely. After the Islamic Revolution of 1979, the Zoroastrian population dwindled, similar to other religions of smaller groups. The Zoroastrian population is estimated to be fewer than 30,000 in Iran at present.

HADI SULTAN-QURRAIE

✦ RUSSIA–IRAN RELATIONS

Of all the nations in the Middle East, Russia's closest relationship is with the Islamic Republic of Iran. While Russia's sale of the Bushehr nuclear power station in 1995 is central to Iranian–Russian relations, there are a number of other facets of the relationship that are of almost equal importance. These include trade, which by 2006 reached the level of $2 billion per year, Russian arms sales to Iran, which include jet fighters and submarines, and diplomatic cooperation in the Caucasus and Central Asia. Both countries also have sought to prevent U.S. hegemony in the world. There are several areas of conflict in the relationship, the most important of which is the legal status of the Caspian Sea. By February 2005, when Moscow and Iran signed an agreement for the supply of Russian uranium to the Bushehr reactor, the two countries could be said to have reached the level of a tactical, if not yet a strategic, alliance.

RUSSIA AND IRAN: THE YELTSIN LEGACY

The rapid development of Russian–Iranian relations under Yeltsin had its origins in the latter part of the Gorbachev era. After alternately supporting first Iran, and then Iraq, during the Iran–Iraq War, by the end of the war Gorbachev had clearly tilted his support toward Iran. The relationship between the two countries was solidified in June 1989 with Hashemi

Rafsanjani's visit to Moscow, where a number of major agreements, including one on military cooperation, were signed. The military agreement permitted Iran to purchase highly sophisticated military aircraft from Moscow, including MIG-29s and SU-24s. At a time when its own air force had been badly eroded by the eight-year-long Iran–Iraq War, and by the refusal of the United States to supply spare parts, let alone new planes to replace losses in the F-14s and other aircraft, which the United States had sold to the Shah's regime, the Soviet military equipment was badly needed.

Iran's military dependence on Moscow grew as a result of the 1990–1991 Gulf War. Not only did the United States, which had now become Iran's primary enemy, become the dominant military power in the Gulf, by formulating defense agreements with a number of GCC states—which included repositioning arrangements for U.S. military equipment—but Saudi Arabia, Iran's most important Islamic challenger, also acquired massive amounts of U.S. weaponry. Given Iran's need for sophisticated arms, the pragmatic Iranian leader, Hashemi Rafsanjani, was careful not to alienate either the Soviet Union or Russia. Thus, when Azerbaijan declared its independence from the Soviet Union in November 1991, Iran, unlike Turkey, did not recognize its independence until after the U.S.S.R. collapsed.

Similarly, despite occasional rhetoric from Iranian officials, Rafsanjani ensured that Iran kept a relatively low profile in Azerbaijan and the other newly independent states of Central Asia, emphasizing cultural and economic ties rather than Islam as the centerpiece of their relations. This was due, in part, to the fact that after more than seventy years of Soviet rule, Islam was in a weak condition in the countries of the former Soviet Union; the leaders of the Muslim successor states were all secular Muslims, and the chances for an Iranian-style Islamic Revolution were very low. Indeed, some skeptics argued that Iran was simply waiting for mosques to be built and Islam to mature before trying to bring about Islamic Revolutions. Nonetheless, the Russian leadership considered Iran a responsible actor in Central Asia and Transcaucasia, and was therefore encouraged to continue supplying it with modern weaponry—including submarines—despite strong protests from the United States.

Indeed, the Russian supply of weapons to Iran became an issue of increasing concern to the United States, and in 1995 U.S. Vice President Al Gore and Russian Prime Minister Viktor Chernomydin signed an agreement under which Moscow would cease supplying Iran with weapons, once existing contracts were fulfilled in the year 1999. At the same time Yeltsin promised American President Bill Clinton that Russia, which had agreed to sell Iran an atomic reactor, would not build a nuclear centrifuge plant for Iran.

During Kozyrev's period as Russia's foreign minister (1991–1995) Russian–Iranian relations quickly progressed. Russia was selling Iran not only arms, but also nuclear reactors and other industrial equipment. Yet economic gain was only one of Russia's many interests in Iran. As in the case of Russian–Iraqi relations, Yeltsin could use the close Russian–Iranian relationship to demonstrate to the nationalists in his Duma that he was independent of the United States. Oil and natural gas development was a third major Russian interest in Iran. Again, despite U.S. objections, in 1997, GASPROM, along with the French company Total, signed a major agreement with Iran to develop the South Pars gas field. Finally, a greatly weakened Russia had found Iran a useful ally in dealing with a number of very sensitive Middle Eastern, Caucasian, Transcaucasian, and Central and Southwest Asian political hot spots. During the Yeltsin era these included Chechnya, where Iran kept a very low profile in the first Chechen war despite the use of Islamic themes by the Chechen rebels in their conflict with Russia; Tajikistan, where Iran helped Russia achieve a political settlement, albeit a shaky one; Afghanistan, where both Russia and Iran stood together against Taliban efforts to seize control over the entire country; and Azerbaijan, which neither Iran, with a sizeable Azeri population of its own, nor Russia under Yeltsin wished to see emerge as a significant economic and military power. In addition, as NATO expanded eastward, many Russian nationalists called for a closer Russian–Iranian relationship as a counterbalance, especially as Turkey was seen by some Russians as closely cooperating with its NATO allies, in expanding its influence in both Transcaucasia and Central Asia.

Excerpt from an Article in the Newspaper *Segodnia*, May 1995

✦

Cooperation with Iran is more than just a question of money and orders for the Russian atomic industry. Today a hostile Tehran could cause a great deal of unpleasantness for Russia in the North Caucasus and in Tajikistan if it were really to set its mind to supporting the Muslim insurgents with weapons, money and volunteers. On the other hand, a friendly Iran could become an important strategic ally in the future. NATO's expansion eastward is making Russia look around hurriedly for at least some kind of strategic allies. In this situation the anti-Western and anti-American regime in Iran would be a natural and very important partner.

These interests and policies were already in place when Yevgeny Primakov became Foreign Minister in January 1996, and he sought to further deepen the relationship. Nonetheless, he also had to cope with increasing frictions in Russian–Iranian relations. First, in December 1996, then Russian Defense Minister Igor Rodionov—while Primakov was in Tehran—described Iran as a possible military threat to Russia, given Russia's weakened position. Second, because of Iran's economic problems, it did not have enough hard currency to pay for the weapons and industrial equipment it wanted to import from Russia. Indeed, despite predictions of several billions of dollars in trade, Russian–Iranian trade was only $415 million in 1996, less than Russia's trade with Israel. Third, Russian supplies of missile technology to Iran caused increasing conflict with the United States (and Israel). Although Russia, in late 1997, very publicly expelled an Iranian diplomat for trying to smuggle missile technology, and in January 1998 promised to stop selling "dual use" equipment to Tehran, by 1999 the issue had become a serious irritant in Russian–American relations, with particularly sharp criticism of Moscow coming from the U.S. Congress. Fourth, since 1995, Iran has increasingly thrust itself forward as an alternative export route for Central Asian oil and natural gas. This came into direct conflict with the efforts of the hardliners in the Russian government to control the oil and gas exports of Azerbaijan, Uzbekistan, Turkmenistan, and Kazakhstan, so as to limit their freedom as Yeltsin sought to dominate the states of the CIS.

While Iran, which remained dependent on Russian exports of military equipment, sought to defuse this problem by trying to organize tripartite projects with Russia and the Central Asian states, Iranian availability as an alternate export route was a concern for Moscow, one that threatened to become even more severe if there was a rapprochement between the United States and Iran, which might lead to the termination of U.S. efforts to prevent foreign investments in Iran's oil and natural gas pipelines as well as infrastructure. Finally, the two countries disputed the division of the Caspian Sea. Iran, with little oil of its own in its Caspian coastal shelf, had opposed the Russian–Kazakh agreement of July 1998, which partially divided the Caspian Sea and continued to call for an equal sharing of the sea's resources, asking for a 20% share instead of the 12% to 13% for which the length of its coastline would have qualified it.

In addition, the election of Mohamed Khatami as Iran's President in May 1997 gave rise to the possibility of a rapprochement with the United States, although the rapprochement was quickly aborted. Khatami, following his election, began to promote a policy of domestic reform and liberalization, along with a policy of rapprochement with the Arab world, Europe, and the

United States. While conservative forces in Iran did not strongly oppose the rapprochements with the Arab world and Europe, as both were aimed at strengthening Iran's diplomatic position, they did take exception to Khatami's policy of domestic liberalization and to his policy of rapprochement with the United States, which held out the possibility of lifting U.S. sanctions against Iran under the 1996 Iran–Libya Sanctions Act. Unfortunately for Khatami and the possibility of an improvement in U.S.–Iranian relations, a conservative counterattack in the summer of 1998 forced an end to his efforts toward a rapprochement. Meanwhile, during the summer of 1998, a successful Iranian missile test strengthened the position of those in the United States who called for the sanctioning of Russian companies that provided Iran with missile help. With the collapse of the Russian economy in August 1998, Russia's government was hard put to resist the U.S. pressure and indeed promised it would do its utmost to prevent the transmission of missile technology to Iran. A further complication to the U.S.–Russian relationship came with what proved to be a temporary elevation of Primakov to the position of Russian Prime Minister in September 1998, following the economic crisis and the ouster of Prime Minister Sergei Kiriyenko. Primakov, and the communist forces in the Duma who supported him, wanted a tougher line toward the United States, and their advocacy became increasingly harsh following the U.S. bombing of Iraq in December 1998 and it's bombing of Serbia in the spring of 1999.

At the same time Yevgeny Adamov, then head of Russia's Atomic Energy Ministry, continued to press for the sale of additional nuclear reactors to Iran, something the United States strongly opposed. In November 1998, Adamov visited Tehran, and, to spur the lagging Bushehr nuclear reactor construction project, signed an agreement which transformed Bushehr into a turnkey project in which Russian technicians, not Iranians, would build the project, whose target date for completion was set for May 2003. However, Russian–Iranian relations were then complicated by the Kosovo crisis, where Iran championed the Albanian Kosovars and Russia the Serbs, and even more so by Russia's decision to invade Chechnya in August 1999, leading to the killing of numerous Muslim Chechens, something which Iran, which was now head of the Islamic Conference, had to protest, albeit mildly.

PUTIN AND IRAN
Policy before 9/11

Chechnya was only one of the problems in Russian–Iranian relations facing Putin when he became Russia's President in January 2000 after Yeltsin abruptly stepped down. Another problem was the overwhelming victory of the moderates in Iran's Majlis (Parliamentary) elections in February 2000. This was of stark concern to Moscow, because many of the elected reformers were interested in improving U.S.–Iranian relations

Furthermore, the Iranian economy, which had been continually beset by high unemployment and inflation, and subjected to American-imposed economic sanctions, would improve alongside stronger political relations with the United States.

Yet the moderate Parliament found itself checkmated by both the conservative forces in the government and by the Iranian supreme religious authority, Ayatollah Khamenei, who opposed their reform efforts, and Iranian President Khatami was not able to overcome them. Indeed, in a speech at the U.N. in September 2000, Khatami berated the United States for its condemnation of Iran for the arrest and conviction of ten Iranian Jews as spies—a development which had further strained U.S.–Iranian relations. The Iranian President, who had met Putin the previous day, also stated that he hoped to forge a closer relationship with Russia.

This Khatami statement seemed to put aside, at least in the short run, the possibilities of a U.S.–Iranian rapprochement, and together with Iran's low profile in the rapidly escalating Chechen war may have led Putin to unilaterally abrogate the Gore–Chernomyrdin agreement of June 30, 1995. Under this agreement, Russia was to have ended all military sales to Tehran by December 31, 1999, once existing arms sales contracts had been completed. This decision risked U.S. sanctions, ranging from a ban on the use of Russian rockets for satellite launches to the discouragement of U.S. investments in Russia, to U.S. pressure on the IMF not to reschedule Russian debts. While improving Russian–Iranian relations and clearly benefiting Rosoboronoexport, Putin's new consolidated arms sales agency, the decision to abrogate the Gore–Chenomyrdin agreement was clearly a blow to U.S.–Russian relations. On the other hand, Putin's decision set the stage for Khatami's visit to Moscow in March 2001.

The Caspian Sea dispute, along with military cooperation, was high on the agenda of Khatami's visit to Moscow. The Iranian ambassador to Moscow, Mehdi Safari, in an apparent attempt to solicit support from Rosoboronoexport, dangled the prospect of $7 billion in arms sales to Iran, prior to the Khatami visit. This followed an estimate of up to $300 million in annual sales by Rosoboronoexport director, Viktor Komardin.

Meanwhile, U.S.–Russian relations sharply deteriorated, as the new (George W.) Bush Administration had called for the abrogation of the ABM Treaty and for the expansion of NATO into the Baltic states. Making matters worse, soon after taking office, the Administration had angered Moscow by bombing Iraqi anti-aircraft installations and by expelling a number of alleged Russian spies. Given this background of deteriorating U.S.–Russian relations, one might have expected more to come out of the Putin–Khatami summit than actually happened. To be sure, Putin formally announced the resumption of arms sales, Khatami was awarded an honorary degree in philosophy from Moscow State University, and the Iranian President was invited to tour Moscow's contribution to the international space station. Former Russian Foreign Minister and Prime Minister Yevgeny Primakov waxed eloquent over the Khatami visit, calling it the biggest event in the history of relations between Tehran and Moscow. Yet the treaty which emerged from the meeting (titled "The Treaty on Foundations of Relations and Principles of Cooperation") merely stated that "if one of the sides will be exposed to an aggression of some state, the other side must not give any help to the aggressor." This was far from a mutual defense treaty, and something that would allow Moscow to stand aside should the United States, one day, attack Iran. No specific mention was made of any military agreements during the summit, and Russian deputy defense minister Alexander Lushkov, possibly in a gesture to the United States, stated, "The planned treaty will not make Russia and Iran strategic partners, but will further strengthen partner-like, neighborly relations."

Following the Khatami visit to Moscow, the Caspian Sea issue again generated problems for Russian–Iranian relations. On July 23, 2001, Iranian gunboats, with fighter escorts, harassed a British Petroleum research ship, forcing BP to suspend its activities in the region, which was located within the sea boundary of Azerbaijan according to a Russian–Azeri agreement, but according to Tehran, lay in the 20% share of the Caspian that it unilaterally claimed. The fact that Turkey subsequently sent combat aircraft to Baku (the arrangement to send the aircraft, however, predated the Caspian Sea incident) complicated matters for Moscow, since Moscow did not want a conflict to arise between Turkey and Iran, both of which Putin was cultivating.

The Impact of September 11

Putin's decision to draw closer to the U.S. after September 11, and particularly, his acquiescence in the deployment of U.S. troops in Central Asia, was scorned by Tehran. Iranian radio noted on December 18, following the U.S. military victory in Afghanistan, "some political observers say that the aim of the U.S. diplomatic activities in the region is to carry out certain parts of U.S. foreign policy, so as to expand its sphere of influence in Central Asia and the Caucasus, and this is to lessen Russia's traditional influence in the region."

A second problem in post-September 11 Russian–Iranian relations dealt with the Caspian Sea. When, again due to Iranian obstinacy, the April 2002

Caspian summit failed, Putin moved to assert Russian authority in the Caspian. This took three forms: first, there was a May 2002 agreement with Kazakhstan to jointly develop the oil fields lying in disputed waters between them; second, a major Russian naval exercise took place in the Caspian in early August 2002 with 60 ships and 10,000 troops. It was witnessed by Russian defense minister Sergei Ivanov. The exercises took place on the 280th anniversary of Peter the Great's naval campaign in the Caspian, both Kazakhstan and Azerbaijan participated, and Putin called the purpose of the exercise "part of the war against terrorism." Finally, in September 2002 Putin and Azeri leader Gaidar Aliev signed an agreement dividing the seabed between them but holding the water in common.

Iran, however, sought to demonstrate that it would not be cowed by the Russian military move, and in September 2003, while the Iranian foreign ministry spokesman Hamid-Reza Asefi was stressing that the militarization of the Caspian Sea would never ensure the security of littoral states, Iran launched its "Paykan" missile boat into the Caspian "to protect the interests of the Iranian nation."

Nuclear Issues Take Center Stage in the Relationship: 2002–2006

Interestingly enough, while Russian–Iranian tension rose over the Caspian, Russian nuclear reactor sales and arms sales continued. In July 2002, just a few weeks before the major military exercises on the Caspian, Moscow announced that not only would it finish Bushehr (despite U.S. opposition) but also stated it had begun discussions on the building of five additional reactors for Iran. It remained unclear at the time, however, whether the spent fuel would be sent back to Russia in order to prevent Iran from making it into nuclear weapons.

As Moscow stepped up its nuclear sales to Tehran, the United States sought to dissuade Russia through both a carrot-and-stick approach, threatening on one hand to withhold $20 billion in aid for the dismantling of the old Soviet military arsenal, while simultaneously promising $10 billion in additional aid for Moscow. Meanwhile support for the Chechens, who had seized a theater in Moscow in October 2002, by Iranian newspapers, including those close to Khamenei, raised questions in the minds of at least some Russians as to whether Moscow was backing the wrong side in the U.S.–Iranian dispute over the Iranian nuclear program.

There are four central reasons why Moscow was unwilling to cooperate with Washington on the nuclear issue. First, the sale of the reactor earns hard currency for Russia, and Putin could not be sure that at a time of escalating deficits in the United States, Congress would be willing to allocate large sums of money to Russia, even if President Bush promised as such. Second, Iran had repeatedly hinted to Moscow that it would purchase a number of additional reactors once the first one was operating. Third, the Bushehr reactor, and the factories in Russia which supply it, employ a large number of Russian engineers and technicians and help keep Russia's nuclear industry alive—something Putin hopes will not only earn Russia much-needed hard currency but also help in the high-tech development of the Russian economy. Finally, by standing firm on Bushehr, Putin could demonstrate to domestic audiences Russia's independent policy *vis-à-vis* the United States, as both the Duma and presidential elections neared.

However, Putin had a dilemma. Throughout 2003 and 2004 either the IAEA continued to find that Iran was hiding information about its nuclear activities, or Iran was reneging on agreements it had already made with the IAEA and/or the EU-3 (Germany, France, and England). This, in turn, induced heavy U.S. pressure on Russia to hold off supplying nuclear fuel to the Bushehr reactor project it was constructing in Iran, lest Iranian efforts to develop a nuclear bomb be enhanced, and Moscow, at least rhetorically, began to criticize Tehran.

MOSCOW'S CHANGED POSITION: 2005–2006

Moscow's rhetoric *vis-à-vis* Tehran began to fade in 2005. In the latter part of 2004, Putin had suffered a number of embarrassing failures both internally and externally with the debacle in Beslan demonstrating just how far Putin was from "normalizing" the situation in Chechnya, and the pro-Western "Orange Revolution" in the Ukraine, apparently indicating the defection of Russia's most important CIS neighbor. Consequently, Putin seems to have decided that he had to demonstrate both his own and Russia's continuing importance in world affairs, and asserting Russia's role in the Middle East and reinforcing his alliance with Iran were ways to do this. In the case of Iran, the process included inviting Iran to join the Shanghai Cooperation Organization as an observer, and also inviting Iran to join the planned Caspian Sea security organization (Iran, under heavy pressure both from the United States and the European Union, eagerly accepted both invitations.) The two countries also stepped up their planning for a North–South transportation corridor through Azerbaijan. In addition, Moscow launched a satellite for Iran and discussed the possibility of the sale of submarine-launched missiles with a range of 200 kilometers to be fitted on the submarines Russia had sold to Iran.

While all these developments demonstrated a reinforced Russian–Iranian tie, the nuclear issue continued to occupy first place in the relationship. Putin realized that in order to cement the relationship with Iran, which he saw as a foreign policy priority, for aforementioned reasons, he had to finalize the nuclear fuel agreement. Consequently, in late February 2005, Russia signed the final agreement for the supply of nuclear fuel to the Bushehr reactor. Under the agreement all spent fuel was to be returned to Russia, thus, in theory at least, preventing its diversion into atomic weapons. The agreement came after a Bush–Putin summit in which the United States and Russia pledged to work together against nuclear proliferation, and, as might be expected, the United States took a dim view of the Russian–Iranian agreement, and an even dimmer view of the election of Iranian President Ahmadinejad in July 2005 and by his abrogation of the treaty with the EU-3 by which Iran had agreed to suspend work on nuclear enrichment.

Russia itself was discomfitted by Ahmadinejad's denial of the Holocaust—just as Russian Foreign minister Lavrov was visiting Israel in October 2005. Nonetheless, despite Iranian defiance over the nuclear issue by insisting it would enrich uranium despite international calls for it to desist, in November 2005 Russia moved much closer to Iran by signing a $1 billion dollar arms deal with it, which included $700 million for surface-to-air missiles that could be deployed to protect Iran's nuclear installations. Such an air defense system, once installed, would seriously inhibit a possible U.S. or Israeli attack. By moving to help Iran to protect its nuclear installations, Moscow sent a clear signal that it would stand by Iran, whatever its nuclear policies.

Russian efforts to protect Iran continued in 2006 as Iran continued to defy not only the International Atomic Energy Agency but also the U.N. Security Council. Finally, in December 2006, the Security Council voted on very mild sanctions against Iran, with Russia again working not only to prevent more severe sanctions but also insisting that the dispute over Iran's nuclear program had to be solved by negotiations and not by force.

ROBERT O. FREEDMAN

✦ SHI'A HIERARCHY

Theoretically, religious hierarchy is an exception to the rule in the teachings of Islam. God explicitly stated that no prophet could or should claim any sanctity for himself or his office. The oneness of God lies at the heart of the revelation of Islam, and therefore considering any other institution or person sacred could be seen as apostasy. Shi'ism in Islam, the official religion of Iran, has developed in such a way that its doctors of law and theology assume a special role with the community, which creates a quasi-clerical hierarchy. It is important to consider where this comes from and the form it takes.

Shi'ism surfaced after the death of Muhammad (d. 632), when his followers disagreed as to who should replace him. The people who insisted that the leadership should go to the prophet's cousin and son in law, Ali, became known as the Shi'a (the party) of Ali, and those who decided to combine the message of Islam with the saying and practices of the Prophet and his close associates became known as the Sunnis. The followers of Ali remained a minority and have had an eventful and embattled history. Within Shi'ism, one could identify various brands and groupings, or, as it is commonly known in religious categories, "sects," depending on whom they followed after Ali. Notable Shi'as are Zaydies, Isma'ilies, and Twelver Shi'ias. The latter formulated a theology according to which legitimate leadership begins with Ali and continues with his descendents until the year 872 when the eleventh Imam died with no apparent successor. It became an accepted view that the Imam had a son who was in hiding for fear of his life. A theology grew around it, claiming that the Twelfth Imam has vanished into an indefinite occultation and will emerge as the savior (*al-Mahdi*) to establish justice and harmony on earth.

When the Iranian dynasty the Buyid—or Buwayid—(932–1055) became the ruling elite, concerned Shi'i scholars collected and edited sayings of Imams and systematically formulated the Shi'i version of Muslim heritage. It was argued that in the absence of a living Imam, scholars and the jurists of Shi'i theology and jurisprudence would assume their role. Part of the principles of jurisprudence is the notion of independent reasoning, which gives enormous power to the Shi'i intelligentsia, as opposed to the Sunni ones who were under the decision of the political elite. The most important office thus became the source of emulation, or *Marja'iyyat*, by which Shi'a Muslims are required to follow someone for proper performance of ones' religious duty. However, the extent of the authority and social position of the scholars continued to be a question of debate as well as historical contingent. For example, politics remained the special prerogative of the hidden Imam who will return and establish a just rule. In his absence, governments were tolerated but not considered ideal or legitimate. Soon, a decentralized religious grouping emerged with no unified or universally recognized titles. Some were known as Sheikh, such as Abu Jafar Tusi (d. 1067), because of the common practice to honor one with this title.

The establishment of the Safavid rule in Iran (1501–1732), which made Shi'ism the official religion of that country, had a paradoxical impact. At one level it strengthened the position of the religious intelligentsia and gave it some organizational structure by linking it to the state. The religious intelligentsia and the state reenforced one another. Many Shi'i seminaries with good endowments were established, the number of people who studied Shi'ism grew, and many titles were assigned to scholars. For example, the highest religious authority came to be known as the Sheikh al-Islam; but there were other titles as well, such as Allameh and Mulla. On another level, two factors undermined the real authority of the religious intelligentsia. First, becoming part of state apparatus left the hierarchy at the behest of politics. Second, to avoid any aberration or limit the misuse of religion by the authorities, concerned and prominent scholars advocated the Akhbari school of jurisprudence, which suggested all decisions should be literal bases of meaning, limiting independent reasoning. This not only limited the power of political rulers, but also limited the authority of the scholars, scribes, and guardians of the sayings of the Imams.

The coming of modernity to Iran did not only fail to limit the authority of the religious hierarchy, but it indirectly strengthened it to the point that they have now become the dominant political elite. The root of this goes back to the history of Iran's encounters with Europe. In the late nineteenth century,

European concessions and influence increased in Iran. The more foreign power gained influence, the more people turned to the religious hierarchy for refuge and protection. Since the 1890s, religious hierarchy has been at the center of all major movements for genuine modernization in Iran such as the Constitutional Revolution (1905–1911), Movement for Nationalization of Oil Industry (1949–1953), and the popular revolution of 1978–1979. In each period, the hierarchy developed more organizations, newer titles, and particular authorities. The last period introduced an idea that some consider an aberration from and innovation in Shi'ism. The idea, proposed by Khomeini, gave religious scholars the mandate not only to assume power, but also the exclusive right to exercise authority. Once again, Shi'ism is directly and intensively mixed with politics. As a result, new functions such as the holding of public Friday prayers were instituted, with the result that the office of Friday prayer leaders has been instituted. Yet many traditional Shi'as take the view that those developments turned Shi'ism into another version of Sunnism in that politics decide the fate of religion, rather than the other way around.

Presently, and partly as a result of the impact of the Islamic Republic, one could talk about three hierarchies in Shi'ism. The first resulted from the introduction of the notion of the Guardianship of the Jurisconsult (*Velayat-e Faqih*) by Khomeini. According to his theory of guardianship, those scholars who have achieved the highest position of scholarship can take the position of leadership of the Muslim community, and Khomeini himself assumed such a role until his death in 1989. An assembly of elected officials, mostly from the ranks of the religious hierarchy, chose his successor, and this practice has continued in case of the death of the present one. The chosen leader, who is the supreme authority and symbolizes the sovereign, will, in turn, choose his own representative (*namayende-ye rahabari*) in each and every branch of the government. Their main task is to make sure that all decisions are within the bounds of the Islamic law.

The second hierarchical system exists within the seminaries and is related to the curriculum of studies. Usually it has three levels. The first is *Moqadamat* (preliminaries), which lasts for two years and is the study of grammar, writing, speech, and Arabic language, logic, hermeneutics, and genealogy. The second also lasts for two years, during which time religious texts and jurisprudence are introduced into the curriculum. During these two phases, the novice is known as *Hojjat al-Islam* (the proof of Islam). Then, the third level is known as *Kharej*, which literally means "out," but here means free seminars on jurisprudence, theology, philosophy, ethics, mysticism, and history. Although the period may change from school to school and from person to person, it usually lasts from four to eight years and the novice is called *Hojjat al-Islamva al-Muslemin* (the proof of Islam and Muslims). The person who has finished all three levels successfully and gained some reputation among his colleagues will be referred to as Ayatollah (the sign of God).

The third hierarchy relates to the social stature of the person. The highest position goes the *Ayatollah al-Uzama* (the Highest Sign), a person who enjoys three characteristics. First, in terms of scholarly achievement, he has completed all courses of studies in the seminaries, has taught jurisprudence and the principles of it, and has acquired notable numbers of students. Second, he has published commentaries on the authoritative texts of Shi'i jurisprudence, particularly the most famous text of jurisprudence in Shi'ism, *Urwa al-Wuthqa* (The firmest bound), written by Ayatollah Seyyed Mohammad Kazem Yazdi (d. 1918). Third, he has many followers in the community and receives special religious taxes, so that his "household" (*bayt*) manages religious inquiries and distributes stipends to religious students. The next position belongs to an Ayatollah, who has achieved the highest stage of scholarship, but has no publication and does not run a "household." The third position is that of *Hojjat al-Islam va al-Muslemin* (the proof of Islam and Muslims). It refers to a person who is studying at the third level and performs religious duties such as marriage and funerals. Finally, there is *Hojjat al-Islam* (the proof of Islam), a title given out of respect to the students of the seminaries who are either at the first or second level of studies.

Suggested Reading

Akhavi, S. 1980. *Religion and politics in contemporary Iran: clergy-state relations in the Pahlavi period*. Albany: State University of New York.

Algar, H. 1969. *Religion and state in Iran, 1785-1906; the role of the Ulama in the Qajar period*. Berkeley: University of California Press.

Arjomand, S. A. 1984. *The shadow of God and the hidden Imam: religion, political organization and societal change in Shi'ite Iran from the beginning to l890*. Chicago: University of Chicago Press.

Hairi, A. 1977. *Shi'ism and constitutionalism in Iran: a study of the role played by the Persian residents of Iraq in Iranian politics*. Leiden: Brill.

Litvak, M. 1998. *Shi'i scholars of nineteenth-century Iraq: the 'Ulama of Najaf and Karbala*. Cambridge: Cambridge University Press.

Tunekabuni, M. M. *Qessas al-Ulama* [*The Stories of the Ulama*]. Qom: Elmiyeh.

FARHANG RAJAEE

✦ SOCIALISM, ISLAMIC

Islamic socialism is a political movement with an egalitarian, socialist ideology that was introduced to Iran in the early 1940s. Its short manifesto entitled "God-Worshipping Socialists" (*Sosialist-ye khoda parast*) inspired a range of organizations that in turn helped attract a large number of religious intellectuals (mainly students) to the 1977–1979 Islamic Revolution.

FORMATION OF THE MOVEMENT

The "movement of God-Worshiping Socialists" emerged during the relatively open political atmosphere of post-allied occupation and Reza Shah's abdication in early 1940s when a group of Islamic lay intellectuals explored, for the first time, modern socialism as a viable principle of social organization for Iran. There is scant evidence that the earliest attempts to synthesize Islam and socialism in Iran were influenced by their counterparts in the Arab world. Their brand of socialism, however, purported to be not only anti-Soviet (and its Iranian ally, the Tudeh Party), but inimical to all forms of foreign domination, domestic tyranny, economic corruption, and class exploitation. Above all, it bore the hallmark of what is today known as "nativism," that is, loyalty to indigenous cultural and religious norms and values.

Founders of this novel social movement were Mohammad Mekanik (1924–1976), who later changed his last name to Nakhshab, and Jalal al Din Ashtiani. Nakhshab, as a precocious senior in Tehran's Dar ol Fonun High School, led a group of like-minded youths in their quest for a progressive plan to rid the country of foreign domination and domestic oppression and corruption. In the meantime, Jalal al Din Ashtiani, a student of mining engineering at the University of Tehran, was running a discussion group with a similar agenda. The two groups eventually became aware of their similarities and merged by 1943 under the umbrella of the League of Patriotic Muslims (*Jam'iat-e Moslemin-e Vatankhah*). Ashtiani, the son of a renowned religious philosopher, Mirza Mahdi Ashtiani, was more philosophically inclined, whereas Nakhsab was a charismatic ideologue and organizer. They performed complementary roles as leaders of the movement. By 1945 the group had changed its name to the "Movement of God-Worshiping Socialists" or *Nehzat e Khoda Parastan e Socialist* (MGWS). There is no doubt that the group's view of Islam as well as socialism was influenced by proponents of the Tudeh Party (Fazlollah Garakani) on the one hand and Islamic scholars (Seyed Kazem Assar) on the other. However, Nakhshab and Ashtiani exhibited considerable deftness in rendering their synthesis more plausible. They believed that the Western-style theory of democracy, although desirable for its emphasis on freedom, is silent on the question of social justice. Conversely, Marxism, as practiced by Iran's northern neighbor, the Soviet Union, emphasized social justice at the expense of democratic principles. Democracy and social justice, they argued, are organically connected, but only when they are based on a kind of moral faith that belief in God inspires can this synthesis be realized—hence the "inverted triangle" in which belief in "God" undergirds both respect for "democratic rights" and struggle for "social justice."

The movement called for articulating the ideals of justice and equality in modern socialism. It also critiqued the trenchant materialism advocated by orthodox or "Soviet" Marxism and its Iranian advocates. Materialism, it argued, provides an insufficient moral basis for the struggle for democracy and justice. Ashtiani described the movement's ideological project as seeking a "middle ground between idealism and materialism." Thus, monotheism, as a defiant posture against earthly corruption and tyrannical domination, was deemed a necessary spiritual component for the worldly ameliorative programs advocated by socialism. The resulting "politicized Islam" thus incorporated nationalism, liberalism, socialism, and nativism. Some have even found similarities between MGWS's brand of socialism and a number of European trends, including humanist Marxism and critical theory. It is noteworthy that, from the outset, MGWS neglected the traditional body of beliefs and rituals that passed as Islam. Instead, MGWS considered the truth of the religion to be contained in its core moral values, which it shared with other monotheistic faiths. Therefore, the members, though affirming their Muslim faith, welcomed Iranian Jews and Christians, and, indeed, there is evidence that at least in one city (Shiraz) the movement had active Jewish members.

MGWS of the 1940s was at once an intellectual discussion group and a political party. As a political formation, it joined the struggle for the nationalization of the oil industry in the late 1940s and early 1950s. In its attempt to play a greater role in the arena of national politics, it first attempted to attract four "independent" members of the Majlis (Makki, Ha'er Zadeh, Bagha'i, and Azad) to form a party. Having failed in that project, it formed a short-lived coalition with a reputable but small party by the name of the Party of Iran (Hezb e Iran). It provided foot soldiers and opened new provincial branches for the party. During the next annual plenary of the party, three of the leaders of MGWS (Nakhshab, Razi, and Nooshin) were elected to central positions, but this move alarmed the party's leadership, and in the power struggle that ensued MGWS voluntarily left the party and formed the "Society for the Liberation of the People of Iran" ("Jam'iat e Azadi e Mardom e Iran"), which was affiliated with the National Front. Publications of the organization that had commenced at Darl ol Fonoun High School as carbon-copied sheets now evolved into a daily newspaper entitled *Mardom-e Iran (The People of Iran)*. Mohammad Nakhshab's main writings, which later appeared as volumes with titles such as *The Worldly Man (Bashar e Maddi)*, *What is Party (Hezb Chist)*, and *The Clash of the Church with Materialism (Neza'-e Kelisa va Materialism)*, were first published in this newspaper. Hours after the coup d'état of 1953, the leadership of MGWS met in secret and, inspired by the French reaction to the Nazi occupation, formed an underground political confederation of all nationalist formations called "The National Resistance Movement" ("Nehzat e Moghavemat e Melli"). Mohammad Nakhshab was elected the first coordinator of the movement. With his arrest, days later, Hossein Razi took over and coordinated protests and strikes in the months following the coup. In the meantime, the movement itself maintained its affiliation with a reconstituted "National Front II."

Mohammad Nakhshab, who had been arrested several times in the course of a decade of intense political activity, now returned to academic life and received his Masters degree in public administration in 1958 from the University of Tehran. He then left the country to complete his studies in public administration in the United States and eventually received his PhD from New York University in the same field. (Ashtiani, who had gone abroad before Nakhshab, eventually abandoned both the intellectual and political aspect of the MGWS project and engaged in a fairly conventional positivist critique of religion.) While abroad, Nakhshab played a pivotal role first in forming the Confederation of Iranian Students Abroad and later in founding the Iranian Students' Islamic Association in North America. In addition, while in the United States, he became a member of the Executive Committee of the U.S. branch of the National Front II and wrote for the Front's quarterly journal *Andishe-I Jebheh* (*The Front's Thought*). Nakhshab spent his last years in the United States working for the United Nations. He was somewhat despondent about the prospects of political reform in Iran. Nakhshab died of a massive heart attack in the United States in September of 1976, two years before the first signs of the Islamic Revolution became palpable in Iran.

MGWS is historically significant as much for its innovative synthetic project as for the long-lasting effect it has had on the subsequent generations of Iran's religious lay elites. For instance, the greatest pre-revolutionary Iranian religious intellectual, Ali Shariati, was affiliated with the movement. He entitled one of his translations on the life of one of the companions of the Prophet of Islam as "Abouzar, The God-Worshiping Socialist," thus obliquely paying tribute to MGWS. The essay reinforced the MGWS's thesis that pristine Islam was compatible with socialism.

MGWS had, in the post-coup d'état years, reconstituted itself as "the party of the People of Iran" ("Hezb-e Mellat-e Iran"), and it was from within the ranks of this party that the second generation of MGWS emerged. They included Kazem Sami, a physician who later became the health minister in the first post-revolutionary government of Mehdi Bazargan, and Habibollah Peyman, a dentist by training and an energetic political activist who, in collaboration with

Sami, formed a more radical splinter group after some of their proposals were rejected by the more moderate leadership of the party. The new organization bore the acronym JAMA, "The Revolutionary Movement of the People of Iran" ("Jonbesh e Azadibakhsh e Mardom e Iran"). When the leaders of the above organization and its affiliates were arrested, the active political phase of the MGWS and its myriad political permutations in Iran drew to a close. However, the nucleus of these political formations continued their diminished clandestine activities and emerged after the revolution with new vigor.

In the meantime, a significant watershed in the history of Islamic radicalism was reached when a small group of radical youths splintered from the religious, nationalist, and liberal organization "the Freedom Movement of Iran" ("Nehzat e Azadi e Iran"). Their departure was on tactical grounds, as they favored armed struggle and were critical of the conventional brand of the opposition politics that the "Movement" pursued. The eventual closure of the Freedom Movement and the incarceration of its founders seemed to confirm the belief of these young radicals in their chosen path of armed struggle. In 1963 the founding members, Mohammad Hanifzezhad, Said Mohsen, and Ali-Asghar Badizadegan, who had been students in the University of Tehran together, formed a study group dedicated to the interpretation of Islamic texts as well as Marxist and socialist history and literature. Two years later, on September 6, 1965, they brought together some twenty trusted friends to form a full-fledged guerilla organization, which remained nameless for the time being. Three years later, after a period of intense theoretical and organizational work, the group set up a central committee that included, in addition to the original founders, nine other members, including the current leader of Mojahedin organization, Masoud Rajavi. Ideological tracts from this period, the volumes entitled "Shenakht" (epistemology) and "Takamol" (evolution), indicate an impressive, if eclectic, synthesis of science, Marxist ideology, Arab socialism, and radical interpretations of the Islamic texts that posited that "the true essence of the Koran was absolute equality: equality between masters and slaves; between men and women; between whites and blacks." It was not until 1972 that the organization officially adopted the name "The Organization of the Warriors of the People of Iran" ("Sazman e Mojahedin-e Khalgh-e Iran") and designed an emblem that reveals its nationalist, socialist, and Islamic nature. Social and class origins of the organization were urban and traditional middle class. They were mostly college-educated professionals or university students. While planning their first major operation, blowing up the central electric plant in Tehran during a major state celebration, the bulk of the organization, sixty-nine individuals, including the three founding members, were arrested and put on trial. Of these, nine were executed, and the rest received various prison terms, including sixteen life sentences. Between 1972 and 1975, the remainder of the members of the organization who had escaped arrest reorganized themselves in three groups that remained unknown to each other except through a three-man central committee. They engaged in limited guerilla activities but continued ideological work. This is the group that, after a bloody purge of one of its leaders, Majid Sharif Vaghefi, initiated a complete disavowal of Islam and formed two purely laic Marxist guerrilla organizations: Pyekar dar Rah-e Azadi-e Taba-qeh-ye Kargar and Rah e Kargar. The group in prison, in the meantime, particularly the members in Qasr prison, huddled around Masoud Rajavi. This was the beginning of Rajavi's "cult of personality," which reached its zenith in the mid-1980s. Between 1975 and 1978, the two Mojahedin organizations, the Muslim one and the Marxist one, operated separately and traded charges of treason and reaction. During that period, the former lost forty-two and the latter forty-seven members to various armed confrontations with the security forces. Despite these activities, the Pahlavi regime could claim, with some justification, that it had effectively neutralized armed guerilla activities (both Marxist, like Fedayian e Khalgh, and Muslim, like Mojahedin e Khalgh) in Iran. The same fate befell the political radical Islamic groups such as JAMA. They were apprehended or placed under house arrest. By the early 1970s, the socialist Islamic movement in Iran seemed effectively neutralized.

Post-revolutionary Iran provided fertile ground for the entire spectrum of leftist politics in Iran. The proponents of the various brands of radical Islam and Islamic socialism were no exception. Among these, four groups are noteworthy. A group of young socialist Islamic ideologues briefly ascended to power in the early years of the revolution. They came to occupy various positions in Prime Minister Hossein Mousavi's government. Most of these individuals eventually abandoned socialist ideologies and reemerged as advocates of development and democracy in 1990s during the popular liberal movement that brought President Khatami to the presidency.

A second group was the newly freed remnants of the Muslim Mojahedin-e Khalgh organization, under the leadership of Mas'oud Rajavi, which claimed the imprimatur of the original group "The Organization of the Warriors of the People of Iran" ("Sazman e Mojahedin-e Khalgh-e Iran"). Having been freed from prison in 1977 under pressure from the international community, they subsequently launched a full-fledged political campaign, paramilitary training camps, and detailed ideological critiques of the political developments in Iran. After the success of the revolution, they created a nationwide organization with electoral ambitions. They also forged a fragile alliance with the first Iranian president, Abolhasan Bani Sadr, after the revolution. Their rocky relationship with the clerical revolutionary establishment led to an armed uprising on June 19, 1981, which faced decisive and brutal crackdown by the security forces. In the wake of that confrontation, the leadership of the organization fled the country and established itself first in France and later in Iraq. The decision to seek refuge in a neighboring county, Iraq, at war with Iran, severely damaged the popularity of the organization in Iran and caused it to revert back into "an inward-looking sect."

A third group, the remnants of the original Mojahedin guerilla organization, splintered from the post-revolutionary reconstituted Mojahedin-e Khalgh organization. They chose the name "Warriors of the Islamic Revolution" ("Sazman e Mojahdin e Enghelab e Eslami") and have operated as loyal opposition. They have continued this path in recent decades and have been vocal in opposing right-wing governmental policies in Iran. A smaller splinter group under the guidance of a young engineer, Lotfollah Meythami, who had been blinded in an explosion while constructing a bomb, pursued a more cerebral course that claims descent from the original ideas of the Mojahedin e Khalgh founders. His group continues to publish the bimonthly political-strategic journal *Cheshm Andaz e Iran* in Tehran.

A fourth group, composed of Habibollah Peyman, Kazem Sami, and a few others, reconstituted JAMA after the revolution with a slight change of name, "Jonbesh e Enghelabi ye Mardom e Iran," which left the acronym intact. After the assassination of Sami in 1998, Peyman pioneered a new political formation known as the "Movement of Militant Muslims" ("Jonbesh-e Mosalmanan-e Mobarez") and encouraged a loose confederation of like-minded individuals and organizations to join the movement. By the 2000 Majlis elections a broad coalition of leftist Islamic groups started to consult and coordinate activities with the intention of affecting the outcome of the elections. This coalition included the remnants of JAMA, Azam Taleghani's women's rights organization, and a number of political personages such as Ezatollah Sahabi, Hasan Yousefi Eshkevari, Hossein Shah Hosseini, Mohammad Basteh Negar, and others. This coalition was called, rather spontaneously, "Melli-Mazhabi ha" ("The Nationalist-Religious Ones"). Although the latter has never declared itself as a political organization with declared principles, it has continued to play a role in Iran's opposition politics. The group maintains an eponymous website and has been a target of political persecution on behalf of Iranian security and judicial authorities. The Melli-Mazhabi group is the only extant political formation in Iran that explicitly traces its political lineage to the MGWS in the 1940s. It even claims a rediscovery of the original ecumenical and liberal reading of Islam evident in the works of Mohammad Nakhshab in the 1940s.

Suggested Reading

Abrahamian, E. 1982. *Iran between two revolutions*. Princeton: Princeton University Press.

Abrahamian, E. 1989. *The Iranian Mojahedin*. New Haven: Yale University Press.

Amou'i, M. A. 2005. Interview with Cheshm Andaz e Iran. No. 35, December, January.

Behrooz, M. 2000. *Rebels with a cause: the failure of the left in Iran*. New York: I. B. Tauris.

Boroujerdi, M. 1996. *Iranian intellectuals and the West: the tormented triumph of nativism*. Syracuse: Syracuse University Press.

Taghavi, S. M. 2004. " 'Fadaeeyan-i Islam': the prototype of Islamic hard-liners in Iran," in: *Middle Eastern Studies*. 40. January, pp 151–165.

Taghavi, S. M. 2005. *The flourishing of Islamic reformation in Iran: political Islamic groups in Iran (1941–1961)*. New York: Routledge Curzon.

Web Sources

http://www.ehsanshariati.com/articles/Azadeh/SosIrIs/Nakhshab.htm

http://www.hrw.org/press98/dec/iranback.htm

http://www.iran57.com/Marjaani,Fareed.html

http://www.mellimazhabi.org

MAHMOUD SADRI

✦ SPORTS

Athletes and sport did not play a role in the Islamic Revolution, and when the Islamic Republic was established, its leaders did not give much thought to sport. However, the new regime's ideological premise, namely that all state policies had to be congruent with Islam, had certain repercussions for sports.

Athletic contests are not expressly mentioned in the Koran. Compendia of jurisprudence only mention two athletic activities: horse racing and archery, the reason being that for these it is permissible for the competitors to bet on the outcome and for third parties to set a prize, an exception to the general prohibition of gambling. At the popular level, the first Shiite Imam, Ali b. Abi Talib, has a formidable reputation as an athlete, making him the major patron saint of the traditional *zurkhaneh* (house of strength) sports. But these facts by themselves could not furnish the bases for a coherent policy on sports, nor could Khomeini's by now famous statement: "I am not an athlete, but I like athletes." And so in the years immediately following the revolution, official sports policies were more influenced by populism and the

Iran's national team, right, and the U.A.E. national team listen to their countries' national anthems before a playoff game, 2001. (AP Photo/Vahid Salemi)

revolutionaries' puritanical outlook on life in general than by scripture or tradition. Elite sports such as horse racing, polo, fencing, and bowling were (temporarily) eliminated. Given the affiliation of many owners of sports clubs with the previous regime, all private clubs were nationalized and Tehran's two major soccer teams were renamed: Persepolis became Piruzi (Victory), and Taj (Crown) became Esteqlal (Independence). Chess, boxing, and Kung fu were forbidden, the first because most Muslim jurists associate it with gambling, the latter two because they inflict physical injury, which is contrary to the *shari'a*. At the same time martial arts like Karate and Taekwondo were positively encouraged, to the point that training facilities were provided in mosques. Women's sports competitions were discontinued until further notice, as athletes' official sports uniforms obviously did not satisfy the requirements of *hejab* (veiling), which was imposed on women beginning in 1981.

By the 1970s soccer had replaced wrestling as the favorite spectator sport of Iranians, a professional soccer league had been established (the Takht-e Jamshid Cup), and soccer players were earning a lot of money and receiving a lot of popular attention. Soccer remained popular after the revolution, which riled the fundamentalists. Consequently for most of the 1980s the official view suggested that the cult of champions was a legacy of imperialism and that in a revolutionary society like Iran sports should be a means to achieve greater health. While the revolution put an end to the Takht-e Jamshid Cup, in 1981 a series of provincial leagues were formed, whose champions would then play each other for the national championship. Reflecting the ideology of the new regime, the cup was called the Quds (Jerusalem) Cup.

Major soccer games presented difficulties for the regime. In a country from which most public entertainment had been banished, attending football matches was one of the few remaining leisure activities for young men. They often led to scuffles, one of the worst of which occurred on October 9, 1984, when a major game had to be stopped midway, spectators went on a rampage, and nineteen were injured in clashes with security forces. However, if the regime tried to stop football, it would antagonize precisely the popular classes on whose support it depended most. The result was constant attempts in the press to contrast the commercialization, exploitation, and hooliganism that characterize sports in the corrupt West with the traditional Iranian values of chivalry (*javanmardi*) which, at least ideally, permeated Iran's native athletic traditions.

The traditional exercises that in theory embody these noble values in its ideals and rituals are performed in a special gymnasium called *zurkhaneh* (house of strength), and since the 1930s these exercises have been called *varzesh-e bastani* ("ancient sports"), implying that they originate in pre-Islamic Iran, for which contention there is no proof. The ceremonies, rituals, and setting of these exercises are laden with religious symbolism, which means that this tradition satisfied the new regime's emphasis on authenticity. In practice, however, full and sustained state support for the propagation and repopularization of Iran's native athletic tradition was fraught with difficulty. One reason was that before the revolution the "ancient sports" establishment had been dominated by a man, Sha'ban Ja'fari, who was hated by the anti-Shah opposition for his role in physically attacking and intimidating opponents of the ruler in the 1950s. Moreover, Ja'fari had organized mass exhibitions involving many hundreds of *zurkhaneh* athletes on such occasions as the Shah's birthday, which meant that in the eyes of many people "ancient sports" were identified with the previous regime, under which they had been interpreted as a manifestation of Iranian anti-Arab patriotism. The association of "ancient sports" with the old regime was overcome by declaring pre-revolutionary practices to have been an aberration and by emphasizing the religious symbolism of the tradition in addition to its patriotic charge. The more serious problem was that Iran's youth showed very little interest in the nation's athletic heritage. While various East Asian martial arts and even recently introduced disciplines such as baseball, cricket, and skateboarding found eager practitioners, "ancient sports" continued to strike most young men as somewhat tacky and out of date. In an attempt to render traditional athletics more popular among the young, competitions in individual exercises were organized at the regional and national levels while the ritualistic aspects of *zurkhaneh* sessions were played down.

The one modern discipline in which the old traditions lived on is wrestling, which had been practiced in *zurkhaneh*s until the 1940s but lost its organizational link with "ancient sports" after international freestyle and Greco–Roman wrestling were introduced. Gholam-Reza Takhti, a legendary champion of the 1950s who had supported the National Front and committed suicide for personal reasons in 1968, was appropriated by the Islamic regime as a forerunner of the Islamic Revolutionaries' struggle against the Shah. All over the country streets, stadiums, sports halls, and *zurkhaneh*s were named after him. In spite of official support, the popularity of wrestling as a spectator sport has continued to decline, and in terms of participants it has faced stiff competition from East Asian martial arts, in particular taekwondo.

In the late 1980s some of Iran's leaders began to realize that the postrevolutionary policy of frowning on all forms of entertainment was self-defeating, as it gave rise to illicit practices far more objectionable than the ones outlawed. Iranian television was hard pressed to produce programs that people actually liked, and sporting events seemed innocuous enough—except that neither football players nor wrestlers cover their legs between the navel and the knee, the minimum male coverage prescribed by the *shari`a*. This led conservatives constantly to criticize the state radio and television organization for not following Muslim strictures in its TV programming. In the end, the matter of sports broadcasts was referred to Imam Khomeini himself, who in late 1987 issued a fatwa authorizing television not only to broadcast films featuring not totally covered women, but also sports events, provided viewers watched without lust. After this ruling sports coverage expanded to the point where in 1993 a third TV channel was set up which broadcasts mainly sports. In 1988 Khomeini issued another fatwa legalizing chess, provided the players did not gamble on the outcome. Soon the ban on boxing was lifted as well.

The death of Khomeini in 1989 and the assumption of the presidency by the pragmatic Ali Akbar Hashemi Rafsanjani a few weeks later heralded a more conciliatory approach of the authorities toward sport. The war with Iraq having ended in 1988, the state was now able to channel more money into sports as well, leading to improved performances of Iranian athletes at the international level. In 1989 a new national soccer league was formed, and it was named *Lig-e Azadegan*, after the POWs who had come home. At the 1990 Asian Games in Beijing the Iranian soccer team won the gold medal, which was a turning point for the sport. By the early 1990s private clubs were allowed again, and a number of companies were specializing in selling international soccer videos, posters, and magazines. International soccer lore was eagerly adopted by young Iranians in spite of the government's exhortations to resist the West's "cultural aggression," and even newspapers published by regime figures began reporting extensively on international soccer. By the late 1990s the quality of the game had improved to the point where many Iranian star players such a Mehdi Mahdavi-Kia and Ali Da'i were playing professionally abroad, with the German *Bundesliga* being the most popular national league.

Women's sports were also positively affected by the new climate. President Rafsanjani's daughter, Fa'ezeh Rafsanjani, took an interest in the expansion of opportunities for women and successfully lobbied the government to provide greater budgetary resources. To enable women to compete according to international rules and regulations, facilities had to be provided from which men would be totally absent. As a result, some sports halls and swimming pools were put at the disposal of women only, and others were built specially for them. Women became officials, referees, coaches, and administrators, resulting in a spectacular growth in the participation of women in sports at all levels. When Fa'ezeh Rafsanjani succeeded to have a park set aside for women to bicycle in, she was attacked by conservatives and the issue of women riding bicycles became an affair of state.

With the country's national sports organizations in disarray as a result of the purges occasioned by the revolution, the Soviet occupation of Afghanistan provided a welcome pretext to boycott the 1980 Olympic Games in Moscow. Four years later, the Olympic Games in Los Angeles were also boycotted to signify opposition to the United States, and it was only in 1988 in Seoul that Iran fielded a team. By contrast, Iran continued sending teams to various regional and world championships in different disciplines, although in the early years of the revolution many athletes used these trips abroad to defect.

In 1998 the national Iranian soccer time for the first time since 1978 qualified for the Football World Cup, which was held in France that year. The qualification after a game against Australia, and the subsequent victory in Lyons against the U.S. team, generated unprecedented enthusiasm, and coming in the wake of reformist President Mohammad Khatami's election in 1997, people were allowed to be celebrated publicly. For Iranian youth, their country's participation at the World Cup meant that their pariah nation had rejoined the international community, and parallels were drawn between *Jam-e jahani* (World Cup) and *Jame'eh-ye jahani* (world society). When in the autumn of 2001 the Iranian national team fared badly in the qualifying matches for the 2002 World Cup, people again poured into the streets, this time to vent their frustrations. Disappointment over the team's loss mingled with disappointment over the stalled reform in Iran, and, fuelled by Persian language radio broadcasts from Los Angeles, rumors circulated that the government had deliberately instructed the national team to lose so as to prevent a repetition of the celebrations of 1998. The demonstrations turned into riots in which a number of buildings were ransacked; hundreds were arrested.

While Iran's national soccer team has on the whole not done well in international competitions, Iranians have continued gaining medals in individual sports, as if to confirm the widespread perception inside and outside Iran that Iranians are inveterate individualists who are incapable of teamwork. Iranian wrestlers have continued to shine on mats around the world, and at the 2000 Olympic Games in Sydney, Iran returned to the forefront of international competition in a discipline in which Iranians had won many medals from the 1940s to the 1960s but had been eclipsed thereafter: weightlifting. Hossein Rezazadeh won the gold medal in the super heavyweight category, a feat he repeated at the 2004 Olympic Games in Athens. Also, Iranians started gaining international medals in taekwondo, constituting serious competition with the Koreans, who, having invented the discipline, had hitherto dominated it.

The international presence of Iranian athletes was mostly confined to men. While women covered with a headscarf could compete internationally for Iran in such disciplines as shooting and archery, women's participation in other disciplines was impossible, given the continued insistence that Iranian women wear the *hejab* in the presence of unrelated men. To provide Iranian women with international competition, Fa'ezeh Rafsanjani founded the Muslim Women's Games, which were first held in Tehran in 1993. On this occasion, female Muslim athletes from around the world competed in a variety of disciplines according to international rules and regulations, but in the total absence of men.

The popularity of international competition among sports-loving Iranians is such that even the officials of the *Zurkhaneh* sports have decided to internationalize "ancient sports" so as to render it more popular among the young. In 2005 an international competition was held in Tehran with teams from neighboring countries and even Korea and Malawi participating. To no one's surprise, Iran won.

Finally, Iranian athletes have gained international success in disabled sports and at the Paralympics. The wealth of talent in the various disciplines is a sad legacy of the Iran–Iraq War.

While most of the country's sports administration has by now settled into a certain routine, one area that remains fraught with disagreement and conflict is the presence of women at men's sports events. Soon after the revolution, women spectators were barred from attending soccer games and other events, the reason being not only the revealing attire of athletes but also the foul language used by supporters in their chants and slogans, which were deemed incompatible with the family values appropriate for women. After the presence of women's sports became an established fact in the early 1990s, the dossier of women's presence at male games was reopened. In July 1994, 500 women were allowed to attend a game between India and Bahrain in a separate section of the stadium in Tehran, but three days later the soccer federation rescinded its decision, stating that unfortunately some football fans had not been able to adapt themselves to the Islamic and humane norms governing society. The controversy would not go away, however, and on February 22, 1995, the head of the Physical Education Organization announced that he was personally in favor of allowing women to attend soccer matches but not wrestling and swimming events, in which men are not "appropriately dressed." To end the controversy, Iran's head of state, Ayatollah Ali Khamenei was asked for a fatwa, and he ruled that "an unrelated women may not look at the naked body of an unrelated man, even if the intent is not deriving lust." But when Iran's footballers returned from their qualifying match against Australia to an enthusiastic welcome at Tehran's main stadium in 1998, hundreds of women stormed the premises to claim an equal right to cheer for the national team. Soon after his election in 2005, President Ahmadinejad declared himself in favor of allowing women to attend men's matches, but he was quickly overruled by Khamenei.

In terms of organizational capacity, Iranian sports under the Islamic Republic evince a certain continuity with pre-Islamic Iran. Personal rivalries, interference by the government, and the all-pervasive *partibazi* (favoritism granted to friends and relatives irrespective of qualifications) hamper the efficiency of the country's large sports bureaucracy. Under President Khatami the government decided to make the presidency of the various federations an elective office, which has had a beneficial effect in the provinces because since then officials have had to campaign across the country for election, allowing provincial federations to extract more budgetary support from the center in exchange for their support for the winning candidate.

H. E. CHEHABI

✦ STATE STRUCTURE

Iran's post-revolutionary state structure is an amalgam of the old, deliberately new, and improvised. Since the multi-class movement that culminated in the Iranian Revolution of 1979 was mostly aimed at decapitating the state, many of the pre-revolutionary institutions have endured despite personnel changes at the top. At the same time, popular forces unleashed during the immediate post-revolutionary period have helped the creation of institutions that at times operate parallel to preexisting institutions. Added to this mix are a number of institutions that deliberately reflect the theocratic nature of the newly formed Iranian state as well as parastatal institutions— some preexisting and some that came into being after the expropriations of property from the elite of the previous regime—which interact with various state institutions and play a very important role in the Iranian political economy. Finally, the Iranian state includes improvised and still-developing institutions that have been added in times of crisis to overcome impasse or avert crisis.

With all these layers and without an organized, ideological party that could bring discipline to contending forces and offer some sort of hierarchical venue for reaching decisions, the Iranian post-revolutionary state has turned into a contested governance structure. Although the Islamic Revolutionaries have been quite capable of consolidating their hold over society, this consolidation has not translated into a centralized system of control over state institutions and political entities. To be sure, looking at the state as both a lever of power and a source of income, they have been able state builders, increasing the size of the state almost 2.5-fold. But rather than joining forces to build a centralized and autonomous state structure, various competing cliques have simply disassembled the state and turned it into a series of multilayered, parallel, and often competing fiefdoms. New parallel institutions have been built in some cases as a means to check institutions with similar objectives, when direct control was deemed impossible.

Today, preexisting state institutions constitute what can be considered the bulk of the administrative apparatus of the state. Most of the preexisting ministries and provincial governments and their bureaucracies have been maintained, even if, as in the case of the Ministry of Culture and Islamic Guidance (previously Ministry of Culture), some of their missions have changed or expanded. Also maintained without much modification are economy-related organizations such as the Central Bank and the Management and Planning Organization, which was created during the Pahlavi period to prepare the country's annual budget and longer term development plans.

The significant changes that have occurred at the administrative level relate to the two sensitive areas of oil and gas production and distribution and intelligence gathering. Since the revolution various firms (*sherkats*) that were involved in oil, gas, and petrochemical production, sales, and distribution have been maintained but have all been brought under the umbrella of the newly created Petroleum Ministry, whose head, like other cabinet ministers, needs to be approved and can be dismissed through a vote of no confidence by the parliament. Intelligence operations, previously performed by the State Security and Intelligence Organization (SAVAK), are now performed by the Ministry of Intelligence, again in a move deliberately intended to make sensitive activities accountable to an elected body and not individuals. But unlike its pre-revolutionary antecedent, this ministry has not been able to centralize all security-related intelligence operations, and often opaque parallel security operations, linked to various revolutionary institutions, have mushroomed.

The political apparatus of the state contains a mixture of the old and new, both deliberate and improvised. The new political arrangement is a republic insofar as personal, hereditary, and lifelong rule is rejected, and popularly elected republican institutions, such as the office of the presidency and the Islamic Consultative Assembly (*majles-e showra-ye eslami* or *majles* for short), as well as the principle of separation of governmental powers based on a complex set of negotiating rules among key players and institutions, have replaced a monarch-dominated system. The republican character of the state was strengthened with the establishment of nationwide elected city and village councils in 1999. This new system of local government created institutions that are intended to move the country in the direction of increased political participation and democracy. In fact, the elected councils brought into the Iranian governmental system more than 200,000 locally elected representatives over-night and helped to solidify the importance of the electoral process in Iran's political setup.

But the political apparatus of the Iranian state is also "Islamic" insofar as the Constitution defines the Islamic Republic as a state overseen by Islamic jurists (*fuqaha*) and creates powerful and non-elective politico-religious institutions, such as the office of the leader (*rahbar*) and the Guardian Council (*showra-ye negahban*), on the side of republican institutions, empowering them with a variety of decision-making, supervisory, and oversight tasks to ensure that the democratic processes enshrined in the Constitution would not result in "un-Islamic" ends and the Islamic character of the state is maintained. Thrown in the mix are institutions like the Assembly of Experts for the Discernment of Leadership (*majles khobregan-e rahbari*), whose task is to oversee the activities of the supreme leader. This institution incorporates re-publican elements through the direct election of its members and yet has an Islamic disposition since standing for election is based on approved knowledge of Islamic principles and laws.

The result of this mix is a political structure that embeds within it sets of dualities that not only rest in uneasy tension next to each other but tend towards constant conflict, hence regularly exposing these contradictory impulses of the Islamic state in public. Extensive public debate about these internal constitutional inconsistencies was initially put on hold or managed by the external threat posed by the eight-year war with Iraq in the 1980s and the forceful presence of the leader of the revolution, Ayatollah Khomeini, who effectively overruled or resolved these contradictions through extra-constitutional personal decrees. The end of the war and the death of the founder and leader of the revolution, however, set the stage for the public exposure of the deep contradictions that exist within the Iranian state structure.

In order to address them, the 1989 amendment to the Constitution recognized the 36 member (expanded to 41 in 2006) Expediency Council (*majma'-e tashkhis-e maslahat-e Nezam*) as an advisory board to the leader, and empowered it to be the final arbiter of what constitutes the "interest of the ruling order" as well as to advise the leader on his task of setting the country's general policies. The Expediency Council had been set up the year before, on a temporary basis, by Ayatollah Khomeini to break the deadlock between the left-leaning Iranian parliament and the conservative Guardian Council, which has veto power over all legislation. With the 1989 amendment to the constitution, the Expediency Council developed into a permanent feature of the system, adding yet another layer to the already very complicated decision-making system. In 2005 the leader also delegated to this council his task of supervising the good performance of the system's general policies, further enhancing the power of this body, again without clearly specifying the range and content of this new responsibility.

The conflicting tendencies and aspirations the Iranian state embodies helps fuel rather than tame conflict among various political forces in Iran because of its silence on how competing institutions should coexist. The result has been continuing tension between competing institutions at the level of everyday politics, so far leading to at least one major constitutional revision (not overhaul) in 1989.

Complicating the political arrangement of the country are a number of revolutionary organizations that sprang up during the heat of the revolution, such as the revolutionary committees in the neighborhoods and the Islamic Revolutionary Guard Corps (IRGC), initially created to fight counter-revolutionaries and then put to use during the Iran–Iraq War. In the early 1990s, the revolutionary committees were incorporated into Iran's newly expanded and reorganized Security Forces (*niruha-ye entezami*) responsible for domestic security. But attempts to coalesce the IRGC and the standing military failed. IRGC has continued to thrive and establish its own parallel branches of the military.

Added to this mix are some 40 mostly economic and religious charity foundations, many of which, like the Foundation for the Oppressed (*Bonyad-e*

Mostas'afan), found their origins in the property confiscated from the extended royal family as well as many other well-to-do Iranians. Not all of these foundations are post-revolutionary institutions. Some religious foundations, such as *Astan-e Qods-e Razavi*, which operates the Imam Reza Shrine in Khorasan-e Razavi Province (a major pilgrimage destination for world's Shi'-ites), are rich pre-revolutionary religious endowments. The Islamic state, however, afforded these religious endowments much leeway to expand their economic, political, and social service activities. Claiming to be non-profit organizations, all these foundations, some of which are run by influential clerics, until very recently have been tax-exempt and even outside of the purview of state audits. They are funded by net incomes of their asset holdings, government transfers, and charitable contributions. Some of these organizations, originally intended to serve a particular clientele based on their needs, have developed into giant business conglomerates, benefiting from favorable government exchange rates, regulations, and contacts without much government oversight. Vastly unrelated and badly diversified, these conglomerates own and operate firms in agriculture, industry, commerce, transportation, construction, and others with absolutely no synergy or externalities. Most of them produce only a fraction of normal returns on their assets, but they are said to bankroll various clerical fiefdoms, or specific non-governmental activities, which have so far been immune from state encroachment.

Further complicating this picture is a vast network of highly non-transparent economic and political activities connected to the trafficking of drugs, arms, contraband commodities, and even artifacts that are rumored to be at least partly linked to, if not controlled by, military and paramilitary wings of the Iranian state (i.e., IRGC and related basij militia). These rumors are reinforced by the fact that, for instance, the IRGC has its own airport terminals and ports where smuggled goods can be brought into the country. The military and paramilitary sectors are further buttressed through their control of the arms industry and heavy involvement in development projects through interlocking construction companies.

Amidst all this, it is a wonder how post-revolutionary authority has been maintained. In fact, it has been maintained through a divided state structure that entrenches political and economic competition among social and political groups that range from traditional trade-centered interests located in the bazaars, to modern professional middle classes tied to more service-oriented interests of a new Iranian political economy, to those whose economic power comes from smuggling, development projects, and the arms industry. The state, rather than becoming the autonomous medium through which competition among these groups becomes regulated and hence controlled, has itself developed into an institutional repository of these varied interests and an arena in which multiple claims over various parts of the state and resources are constantly negotiated, sometimes very acrimoniously, rather than resolved. Meanwhile, the heavy hand of the state's ideological and repressive apparatus is used in coordination to make legitimate the clerical claim to state power.

Suggested Reading

Buchta, W. 2000. *Who rules Iran? The structure of power in the Islamic Republic.* Washington: The Washington Institute for Near East Policy.

Chehabi, H. 1996. The impossible state: contradictions of the Islamic state in Iran. *Contention* 5: 135–154.

Ehteshami, A. 1995. *After Khomeini: the Iranian Second Republic.* London: Routledge.

Schirazi, A. 1997. *The constitution of Iran: politics and the state in the Islamic Republic,* trans. by John O'Kane. London: I. B. Tauris.

Tajbakhsh, K. 2000. Political decentralization and the creation of local government in Iran: consolidation or transformation of the theocratic state? *Social Research* 67: 377–404.

FARIDEH FARHI

✦ TRADE

With the onset of the Iranian Revolution of 1979, the rhetoric of the revolutionary leadership called for freeing Iran from imperialist domination and for redirecting the country's trade and cooperative ventures toward the oppressed and exploited third world countries. It was argued that by doing so, Iran's resources would be immune from exploitation by more powerful transnational and multinational corporations. At the same time, it would enhance Iran's prestige and leadership among other third-world countries while improving prospects for prosperity, fair trade, and mutual cooperation. This, in turn, would promote Islamic ideology and an Islamic economic system that would better meet the moral, spiritual, and materialistic needs of the deprived and repressed masses of the third world.

Now, from the perspective of nearly three decades later, several questions might be raised in regard to Iran's international trade. Have the ideology and rhetoric, so adamantly proclaimed during the revolution, in fact played a significant role in shaping the country's international trade? How has this ideology evolved over the years, before and after the revolution? Has the regime succeeded in advancing Iran's economic independence? Has the direction of trade changed?

The Evolution of Revolutionary Rhetoric and Ideology

The revolutionary rhetoric drew upon two sources—the *Qur'anic* tradition and Marxist literature. It was a rhetoric which appealed to the Iranian sense of nationalism, religion, equity, and pride; a rhetoric that had been tested and sharpened in the earlier revolutionary movements of Iran as well as in other countries such as the former Soviet Union, China, Cuba, Vietnam, and Algeria, among others. The revolutionary rhetoric set a high standard and held out promise for all participants.

In many instances, anti-colonialism and anti-imperialism were advanced as religious duties. However, since Islam considers international and domestic trade as a respectable and honorable profession, many clerics provided interpretations of its potentially "undesirable" aspects. That is, they warned their audiences of the shortsightedness of "colonialism" and those they considered "colonialists."

At the time that the world was turning toward liberal democracy of market economies and free trade, Marxist rhetoric continuously and unceasingly hammered upon their audiences the notion of an "imperialist conspiracy" designed to exploit and plunder the resources of developing countries such as Iran. Accordingly, Marxists impressed upon their constituents that multinational corporations of industrially advanced countries were given free rein to invest in the exploration, extraction, and exportation of primary commodities while contributing little to the health and wealth of the host country through forward and backward linkages to the local economies that are needed for balanced economic growth and development. The revolutionary religious and Marxists rhetoric came to fruition in the post-revolutionary Islamic Republic's Constitution.

REALIZATION OF REVOLUTIONARY RHETORIC

In order to safeguard the country, the revolutionary leaders produced a Constitution, which proved to be less than friendly toward any group or organization that was perceived to be a potential foreign exploiter or an imperialist in disguise. Therefore, international trade was placed under the control of the public sector. This put severe restrictions on activities of foreign companies in Iran. Evidence (Figures 6 and 7) shows that Iran's exports, oil and gas included, as a percentage of world exports, have dropped over the span of 1953–2005. This development has been a consequence of sanctions and policy decisions of the Islamic Republic at the onset of its formation.

COMPOSITION OF NON-OIL EXPORTS

The best performance of the economy in terms of Iran's ability to pay for its imports was recorded in 1996 when Iran could pay for 46% of its imports by non-oil exports. However, subsequent data proved that year's performance to be an outlier. In the following years the ratio fell to seemingly more

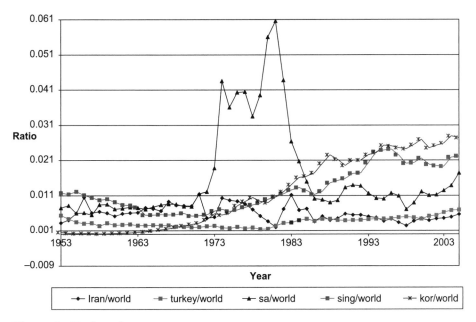

Figure 6 Trade ratios.

sustainable levels. The decline in the ratio of non-oil exports to total imports has been at its worst levels in the post-revolutionary era. For many years (1975–1986), Iran was able to pay for 2% to 9% of its imports. This should not be too surprising considering the Iran–Iraq War, which caused much destruction and required reallocating resources to the war effort and mitigating sanctions' impacts. Nonetheless, economically speaking, the inability to pay for imports has been and remains the most critical vulnerability of Iran.

In order to encourage and expand non-oil exports, a major turn in policy toward a free foreign exchange market occurred in the month of Azar 1994. Bank Markazi Iran announced that exporters could use foreign currency for importation purposes. Accordingly, exporters no longer had to sell their foreign currency to the banking system at the official rate as they had done prior to that time. However, this led to a great deal of chaotic trading, and the central bank abandoned the policy shortly after it was enacted. In the last decade and a half, the trade policies of the Islamic Republic have been, at best, ad hoc and therefore erratic.

Geographical Distribution of Imports and Exports

The geographical distribution of imports and exports has gone through a noticeable transformation since the 1980s. There has been a considerable

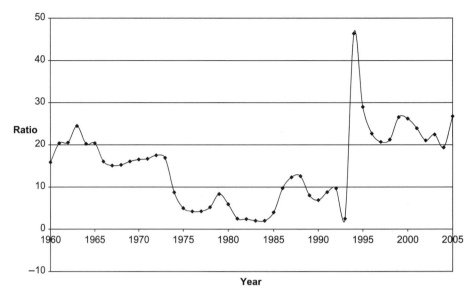

Figure 7   Ratio of non-oil exports to imports.

shift in Iranian trade away from developed countries and in favor of other oil-producing and non-oil-producing less-developed countries. These trends could be due to conscious policies of the Islamic Republic or political forces that have been pushing for the country's political and economic isolation.

There are two periods when trade relations with the developed countries showed precipitous decline. The first period of note encompasses the years during and immediately following the revolution when the country was mulling over its future—1357–1361 (1978–1982). During this period imports from developed countries ranged from 84.79% ($17.004 billion) in 1978 to a low level of 59.79% ($6.661 billion) in 1982, while exports fell from 82.62% ($18.025 billion) in 1978 to a low of 53.93% ($8.630 billion) of total exports in 1981. Even though the direction of trade with developed countries recovered somewhat, it never reached the level attained during the pre-revolutionary period. Trade with developed countries hovered around 60%–70% during the rest of 1980s.

The second notable period reveals more drastic changes. Starting in 1990, exports to developed countries fell precipitously from 71.03% ($13.712 billion) to a low of 43.7% ($8.037 billion) of total exports in 1994. This happened despite the fact that ever since the passing of the late Ayatollah Khomeini, the Iranian government has struggled to reverse its socioeconomic and political policies as well its image on both the domestic and international fronts.

All in all, there has been a marked shift in Iran's total trade away from the developed countries and toward oil-producing and non-oil-producing less-developed countries. However, despite the sharp decline in Iran's trade with the West, one could argue that Iran's trade with the West did not decrease at all, but that it is taking a detour through the Persian Gulf littoral Arab Sheikhdoms. Much of this trade is informal or takes place through the private sector, whereby Iranian intrapreneurs conduct business with Western companies through Persian Gulf intermediaries. Many-fold increases in trade of these Sheikhdoms with the rest of the world supports that argument. This could also be considered as the cost of economic sanctions.

Developments in the Post-Khomeini Era: Free Trade Zones Policy

In order to break with the past, the revolutionary leadership initially embarked on a path of nationalization of private enterprises to curtail the dominance of the wealthy domestic and foreign capitalists. The impact of this disposition was most obvious in regard to international trade and banking. After the revolution, the banking system was completely nationalized and international trade was delegated to government control by the Constitution.

The purpose of nationalization of international trade was to extract the presumed economic rent from foreign trade. Also, the regime believed that Iran could not free itself from foreign domination as long as international trade was not controlled by the government. In other words, it was believed that as long as international trade is controlled by the private sector, foreign domination is inevitable. In the absence of government monopoly of foreign trade, foreigners, in pursuit of their self interests, would exploit Iranian resources and jeopardize the balanced development of the economy as a whole. This was precisely the situation that had existed under the regime of the Shah. Therefore, if foreign trade were kept under the public domain, a more favorable and appropriate trading pattern would emerge. The emerging pattern would depend, to a lesser extent, on oil exports than had been the case during previous decades.

In the 1990s, the government, in a complete reversal of its revolutionary rhetoric, invited foreign companies to initiate joint venture investments in Iran. This new direction is based on the finding issued by the Council of Guardians of the Constitution that: "foreign corporations having concluded legal contracts with Iranian governmental departments can, with the purposes of performing legal affairs and their activities within the framework of concluded contracts, register their offices in Iran, in accordance with Article 3 of the registration of Companies Act. This shall not contradict Principle 81 of the Constitution."

In 1993, the government designated two islands, *Kish* and *Qeshm* in the Persian Gulf, as well as two other mainland locations, *Sirjan* (central Iran) and *Chabahar* (near the Pakistani border), as free trade zones. An objective of the Free Trade Zones policy was to increase and encourage foreign direct investment in the form of joint ventures. The government assumed that the two Persian Gulf islands would serve as a safe environment for those who perceived investment in Iran as too risky. Therefore, by making these two islands free of the laws, rules, bureaucratic red tape, and regulations, the government expected that the perceived risk would be diminished, or in a best case scenario, eliminated.

The lukewarm reception of the Free Trade Zones by the international business community, however, should not have come as a surprise to many people. Both economic and social factors have contributed to the limited enthusiasm. In the aftermath of the 1979 Iranian Revolution and also after the 1982 Mexican debt problems, multinational enterprises have become more cautious in their foreign direct investment in less-developed countries and have begun to pay more attention to country risk evaluation.

Due to the excesses of the revolutionary government, and because the United States has successfully portrayed it as a pariah state, Iran has suffered from an image problem in the international community. In spite of Rafsanjani and Khatami's charm offensives, Iran has not been able to shed certain attributes associated with its immediate post-revolutionary conduct.

CONCLUDING OBSERVATIONS

In the first decade after the revolution, while the late Ayatollah Khomeini was in control of the country, almost every policy was based on furthering Islamic ideology, independence, and self-sufficiency at any cost. The government's stance toward international trade and the presence of foreign-owned companies has been a striking reversal in rhetoric and policy. Immediately after the revolution, international trade was assumed to be a Trojan horse used by imperialists to plunder the country's wealth. However, decades of struggle and political posturing have not resulted in domestic and international economic achievements that could serve as a model for others. Rather, Iran's economic policies have brought consternation and bewilderment.

The Iranian government in the post-Khomeini era has recognized that international trade should bypass ideology. Thus, the government has embarked upon a course which conforms more to the realities of the world. However, as shown by the results of the free trade zone policy, for example, policy reversal in the international trade areas has been less than adequate. The government's main intention in nationalizing international trade has been the elimination of the economic rent that accrued to the *bazaaris*—the import–export merchants. Yet it has not been successful in eliminating the *bazaaris* nor has it been successful in eliminating the economic rent that accompanies the import and export business. All that has happened has been replacement of the old familiar merchants with a new group of recently empowered merchants. Although it is reasonable to assume that the government has the right and responsibility to control and choose the direction of the country, it is also reasonable to assume that the government must forsake policies that are based on a premise that has not been fruitful.

As for non-oil trade, the government made an explicit turn in policy. The government made it a priority to increase trade with the Asian, African, and 'non-allied' countries of the third world, especially the Muslim countries. Whether intentional or a result of international political pressure, Iran's trade has been reshaped. It has shifted from developed countries to less developed countries.

Suggested Reading
Bina, C., and H. Zangeneh, eds. 1991. *Modern capitalism and Islamic ideology in Iran*. New York: St. Martin's.
Economic Analysis Office. 1362 [1983]. *Analysis of economic development of the country after the revolution*. Tehran: Central Bank of Islamic Republic of Iran.
Zangeneh, H. 1994. *Islam, Iran, and world stability*. New York: Palgrave Macmillan.

HAMID ZANGENEH

✦ TRIBES

The tribes and tribal groups of Iran have played important roles throughout Iranian history, and they continue to be a significant component of Iranian society in the revolutionary and post-revolutionary periods. In times of political turmoil and unstable and unpopular central governments, tribal groups offered their members some degree of autonomy and protection. They attracted the loyalty of their members, whose primary allegiance might not have been to the state.

People in Iran commonly used the terms *il* (*ilat*, pl.), *tayefeh*, and *qabileh* for tribes and tribal groups. These terms, among others, were sometimes interchangeable and also referred to more complex and less complex entities, depending on the circumstances. Most tribal people deployed a hierarchy of terms to indicate the groups to which they belonged. The Qashqa'i, for example, used *il* for the tribal confederacy, *tayefeh* for each component tribe, *tireh* for each subtribal group, and *beley* or *bunku* for each extended family. Each level possessed its own type of leaders. Often the adjective "tribal," which refers to sociopolitical traits, is more appropriate than the noun "tribe," because drawing boundaries around specific groups may be difficult.

The tribal groups of contemporary Iran ranged from small, localized groups with only local-level elders as leaders to large tribal confederacies with hierarchical leadership. Their ability to play political and military roles depended on the power of the central government and its interest in establishing control over the territories and resources it claimed. Where the state held vested interests, such as the areas in southwestern Iran that produced oil and natural gas, its agents attempted to exercise surveillance and control over the tribal people there (on the assumption that they might pose threats). Where state interests seemed less crucial, such as in the central deserts distant from international borders, governmental agents made fewer efforts to assert centralized control. Similarly, where tribal groups held wide economic and strategic interests in certain territories (such as control over trade routes), their leaders were apt to be well organized and articulated with their supporters. Where tribal groups focused primarily on local-level issues (such as sufficient vegetation and water for productive pastoralism), leaders may have been less developed and were more apt to represent local communities only. Such situations were dynamic, and the structure and functioning of the central government and the tribal groups expressed the changes that each polity experienced.

A tribe is a named sociopolitical entity that formed in response to external and internal pressures and circumstances. Some scholars define tribes in terms of kinship, by which they usually mean descent. Notions of kinship (a symbolic system of classification) were important in relationships among tribal people at the local level, but kinship ties alone did not form tribal polities. Hence a definition of a tribe as a kinship or kinship-based group is not sufficient or accurate because it places too much weight on the factor of kinship and neglects other, more significant factors. Kinship principles often gave tribal people a sense of solidarity, especially at the local level, but many non-tribal societies, both rural and urban, functioned equivalently this way. In addition, all tribal polities contained people whose links to local and wider groups were not defined by actual or fictive kinship ties. In the larger tribal polities, no kinship system was elaborate enough to encompass all members. Tribal people asserting connections to a genealogy or a common ancestor were issuing a political statement; such genealogies were charters of organization, not maps of actual kinship ties. Some tribal people may have conceptualized political relationships within and between tribal societies in terms of kinship bonds. By these strategies, which should not be glossed over simply as "kinship," people aimed to create a political context and act within it.

All tribal people operated within different spheres: residential and socio-territorial groups (in which they recruited members voluntarily), kinship groups (which they defined on notions of descent—actual or fictive—and marriage), and sociopolitical or "tribal" groups (in which they recruited members through political allegiance). Their ties in any one of these groups could link them to the others. Each tribal person drew on these residential, kinship, and political ties in different ways, depending on the circumstances. Upon hearing the news of an elder's death, for example, individuals would decide to attend the possibly distant funeral based on the strength of their bonds with the person and his family and group. Socio-territorial and kinship ties may or may not have connected them to the deceased person; tribal links, which the attendees sought to enhance, may have played a more significant role.

Scholars and other writers often misuse the terms "tribe" and "tribal." Many equate the words with a pattern of mobility (nomadism) and a particular livelihood (pastoralism, the dependence on livestock production). The *Encyclopaedia Iranica* (1987) entry on *ashayer* (nomads) translates the term as "tribes." The literature in Persian often uses the phrase "*ilat va ashayer*" (tribes and nomads) to convey the link between tribal organization and nomadism. Although many tribes held members who were mobile pastoralists, other members were not. Tribal people were not necessarily nomadic or pastoral, and some nomads and pastoralists (such as the Sangsari in north-central Iran) were not tribally organized.

Many scholars and others also assume that certain cultural, ethnic, and linguistic characteristics are inherent components of tribes and tribal groups, which they may define in these terms. An historian, for example, may write that Iran's paramilitary forces recruited soldiers from among the tribes during the Iraq–Iran war (1980–1988). Yet the evidence on which the person bases this statement derives from a news report stating that the recruits in question wore "tribal" garb. The initial assertion is correct, but the attire would have represented a cultural or ethnic affiliation and not necessarily a tribal one.

The tribal groups of Iran were located primarily in the border regions and in steppe, semi-desert, desert, and mountainous zones. The geography and ecology of these areas were especially suited to the primary pursuit (nomadic pastoralism) of many tribal people, and the marginality of their territories contributed to their often successful efforts to achieve some degree of political autonomy. Mobile pastoralism was often the only sustainable livelihood possible in these locales, and its practitioners contributed to Iran's economy by producing meat and dairy products and textiles for the market.

The largest and most prominent tribal groups in Iran in the twentieth and early twenty-first centuries can be listed geographically. In the northwest, they include Shahsevan and Kurds. In the central west, Kurds, Lurs, Laks, Arabs, and Bakhtiyari. In the southwest, Arabs, Bakhtiyari, Lurs, Qashqa'i, and Khamseh. In the central south, Afshar and Arabs. In the south, Arabs. In the southeast, Baluch and Brahui. In the east, Baluch and Timuris. In the northeast, Turkmans, other Turks, and Kurds. In the north (the Caspian Sea littoral), Turks. Some tribal groups inhabited border regions (and identified with compatriots in neighboring countries), while others were encircled within Iranian territory.

Each of these names represents a composite group, the parts of which also held their own identifying names. "Lur," for example, is a general term indicating broad ethnolinguistic traits, while Mamassani and Boir Ahmad (each also having its own named sections) are examples of groups under the Lur category. The Bakhtiyari are also Lurs, in language and culture, yet the national prominence of Bakhtiyari leaders in the late nineteenth and early twentieth centuries enhanced the significance of the Bakhtiyari name to the extent that many scholars do not know that this tribal group is also Lur. "Afshar," as another example of a broad term, includes diverse groups, primarily in Kerman province. The area's tribal people referred to themselves by other names often relating to their histories, ancestors, and territories.

A scholar who conducted ethno-archeological research in a village in western Iran remained perplexed throughout her stay about the tribal and ethnic identities of the people living there. The labels they gave for themselves—Kurd, Lak, and Lur—varied according to the circumstances.

The Khamseh tribal confederacy in southwestern Iran contained what outsiders often listed as three Turkish tribes, one Arab tribe, and one Persian tribe, yet each of these five tribes was ethnolinguistically mixed. People in the area often spoke of the Khamseh as an "Arab" group, as compared to its neighbor, the Qashqa'i, who people labeled as "Turks." Still, both confederacies were diverse in composition.

Small tribal groups, identified by all these names and many others, were located throughout Iran, and many of them had once formed part of larger polities. The larger polities themselves were conglomerates of small tribal groups. The most dispersed groups in Iran were various Turks (especially Afshars), Kurds, and Arabs. Shahs and other rulers in past centuries had divided large groups and relocated some of their sections to new territories for the purpose of security, punishment, and economics. The names of the subtribes (*tireh*s) of the Qashqa'i confederacy represent many prominent tribes in Iran's past, yet historians and others cannot usually document actual connections between the historical groups and the twentieth-century *tireh*s (for example, Qizilbash, Aqquyunlu, and Zand). Various Persian-speaking peoples, who may have been Persian in origin (that is, not recently assimilated as Persians), were also found among most tribes. Only some of the Kurdish and Arab peoples of Iran were tribally organized.

Half of Iran's population in the twentieth century consisted of Persians; the other half held Turks, Kurds, Lurs, Arabs, Baluch, and others, many of whom were tribally affiliated.

In the case of all of these large and small groups, political and socioeconomic change in the twentieth and early twenty-first centuries often resulted in the loss or decrease in importance of tribal (that is, sociopolitical) traits. For some, the change meant a rise in significance of ethnic and national-minority characteristics. Many Baluch in Iran, for example, asserted their connections with the Baluch in Afghanistan and Pakistan when outside forces drew these territories into conflict in the late twentieth century.

Other ways of categorizing the tribal groups of Iran also exist. Some scholars divide Iran's tribes into two groups: those of perceived Iranian origins (such as Kurds, Lurs, and Baluch) and those who originated from "outside" (such as Turks and Arabs). Tribes can be grouped ethnolinguistically, such as Turks and Baluch, and may be included in larger ethnic and national-minority groups, such as Kurds and Qashqa'i. Some tribal groups were more Persianized and assimilated in Iran than others, a situation also holding true for members of each group, some being more assimilated than others. Many of Iran's tribal groups were Sunni Muslim, especially those in border regions, while others were Shi'i Muslim. Some groups, including some Ahl-e Haqq (a Shi'i sect) in western Iran, affiliated with popular forms of Islam, such as sufi brotherhoods and saintly lineages. Tribal groups can also be characterized by relative size and by the complexity of their political organizations and leadership systems.

Iran's tribal groups demonstrated a range of economic livelihoods, in part depending on the local geography and ecology. They include nomadic and settled pastoralists, settled agriculturalists (often living in villages), and town and city dwellers who engaged in diverse occupations. For those tribes relying on mobility, their patterns of migration characterize them. In search of vegetation, water, and suitable climates, some groups moved year-round within relatively similar terrains, while others traveled long distances seasonally between low and high altitudes. Some were mobile for part of the year and settled for the rest. Transhumance, in which people occupied settlements for one or several seasons and then moved their animals to higher elevations for grazing there, was common. For people who were pastoralists, the kind of livestock that dominated their livelihoods (camels, sheep, goats, cattle, and water buffalo) differentiates them.

The tribes and tribal groups of Iran played little or no role in revolutionary activities in 1978–1979. The revolution was primarily an urban phenomenon, stemming from urban-based institutions and social groups. Some tribal people who lived in towns and cities participated in or observed political demonstrations there, but they acted as urban students and workers and not as tribal members per se. They may have shared similar interests with other protesters in wanting to rid Iran of Mohammad Reza Shah and his corrupt monarchy. "Tribal" interests (whatever these may have been) were not an articulated component of the revolutionary process.

Just after the revolution, when the Ayatollah Khomeini, other Muslim clergy, and their supporters began to establish the apparatus of an Islamic government, some tribal people grew uneasy about their own local interests. They worried that the emerging central government would impose its own security forces in tribal territory, and they wondered how the state would handle the issue of land rights. Mohammad Reza Shah had enacted land reform throughout Iran in the 1960s, and many people in the country (not only among the tribes) questioned whether the Islamic Republic would uphold the shah's changes or whether the new regime would reverse or undercut them. Some new state leaders, inspired by the populist sentiments of a revolutionary Shi'i Islam, urged a redistribution of land to benefit Iran's "deprived" and underprivileged citizens (including nomads). Other leaders, often large landowners themselves, stressed the Qur'an's assertion of the inviolability of private property and urged the preservation of the status quo.

Professing their own ideologically based agendas, urban, middle-class, Persian leftists of various political affiliations traveled to tribal areas (particularly in Khorasan, Azerbaijan, Kurdistan, and Khuzistan) to urge people there to unite against the local landed elite (some of whom were tribally affiliated and were current or former tribal leaders) and to seize their land. When the government's revolutionary guards (*pasdaran*) arrived to suppress the activity, armed conflict erupted. Needing to apply centralized authority quickly, leaders in Tehran sent reinforcements, and agitation at the local level subsided.

In Fars province in southwestern Iran, several hundred Qashqa'i men and women formed a tribal insurgency in 1980. A more accurate label for this event is a "defensive resistance" because the group aimed to prevent the government from capturing Qashqa'i leaders, not to initiate their own aggressive maneuvers. Opponents of the tribal khans labeled them as feudal landlords who had returned to Iran, after twenty-five years in forced exile abroad, in order to reclaim their vast landed properties. Revolutionary guards had already seized and imprisoned a prominent leader, Khosrow Khan Qashqa'i, who had reentered national politics when he was elected to the Islamic Republic's first parliament. In response, other Qashqa'i khans and their supporters formed small, mobile camps in mountainous territory not easily reached by governmental forces. After a two-year stalemate punctuated by periodic fighting, mediators reached an apparent—but soon violated—compromise. The insurgency ended when revolutionary guards captured, imprisoned, tortured, and executed many of the principal figures.

The formation of Iran's current international borders separated the tribal groups residing there from their compatriots in the adjoining countries. Since 1979, Iran's unstable border regions have experienced unrest, in part because of political disruption in the neighboring countries (Afghanistan and Iraq in particular) and the influx of refugees and others seeking a safer environment. The prevalence of armed smugglers (who trafficked in commodities and assisted Iranians who wanted to flee Iran) also increased the tension along the borders. Iran's government blamed various tribes for the lawless conditions, but the regime's ineffectual rule in the area was probably more at fault. Tribes as such did not create the instability. Rather, organized entrepreneurs (in collaboration with state officials, whom they bribed) exploited the unstable situation in order to profit from lucrative pursuits.

Scholars and others sometimes consider tribes to be part of ethnic groups, especially if these latter entities were large and complexly organized (the Kurds offering an example). Like tribal identities, ethnic identities represent symbolic systems of classification invoked for political reasons under changing circumstances. Ethnicity is a wider, more inclusive construct than that of tribe. As part of the processes of socioeconomic change in the twentieth and early twenty-first centuries, some tribal groups gradually assumed some characteristics of ethnic groups (without necessarily abandoning all tribal—that is, sociopolitical—traits), especially when the state increasingly drew the people under its control and administration. When state or other pressures undermined or eliminated key tribal organizations and institutions (particularly the leadership), the people formerly encompassed by these systems sometimes adopted or enhanced other traits associated with ethnic groups, particularly a self-conscious sense of distinctiveness. For example, when conservative hard-liners within the Islamic Republic undercut the power of the Qashqa'i tribal khans in the 1980s, the Qashqa'i people reasserted the importance of their Turkic language and culture in order to differentiate and unify themselves within the wider Iranian society, where ethnic Persians dominated.

Some tribally organized ethnic populations could also be considered national minorities or parts of them, groups united by a shared political consciousness—a sense of "nation"—and by an interest in achieving political and cultural self-expression. The Baluch in Iran, Pakistan, and Afghanistan provide an example. Baluch at the local and regional levels shared kinship and tribal links; they also held notions of linguistic and ethnic distinctiveness in common; and they formed part of the wider Baluch nation that overlapped these international borders and also included the Baluch in diaspora (in Kuwait and Great Britain, for example).

The tribal and ethnic-minority populations of Iran attracted domestic and international attention, especially if they exhibited colorful, picturesque, and exotic traits. Iranian and foreign filmmakers, photographers, and journalists expressed their fascination with these people and drew the interest of an increasingly widening audience.

Some tribal and ethnic communities, such as the Qashqa'i and Bakhtiyari in southwestern Iran, fell victim to the exploitative visits of uninvited domestic tourists. Urban middle-class Iranians imagined that a trip to the mountains or distant countryside—where reluctant yet still obliging hosts would offer elaborate hospitality—would be entertaining. Tourists also engaged in these excursions in order to evade the stiff social restrictions of the Islamic Republic, which mandated modest Islamic dress (especially for women) and forbade alcoholic beverages, drugs (especially opium), social mixing of unrelated men and women, dancing, and listening to Western and popular music (especially if sung by females). The Islamic Republic had touted the appealing traits of these and other tribal and ethnic minorities in order to moderate the unfriendly, conservative image of Iran for the benefit of foreign audiences. By doing so, the regime ironically helped Iranian citizens to locate spaces for the pursuit of clandestine pleasures forbidden by the state.

See also Nomads; and Qashqa'i.

Suggested Reading
Beck, L. 1990. Tribes and the state in nineteenth- and twentieth-century Iran. In *Tribes and state formation in the Middle East*, eds. P. Khoury and J. Kostiner. Berkeley: University of California Press.

Beck, L., and J. Huang. 2006. Manipulating private lives and public spaces in Qashqa'i society in Iran. *Comparative Studies of South Asia, Africa, and the Middle East.* 26: 303–325.

Cronin, S. 2007. *Tribal politics in Iran: rural conflict and the new state, 1921–1941.* London: Routledge.

Lambton, A. 1971. Ilat [Tribes]. *Encyclopedia of Islam*, new ed., vol. 3, pp. 1095–1110.

Tapper, R., ed. 1983. *The conflict of tribe and state in Iran and Afghanistan.* London: Croom Helm.

LOIS BECK AND JULIA HUANG

✦ TURKMEN AND TURKMAN SAHRA

The history of the Turkman people's settlement of Iran is as old as other Turks' habitation of land. Like other ethnic Iranian groups, Turkmen share the language of an independent country beyond the political borders of Iran. The existence of such independent states in which different Iranian ethnic peoples' culture is preserved and their languages are given formal recognition is a boost in the surviving and thriving of the ethnic identities within the borders of Iran. Turkmen of Iran live in Turkman Sahra, parts of Mazandaran and Golestan provinces. Outside Iran, besides five million Turkmen living in the Republic of Turkmenistan, there are Turkmen living in Iraq and Syria. The Turkman Population of Iran is estimated to be around two million. Like other ethnic groups, Turkman culture and language suffered the suppressions of the Pahlavi era. In the early days of the Islamic Revolution of Iran, the Cultural and Political Center of Turkmen people of Iran was created, and it mobilized the majority of Iranian Turkmen. Most members of Cultural and Political Center of Turkmen People of Iran had leftist proclivities, at that time branching off from Fedaiyan-e Khalq. They withstood the assaults of the Islamic Republic in the early days of the revolution in the city of Qonbad-e Qabus. However, the kidnapping and murdering the leaders of Cultural and Political Center of Turkmen People of Iran—Khalq-e Tukman—was a blow from which Turkmen people's movement has not yet recovered.

HADI SULTAN-QURRAIE

U

♦ U.S.–IRAN RELATIONS

Historically, U.S.–Iran relations can be traced back to the 1830s when Americans traveled to Iran as the first missionaries. During the Naseredin Shah period, direct contacts with Americans helped to create a navy force for Persia in the Bushehr port. Later in the 1870s, a group of American physicians helped establish Urmia University's College of Medicine. By the early twentieth century, relations between the two countries became a major force behind Iranians decision to modernize its economy and liberate it from British and Russian influences.

During the Persian Constitutional Revolution (1905–1911), Morgan Shuster was appointed Treasury General of Persia, to counter Russian and British interests in Iran. Under pressure by both Russia and Great Britain, Shuster resigned. The British proved instrumental in carrying out the 1921 coup that brought Reza Pahlavi to power. World War II and the emergence of the United States as the dominant player on the global scene marginalized the British role in Iran. The abdication of Reza Shah and his son's ascension to power in the early 1940s heralded a new era in U.S.–Iran relations, one that was marked by fast-paced modernization.

OIL NATIONALIZATION AND STRATEGIC ALLIANCE

During the early 1950s, Iran's democratically elected nationalist Prime Minister, Muhammad Mossadeq, rose to unprecedented popularity, forcing the Shah Mohammad Reza Pahlavi into exile. Mossadeq's rise to power and parliament's approval of nationalization of the Anglo-Iranian Oil Company (AIOC) thrilled Iranians but outraged British leaders.

Prime Minister Mossadeq was removed from power in 1953 by a CIA-engineered coup (known as Operation Ajax), which was conducted mainly from the U.S. Embassy in Tehran. U.S. officials helped organize street demonstrations and protests to overthrow Mossadeq and returned the Shah from his brief exile. The 1953 coup ended Iran's fledgling attempts at democracy, giving rise to a modernizing royal dictatorship that, a quarter of a century later, set off an anti-American revolution that brought militant Islamic groups to power. The shah restored his absolute power by eliminating all constitutional obstacles in his way. He repressed opposition newspapers, political parties, trade unions, and civil groups. The real tragedy of American–Iranian relations stemmed from the fact that United States policymakers depended solely upon the Shah's view of the situation and overlooked blatant signs of popular disenchantment and unrest, which ultimately led to the Islamic Revolution. Many U.S. foreign policymakers were caught by surprise at the Khomeini revolution and by the extent of hatred toward the United States. In the long run, U.S. intervention in Iran paved the way for the eventual rupture of U.S.–Iranian relations in the 1979 Islamic Revolution.

U.S.–Iranian relations were largely premised on maintaining stability in the Persian Gulf. The shah received unconditional U.S. support as a pillar of U.S. foreign policy in the region. President Richard Nixon developed a strategy of cooperation with dictators such as the Shah to be the guarantor of U.S. interests in the Persian Gulf region. Despite the pressure on the Shah to open up the country's political space, Jimmy Carter's presidency viewed the Shah as an ally and thus a source of stability that had to be backed by U.S. foreign policy.

The Shah's aggressive modernization and Westernization projects alienated cultural and religious elites in a country where religious values held a tight grip on cultural traditions. Moreover, modernization under the Shah was intimately linked to economic growth and industrialization. Oil-induced growth boosted Iran's GNP per capita from $108 in 1957 to $1,660 in 1978. The pace of economic growth reached its most dramatic peak in the modern history of Iran between 1970 and 1978, when the annual average growth rate of GNP was 13.3%—by far the world's highest figure. Meanwhile, the agricultural sector faced many setbacks as a result of the Shah's program of industrialization at any cost. The Shah's land reform programs, under pressure from the Kennedy administration, altered the class structure in Iran's countryside, creating a new rural bourgeoisie, a new rural propertied class, a new proletariat, and a new landless class that relied on its labor for survival.

Prelude to the Iranian Revolution

From 1960 to 1970, the percentage share of GDP contributed by the agricultural sector dropped from 29% to 9%, the largest decline among Middle Eastern countries during that period. High economic growth rates during the 1960s and the 1970s resulted in a narrow distribution of income. The Shah regime's continued reliance on oil revenues made such growth rates feasible.

At the same time, social mobilization in Iran contributed to higher rates of education, literacy, communication development, and urbanization. The newly mobilized, politically relevant segments of the population had a high propensity for political participation. These social strata were composed of elements of the middle class, the urban working class, and the jobless labor forces in cities. The latter group proved to be highly politicized during the 1979 Iranian Revolution, even as the revolution was not rural overall.

The state reduced religious authorities' spheres of influence, which culminated in a legitimacy crisis that weakened the Shah's regime in the late 1970s. The regime deprived the clerics of their control of the two areas in which their social influence had been dominant—law and education—as well as of their economic and ideological status. The only opposition group allowed to operate was a secular group, the Committee for Defense of Freedom and Human Rights. Established in Tehran in 1977, this committee was the first independent human rights organization in Iran's history. Its membership included Shahpur Bakhtiar and Mahdi Bazargan. The latter became Iran's first prime minister in the Islamic Republic of Iran.

The shah's distraction from civilian politics and his close ties to the Army as well as with the United States alienated him from certain segments of the Iranian population. His notorious security apparatus (SAVAK), in the absence of any viable secular opposition, caused deep resentment against the regime among the vast majority of Iranians. This fact, along with the failure of urban guerrillas to develop the mass base necessary to promote an effective guerrilla war, gave the clergy a unique opportunity to direct the revolution. By the late 1970s, the Shah's violent attempts to curb revolutionary fervor had proven ineffective. The conservative forces, spearheaded by Ayatollah Rouhollah Khomeini, overwhelmed pro-Shah forces and toppled the monarchy.

The Khomeini Era (1979–1989)

Intent on restoring power to the common person and on reinstating the social solidarity of early Islamic communities to urban life, neo-Islamic populism under the Khomeini regime aimed to terminate foreign economic and cultural domination. In the early years of the revolution, the government of

Mehdi Bazargan struggled during a chaotic and troubling era to define its foreign policy. When the Bazargan government tried to approach the U.S. delegation in Algeria, it was heavily criticized at home by the clergy. The November 4, 1979 hostage crisis, in which revolutionary students stormed the U.S. embassy in Tehran and took its fifty-four diplomats hostage for fourteen months, effectively disrupted any diplomatic relations that existed between the two countries.

The ensuing Iran–Iraq War (1980–1988) further intensified U.S.–Iran relations. Many Iranian experts held the view that the Iraqi invasion of Iran was largely instigated by the United States. In 1986, the Reagan administration "reflagged" Kuwaiti and other tankers that shipped oil from the Middle East to the West. This meant that the tankers would be defended by the U.S. Navy. As the war was drawing to a close in 1988, the U.S.S. Vincennes mistakenly shot down an Iranian airliner, killing 290 people aboard.

In a secret deal in 1987, the United States supplied Iran with missiles and other arms to win the release of American hostages in Lebanon as well as to provide funds for the Contras fighting a civil war in Nicaragua, which the U.S. Congress had banned. When this affair, which came to be known as the Iran–Contra Affair, became public, President Reagan rationalized it in the name of building support for the moderates within the Iranian regime.

The challenge of revolutionary Iran in the Persian Gulf became a central preoccupation of U.S. foreign policy. Several factors contributed to the establishment of the Gulf Cooperation Council (GCC) in the early 1980s: the Iranian Revolution, the Soviet invasion of Afghanistan, superpower competition, and the threat of spillover violence from the Iraq–Iran war.

The publication of Salman Rushdie's novel *The Satanic Verses* in 1989 gave Khomeini the necessary ammunition to criticize the West as well as to unify the nation during a period strained by the losses of war with Iraq. Khomeini issued a *fatwa* against Rushdie, putting a bounty on his head. The pragmatists were unprepared for dealing with the furor that erupted in the Muslim community more generally and in Iran more particularly in response to the publication of *The Satanic Verses*.

During the 1990s, however, Iranian officials frequently said that their government had no plans to track down Rushdie and carry out the execution. On September 24, 1998, Iran's foreign minister, Kamal Kharrazi, announced the lifting of the death decree against Rushdie. Speaking to a press conference at the United Nations, Kharrazi stated: "The government of the Islamic Republic of Iran has no intention, nor is it going to take any action whatsoever to threaten the life of the author of *The Satanic Verses* or anybody associated with his work, nor will it encourage or assist anybody to do so" (Esposito, 1999: 124).

Although the *fatwa* remains in force and may not change for some time to come, it has no official backing. In his visit to the United Nations in late September 1998, Mohammad Khatami, Iran's then-president, distanced himself from the *fatwa* by declaring the case against Rushdie "completely finished." Internationally, Khatami's decision was seen by many as part of his emphasis on civilizational dialogue to bring Iran into the international fold. Internally, however, his position was not shared by conservative factions within Iran, revealing the jockeying for power among different factions there. While many hardliners continued to insist that the death sentence against Rushdie be carried out, President Khatami, who sought improving ties with the West, appeared determined to lay the *fatwa* to rest.

By the mid-1980s, the United States had imposed—although not as an official policy—a trade embargo on the Islamic Republic. Since the mid-1990s, however, U.S. sanctions became a principal instrument for pressuring Iran as part of a declared policy of "dual containment" intended to contain both Iran and Iraq. The results have been mixed. The immediate effect of U.S. President Bill Clinton's May 8, 1995 executive order banning trade and investment with Iran was a sudden fall in the value of Iranian currency and, subsequently, a formal devaluation of the rial. The "1996 Iran–Libya Act" under President Clinton continued the sanction policy on Iran's petroleum exports. Such unilateral sanctions proved ineffectual, as they pulled Iran and Russia together and drove the United States and its European and Asian allies apart. In 1995, when Conoco's deal was canceled under the U.S. embargo, the French oil company Total replaced Conoco to develop the Sirri offshore oil fields in the Persian Gulf.

ISLAMIC PRAGMATISM

In the first decade after the 1979 Islamic Revolution, ideological confrontation and plain hostility characterized the tumultuous relations between the United States and Iran. After the death of Ayatollah Khomeini in 1989, this adversarial relationship was replaced with a period of pragmatism about how to best work with the United States. With the ascendancy to power of President Mohammad Khatami, enlightened pragmatism and regional détente came to define Iran's foreign policy orientation. Even then, not much progress toward rapprochement was made.

With the passing away of Khomeini from the Iranian political scene, interfactional disputes and the primacy of the economy over Islamic ideology came to characterize Rafsanjani's two-term presidency (1989–1997). Little was done to normalize the ties between the two countries, as Rafsanjani's most visible programs concerned the country's economy. Reform of foreign trade and correction of the exchange rate were crucial elements of Rafsanjani's liberalization programs.

In a decisive victory on May 23, 1997, Mohammad Khatami became Iran's new reformist president. Formerly a minister of culture and Islamic guidance (1982–1992), Khatami attempted to ease restrictions on private life and open the country to more commercial and cultural influences from abroad. U.S.–Iran relations entered a relaxed phase when the U.S. Secretary of State, Madeleine Albright, apologized for U.S. past actions in Iran and opened the door for rapprochement.

Throughout Khatami's two-term presidency, conservative clerics trumped his efforts to appoint a more open and democratic government or to pursue much-needed reform. Constrained by such obstacles, Khatami could not have initiated a rapprochement with the United States. His rhetoric of normalization of ties with the United States never went far. The Clinton administration approached the normalization talks with a two-track strategy. On the one hand, it continued to insist that if the 1996 Iran–Libya Sanctions Act (ILSA) was to be suspended, Iran must end its efforts to gain access to nuclear weapons, must terminate its support for terrorism, and must forgo denouncing the Middle East Peace Process. On the other hand, it repeatedly expressed its readiness to enter into state-to-state talks with Iran.

For its part, Iran responded with demands such as ending the U.S. military presence in the Persian Gulf, releasing the Iranian assets the United States had frozen from the time of the revolution, repaying Iran the money under dispute at the Hague, and stopping attempts to overthrow its Islamic regime. These issues, along with the lack of political determination and commitment on either side to address genuinely how the barriers to normal diplomatic ties between the two countries could be overcome, have hindered any further progress toward normalization.

The Aftermath of September 11

The tragic events of September 11, 2001, significantly altered U.S. foreign policy toward the region. President George W. Bush included Iran with Iraq and North Korea in the "Axis of Evil," as defined in his 2002 State of the Union address, and bolstered his anti-Iranian rhetoric, especially regarding Iran's nuclear programs and its alleged ties with Hezbollah, Hamas, and Islamic Jihad. It seemed as though any possibility of rapprochement between the United States and Iran was fatally lost. Ironically, the Iraqi war may have drawn the two countries closer. Following a multilateral effort to edge North Korea toward a nuclear non-proliferation treaty, the Islamic Republic of Iran ranks high on the agenda of U.S. foreign policy.

In retaliation to the September 11, 2001, terrorist attacks, the United States invaded Afghanistan and subsequently Iraq. The latter invasion has placed Iranian rulers in a far better position to bargain with the United States. The toppling of the Taliban regime with assistance from Iran and other regional countries, including Pakistan, raised the possibility of an opening in U.S.–Iran relations. Likewise, the Iraqi war brought Iran and the United States closer in the sense that stability in Iraq serves both countries' interests, and that Iran can be a stabilizing factor in the post-war reconstruction, as was the case in Afghanistan.

Yet at the same time, Iranians genuinely fear encirclement by the United States. Rapprochement between the two countries could prove to be a vexing problem for U.S. policymakers. Winning trade and investment concessions from the West would almost certainly reinforce clerical rule. Absent genuine democratic reforms, these trade ties could further deepen the rift between Iranian state and society. U.S.–Iran rapprochement is likely to bypass Iranian civil society, which is one of the most vibrant, explosive, and developed examples of its kind in the Middle East.

THE RETURN OF ISLAMIC POPULISM

In the 2005 presidential elections, Mahmoud Ahmadinejad, Tehran's former mayor, became Iran's new president. Iran's Islamic hardliners swept into power after thousands of pro-reform candidates were barred from running in recent disputed parliamentary elections. The Bush administration seemed less enthusiastic about pushing for regime change in Iran, even as Iranian conservative clerics consolidated political control at home. Some observers insisted that Iran was the next U.S. target of a preemptive strike.

When the conservatives won a new majority, the real question became whether Iran and the United States would work toward improving their relations. Undoubtedly, the sham parliamentary elections have further deepened Iranians' social discontent with clerical rule and have dealt a severe blow to Iranian reformers. U.S. foreign policy faced a classic dilemma: taking into account geopolitical factors or promoting democratic values.

It is clear that considerations of power politics and the regional balance of power will not be subordinated to democratic values enunciated in U.S. foreign policy. In fact, pragmatic conservatives have signaled that they are ready to bargain with the United States when the time comes. Likewise, the Bush administration has found it necessary—if not desirable—to deal with Iran's power-wielding elites who could deliver on the Non-Proliferation Treaty (NPT), stabilization of Iraq, reconstruction of Afghanistan, narcoterrorism, Al Qaeda, and Israeli–Palestinian tensions. With regard to Iran's nuclear program, experts argue that the central problem is not nuclear technology, but rather Iran's foreign policy as a revolutionary state, with nuclear ambitions that collide with the interests of its neighbors and the West.

If the Bush administration's policy toward Iran grows deferential rather than supportive of human rights, the future bodes ill for many reform-minded segments of Iranian society and, by implication, for the rest of the countries in the Middle East. For this reason, some believe that any rapprochement with Iran must be made both politically and ideologically contingent upon its improved human rights and democratic standards. The persistence of the Bush administration in asserting a pragmatic agenda alone is particularly damaging to the youth, women, and reform-minded journalists and activists—in essence, the human capital so essential to any democratic reform in Iran.

Thus far Washington has inconsistently navigated between strategic choices and human rights policy, and has employed double standards in its approach toward Iran, criticizing the Islamic Republic's human rights record while working on normalizing economic and diplomatic ties behind the scenes. Many see that this policy will prove detrimental to the Iranian pro-reform moments. No dramatic breakthroughs in U.S.–Iran relations seem likely unless U.S. policymakers view the new regional security structure as imperative to preventing Iraq from descending into chaos and partition.

It is unknown whether the United States will take a tougher stance toward Iran in sticking to its democratic rhetoric or whether it will pursue a pragmatic course guided solely by geopolitical exigencies. Each of these courses holds profound ramifications for the future of democracy in Iran. Policymakers in both countries face unprecedented challenges and tough choices, as millions of Iranians tend to view with both hope and uncertainty the shape of things to come.

Suggested Reading

Bill, J. A. 1988. *The eagle and the lion: the tragedy of American–Iranian relations*. New Haven: Yale University Press.

Chubin, S. 2006. *Iran's nuclear ambitions*. Washington, D.C.: Carnegie Endowment for International Peace.

Esposito, J. L. 1999. *The Islamic threat: myth or reality*? Third Edition. New York: Oxford University Press.

Friedlander, M. 1991. *Conviction and credence: U.S. policymaking in the Middle East*. Boulder, Colo.: Lynne Rienner Publishers.

Hauss, C. 2006. *Comparative politics: domestic responses to global challenges*, Fifth Edition. Belmont, Calif.: Thomson Wadsworth.

Kinzer, S. 2006. *Overthrow: America's century of regime change from Hawaii to Iraq*. New York: Times Books.

Monshipoure, M. 1998. *Islamism, secularism, and human rights in the Middle East.* Boulder, Colo.: Lynne Rienner Publishers.

Ramazani, R. 1986. *Revolutionary Iran: challenge and response in the Middle East.* Baltimore: The Johns Hopkins University Press.

Yaphe, J. S. 2002. U.S.–Iran relations: normalization in the future? *Strategic Forum*, No. 188. Washington, D.C.: Institute for National Strategic Studies, National Defense University.

MAHMOOD MONSHIPOURI

✦ VEIL AND VEILING

Neither the veil nor the practice of veiling is an invention of Islam. The veil has a long history that predates all the Abrahamic religions of Judaism, Christianity, and Islam. Many different people of other religions, such as Hindus and Sikhs, wear or wore the veil in some form during their history. The veil is also worn by men in different parts of the Sahara in Africa. The Islamic veil is known as *hijab*, a generic term referring to a modest coverage of the entire body and hair (not necessarily the face). The Arabic term *hijab* literally means curtain in addition to divider, coverage, or a shield.

Many cultures had a form of veiling or a form of head coverage for its people prior to the arrival of Islam. A plethora of terms and words for the veil and veiling existed in many non-Arab languages and cultures around the world, which is an indication of the practice of veiling as a cultural norm rather than as a requirement for religious purposes. For example, the following non-Arabic terms such as *parandja* (Uzbek), *purdah* (Urdu), *safsari* (Berber), *haik* (berber term used in Morocco and Algeria), *Ghuunghat* (Punjabi), *Chadderi* (Dari), *Chador* (Persian), *Chuonni* (Hindi), and many more, clearly establish this point of argument.

In Islam there are two specific Qur̀anic chapters that are referred to regarding the mandatory veiling for Muslim women: Chapters XXIV and XXXIII.

Chapter XXIV: 28–31 (*Nur*/Light) is very often quoted for the rules of modesty and specifically verse 31:

And Say to the believing women
That they should lower
Their gaze and guard
Their modesty. That they
Should not display their
Beauty and ornaments, except
What (must ordinarily) appear
Thereof; that they should
Draw their veils over
Their bosoms and not display
Their beauty except
To their husbands, their fathers
Their husbands' sons,
Their brothers or their brothers' sons ...

Chapter XXXIII: 53 (*Ahzab*/Confederates), the middle section of the verse is quoted often to insist on the mandatory status of veiling for Muslim women:

...And when ye Ask (his ladies)
For anything ye want,
Ask them from before
A screen: that makes
For greater purity for
Your hearts and for theirs. (Yusuf 1983)

Earliest Records of Veiling
◆

It is thought that the first known reference to veiling was made in an Assyrian legal text of the 13th century BC, which restricted veiling to respectable women and prohibited it for prostitutes. In the texts of Middle–Assyrian laws dating to 750-612 BC, veiling is mentioned; this predates Islam by more than twelve hundred years. A harlot or slave girl found wearing a veil in the street in Middle–Assyria is ordered to be brought to the palace for punishment.

Orientalists' Views on Veiling

The veil has been a subject of interest of Orientalists, who have given it a layer of mystery, seduction, and sexual connotation. One scholar has noted that "genuine travelogues, tales of imaginary voyages in novels set in exotic places, and 'Oriental' erotica provided European writers with a poetic backdrop of 'Oriental' authenticity"(Faegheh 2003, 44). French novelist Gustave Flaubert wrote in *L'Éducation Sentimentale* of a particular brothel owned by a woman known to her clients as "La Turque"—the Turkish woman. This added to the poetic character of the "Madame's" establishment. Scholar-explorer Sir Richard Burton (1821–1890) also wrote of the veil and harem girls in his translation of *Arabian Nights*. Men did not solely create the Western images of Muslim women/Middle Eastern women. By the end of the nineteenth century, a significant number of European women worked and lived in Middle Eastern countries. It has been contended that these women "contributed to the body of Western literature and imagery on the Middle East, …[but] there is little evidence that gender alone distinguished their views from those of men, except in one respect: the fact that they had many more opportunities to observe the daily lives of Middle Eastern women, even those who lived in seclusion" (Graham-Brown 1988, 18). A prominent scholar today on Middle Eastern women, Leila Ahmadhas, has written about the opinions of Western (Christian) officials and missionaries who seemed to have had a problem with the Muslim women's tradition of veiling, as many equated veiling with one of the evils of Islam. As well, many well-meaning European feminists during the 1890s "earnestly inducted young Muslim women into the European understanding of the meaning of the veil and the need to cast if off as the essential first step in the struggle for female liberation." Ahmad further has stressed the fact that Westerners insisted that all Muslims "had to give up their native religion, customs, and dress, or at least reform their religion and habits along the recommended lines, and for all of them the veil and customs regarding women were the prime matters requiring reform."

IRANIAN WOMEN AND VEILING

The woman's veil in Iranian culture has gone through centuries of change and evolution not only in style but also in meaning and status. The veil has served as a symbol for religious, social, and cultural purposes.

Veiled Iranian woman wears a traditional dress as she smokes a water pipe on Qeshm Island in the Persian Gulf, some 932 miles south of Tehran, 2002. (AP Photo/Hasan Sarbakhshian)

Persian women during the time of the Sassanid Dynasty veiled themselves. The Sassanids were the last dynasty of native rulers to reign in Persia before the Arab conquest. The period of their dominion extended from AD 224, when the Parthians were overthrown and the capital, Ctesiphon, was taken, until c.640, when the country fell under the power of the Arabs. Zoroastrian women wore the veil every day as proper attire; this veil was known as *makhna*. A makhna is a rectangular piece of cloth about two meters long and one meter wide. The manner of wearing it is interesting, as the center of this long cloth is placed under the chin and each end of it is thrown to the crown of the head (covering the ears on either sides) and then tucked in to the corners of the checks.

Wearing some sort of head covering by women in Iran has been a tradition not particularly associated with Islam, but as evident in many regional folk dresses still in use around Iran. Village women in their traditional clothing cover their hair with a large colorful piece of patterned cloth, or unpatterned cloth adorned with other forms of decorations such as sequins or embroidery work. In some regions, this long piece of cloth can be very thin and transparent. Sometimes the head covers are worn with small caps as a complete form of headdress.

Many examples of miniature paintings have survived from the Ilkhanid Dynasty (1256–1353). The founder of the Ilkhanate dynasty was Hulegu Khan, grandson of Genghis Khan and brother of Mongke Khan, taking over from Baiju in 1255 or 1256. The Timurid Dynasty (1363–1506), a Turkic dynasty descended from the conqueror Timur (Tamerlane), was renowned for its brilliant revival of artistic and intellectual life in Iran and Central Asia, and the Safavids (1502–1722) showcase images of women in court costumes with a variety of headscarves and embellishments.

During the Qajar period (1781–1925), women were veiled entirely, including their faces. The Qajar dynasty was founded in 1781 by Agha

Muhammad Khan, of Iranian Turkmen descent. He defeated the last ruler of the Zand dynasty in 1796 but was himself assassinated only a year later. One of the most educated Qajar ladies of the time was Fatimeh, zarrin Taj Barghani, better known as Qurrat al-Ayn (1814–1852) (Nashat 2004, 15), who became involved in the Babi movement (those who followed Sayyid Ali Muhammad, who proclaimed himself as the Bab, the hidden 12th Shi`i Imam in 1844). Qurrat al-Ayn was the first woman who unveiled (removed her face veil) herself publicly. Some European ladies who visited Iran at this time contradicted the image of the stereotypical helpless, oppressed veiled Iranian woman. Seclusion and veiling were not enforced during the Qajar time for women who worked in the fields alongside men. More restrictions were placed upon wealthier women than poorer women.

UNVEILING, RE-VEILING, AND PROPERLY VEILING

During the Constitutional Revolution (1905–1911), a large number of intellectual members of Iranian society pushed for the unveiling of women. The revolution marked the beginning of the end of Iran's feudalistic society and led to the establishment of a parliament in Persia (Iran).

The Persian Constitutional Revolution was the first event of its kind in the Middle East. The revolution prepared Iranian society for stepping into the modern era. Among the many intellectuals involved in the revolution, the Iranian poet Iraj Mirza (1874–1926) championed unveiling. Mirza composed poetry using the image of women and the veil to express his discontent with the social, political, and religious status quo of his time. Another contemporary of Iraj Mirza was Nezam Vafa (1889–1964), who was also influenced by events of the constitutional revolutionary era. He published a magazine called *Vafa* in which he introduced his own poetry and literary works, and he also tried to come to terms with the issue of unveiling of the time.

The genesis of women's literary tradition in Iran coincides with their attempts to unveil. One of the female voices who addresses the issue of the veil is that of Parvin Etesami (1906–1941), a preeminent Persion poet who advocated for women's rights in a male dominated culture. In her poetry, Etesami voices her concerns about the condition of women in Iran prior to Reza Shah's unveiling decree of 1936. In the poem "Zan dar Iran" (Iranian Women), Etesami criticized the chadur/chador (veil). Etesami is often compared with another great Iranian female poet, Forugh Farrokhzad (1935–1967). The difference here is Farrokhzad did not have to go through the unveiling process, because at least officially the veil had been abolished by Reza Shah's unveiling order of 1936. Her poetry is important because it demonstrated that unveiling did not necessarily reduce the influence of tradition and that, according to her, Iranian women continued to remain confined and restricted.

During the era of the Women's Awakening Project, *nahzat-e banouvan* (1936–1941), Reza Shah Pahlavi attempted to radically transform Iranian womanhood to fit a modern society (Pahlavi reigned from 1925–1941). This Women's Awakening was a government feminism project that gave women educational and job opportunities if they would give up wearing the veil in public. After the Women's Awakening true gender equality was demanded, and the campaign for women's suffrage gained momentum. The unveiling of women has been seen as one the most essential symbols of Reza Shah's reign. Many, including the clergy, resented this unveiling order and tried to prevent its execution. However, police were instructed to use force to remove women's veils in the streets. They were also ordered to rid the streets of the most conspicuous sign of "backwardness," and that was, according to Reza Shah, the chador. Many women from traditional families, afraid of being attacked by police, refused to leave their homes. After five years of forced unveiling, Reza Shah was ousted by the Allied Forces (1941), and clerics cried for the return of the veil. Women who had been forced to unveil were now forced by social and religious pressures and by a clerically organized mob to veil again; many older women in the cities voluntarily resumed the veil.

Apparently, as early as 1927, women from a more affluent part of Tehran ventured out unveiled, and this was a secret activity among upper class families in Iran. Reza Shah embarked on his quest to modernize the state by imitating the Western model of men and women's dress. These reform policies continued during the reign of his son, Mohammad Reza Shah Pahlavi (September 16, 1941–February 11, 1979).

In 1979, Ayatollah Khomeini called on women to comply with the religiously sanctioned dress code for Muslim women. During the Iran–Iraq War (1980–1988), the dress of the Iranian woman was under intense scrutiny. Posters, banners, and even postage stamps taught women the correct way of veiling. Also during this period, we find a noticeable semantic fusion of *hijab* and *jihad* (holy war) in the context of martyrdom. In the 1990s, the graffiti in metropolitan towns, sanctioned and perhaps written by members of Hezbollah, showed that the veil was still employed to promote the political agendas of the Iranian clergy.

In 1990, the Iranian government published two documents that had been classified as secret until then. These documents contain correspondence of Reza Shah between 1924 and 1933 and prove most revealing with regard to the process of forceful unveiling under the regime of Reza Shah.

The Islamic Republic of Iran introduced many new rules and regulations concerning all aspects of women's lives. Women were persuaded, often by force, to veil. Women who appeared unveiled in public were assumed to be opposed to the tenets of the Islamic Revolution and were thus not only religiously but also politically suspect. In the eyes of revolutionaries, unveiled women represented Western values, which the Islamic regime wished to eradicate from Iranian society.

Two men were instrumental in defining the ideology of the hijab in the new regime of the Islamic Republic of Iran: the Ayatollah Motahari and the intellectual Ali Shariati. Both rejected Iran's domination by the West by rejecting the concept of the "modern" Iranian woman, the unveiled woman. Motahari in his famous book *Mas`aleh-ye Hejab* [*The Question of Hijab*] discusses the history of the hijab and speculates on the logic and reasons for its existence. He explains that women's sexuality can cause *fitna* (social chaos) unless it is properly controlled. Thus, women should be veiled to control this chaos. Motahari states that the hijab provides a barrier between the sexes and thus serves to uphold the social order. In this way, he makes women responsible for keeping this barrier and preventing *fitna*.

During the earlier years of the Islamic Revolution and the war with Iraq, *comates* (from the French *comite*) patrols, "guardians of the Islamic Revolution," composed of both men and women, safeguarded people's moral conduct in public by looking for women who show a "bad hijab" in public. A "bad hijab" refers to any garment, adornment, or appearance that intentionally or unintentionally might have the potential to draw the male gaze. Bad *hijab* can include letting the hair show from under the veil, wearing clothes that cling to the body or are otherwise ostentatious, using makeup, lipstick, nail polish, or perfume. Sometimes severe, punishments for bad *hijab* were up to the discretion of the *Komiteh*.

One of the new dimensions of the veil was its use as propaganda to promote the Iran–Iraq War. Posters, billboards, and stamps promoted the war by heralding the "ideal" veiled woman. Many slogans and graffiti promoted the *hijab* where the *hijab* symbolized dignity, chastity, duty, piety, and self-worth. Other slogans promise the woman who wears the proper veil safety and protection from the male gaze and from her own sexuality as some clerics claim: "veiling is safety, not restriction." Much rhetoric on the subject of what makes a good or bad *hijab* has transpired throughout the contemporary era of Iranian history since Ayatollah Khomeini came to power. Khomeini preached "Chador as the best form of *Hijab*" and he also stressed the chador as a national costume. Young generations of Iranian women do not wear the chador or other political and conservative forms of the *hijab* such as *maghna`e* (a head cover covering the entire shoulders and chest), promoted by the government of Islamic Republic as the best form of *hijab*. Young urban women in Iran usually follow the fashionable European styles and colors and create their own personal styles of hijab.

Today, nearly thirty years after the success of the revolution, strictures regarding the veil have been slightly loosened up. Nevertheless, there still continue to be occasional, and at times harsh, throwbacks to the earlier days of the revolution when it comes to women's clothing.

Suggested Reading

Ahmad, L. 1992. *Women and gender in Islam: historical roots of a modern debate*. New Haven: Yale University Press.

Amin, C. M. 2002. *The making of the modern Iranian woman: gender, state policy, and popular culture, 1865–1946*. Gainesville: University Press of Florida.

Driver, G. R., and J. C. Miles, eds. 1952. *The Babylonian laws*. Oxford: Clarendon Press.

Graham-Brown, Sarah. 1988. *Images of women, the portrayal of women in photography of the Middle East 1860–1950*. New York: Columbia University Press.

Keddie, N. R., and B. Baron. eds. *Women in Middle Eastern history: shifting boundaries in sex and gender*. New Haven: Yale University Press.

Khoshonat va Farhang: Asnad-e Mahramaneh-e Kashfe Hejab (1313–1322) [Violence and culture: confidential records about the abolition of the hijab, 1313–1322 H.SH.]. Tehran: Department of Research Publication and Education, 1990.

Mernissi, F. 1991. *The veil and the male elite: a feminist interpretation of women's rights in Islam*. New York: Addison-Wesley.

Milani, F. 1992. *Veils and words: the emerging voices of Iranian women writers*. Syracuse: Syracuse University Press.

Shirazi, F. 2001, 2003. *The veil unveiled: Hijab in modern culture*. Gainesville: University Press of Florida.

Vaghe-e Kashfe Hejab, Asnad-e Montasher Nashodeh-e Hejab dar Asr-e Reza Khan [Reality of unveiling: unpublished documents from the time of Reza Khan]. Tehran: Agency of Cultural Documents of the Islamic Revolution, 1990.

Yusuf, A. 1983. *The Holy Qur'an, Text, translation and commentary*. Brentwood: Ammana Corp.

FAEGHEH S. SHIRAZI

✦ VELAYAT-E FAQIH

Since the death of the Prophet Muhammad in AD 632, the question of the leadership of the community of believers has been a central concern to Muslims. The two main branches of Islam—Sunnis and Shi'ism—each follow different patterns in providing guidance for the Muslim community until the Judgment Day, considered to be the end of the world, when Muslims have to account for their deeds in this world.

The followers of 'Ali ('Alids), the son-in-law of Prophet Muhammad, later known as Shi'as, believe that the Prophet had designated 'Ali and his descendents (*ahl al-bayt*) to leadership of the Muslim community. After the disappearance of the twelfth Imam, known as Imam al-Mahdi, who according to Twelver Shi'as (hereafter referred to as Shi'a) tradition went into occultation in 940 and is to reappear at Judgment Day, Shi'as have been left with no apparent heir to lead the community until that day. This vacuum of leadership has caused the largest debate among Shi'a religious scholars (*mujtahid*) over the centuries. Who should lead the community in the absence of a member of the Prophet's family, and what are his duties and responsibilities? Is he confined to give guidance in religious matters or is he a political leader as well? How does one define the relationship between the Shi'a community and the ruling elite? And most importantly, how does one define the boundaries between religious and political issues, considering that the ruling elite have often been non-Shi'as ?

During the seventeenth century a decisive debate broke out between Shi'a religious scholars resulting in the development of two schools of thought regarding the leadership of the community in the absence of the Twelfth Imam known as the Akhbari and the Usuli tradition. According to the Akhbaris, Shi'as should rely directly on the Quran and the Traditions (sayings of the Prophet Muhammad and the Twelve Imams) without any intermediary to interpret those sources, usually the *mujtahids*. However, the Usulis—who became the dominant group in the Shi'a world—argued that until the reappearance of the Twelfth Imam, Shi'a religious scholars should take on the responsibility to interpret these sources for the laity and provide guidance for them. In other words, they considered themselves the indirect deputies of the twelfth Imam (*na'ib al-Imam*). Relying on the concept of *ijtihad*, independent reasoning to elicit the law from the sacred texts, they would engage in activities such as resolving disputes, collecting religious taxes and redistributing them, and providing solutions to novel problems. The religious scholar(s) who would provide this guidance would be called the source of emulation, or *marja'* (plural *maraji*). Ideally, a *marja'* is the most educated and pious among the high ranking religious scholars (*mujtahid*), while ethnic and linguistic identities should not play a role in appointing a *marja'*. The Shi'a community had at times only one *marja'*, and at others there have been two to three (but sometimes even more) providing guidance for the community simultaneously.

It is against this background that Ayatollah Ruhollah Khomeini's (1902–1989) interpretation of the concept of the *velayat-e faqih* or the rule of the jurisprudent is best understood. Although the concept existed prior to Khomeini and other religious scholars had debated the degree of guardians' (*vali/*

plural *awliya*) authority, Khomeini was the first person to argue that in the absence of the Twelfth Imam, the religious scholars, but mainly the jurists (*faqih*/plural *fuqaha*) among them, should not only provide religious guidance but also serve as the political leaders of the community as well, a position associated until then with the Prophet and the Twelve Imams only. The leadership could be limited to one religious scholar or consist of a council (*shura*) of several religious scholars. In fact, in Khomeini's opinion, the distinction between religion and politics did not exist in Islam. The distinction was a Western concept imported to Islamic countries to divide and weaken Muslims. The clerical rule in an Islamic state, in which *shari`a* regulates all aspects of life, would be the only acceptable form of political life for Muslims and should serve as an example for other Muslim countries as well. Thus, he argued that while the *vali* is not infallible like the members of the *ahl al-bayt*, he has the same authority as the Imams.

This was a revolutionary break with former traditions on interpreting the concept of the *velayat-e faqih*, which until then was mainly confined to proving guardianship for children, the mentally ill, and widowed women and functioning as trustees of religious taxes. Khomeini discussed the form of the Islamic state in a series of his writings between the 1940s and 1970s, such as the *Kashf al-Asrar* (Revealing of Secrets) published in 1943, and in *Velayat-e Faqih: Hokumat-i Islami* (The Jurist's Guardianship: Islamic Government), which is a collection of seventeen lectures he delivered in his exile in Najaf in 1969–1970. To prove the validity of his arguments in all these writings, Khomeini relied on interpretations of Shi'a Traditions. However, to many other religious scholars but also to many Western academics, Khomeini's interpretations of these sources seem weak, stretched, and not consistent with the interpretation of jurists prior to him. Khomeini did not have one single vision of an Islamic state, nor did he clarify exactly the extent of the power of the jurists and their relation to the state.

One such example of a shift away from earlier positions in his later writings is his stance toward the constitution of 1906 in Qajar Iran, which sought to limit the power of Qajar rulers, often envisioned as arbitrary, through the creation of a Constituent National Assembly and legal codes resembling those in Western countries. While in his earlier writings Khomeini was sympathetic to the existence of a constitution in his vision of an Islamic Iran, later writings declare the constitutional movement (1906–1911) the result of a foreign, mainly British, plot to weaken Islam in Iran. Similarly, while he was initially sympathetic to the idea of a constitutional monarchy, in later writings he argues that monarchy is an un-Islamic institution and is a form of idolatry, and therefore illegitimate.

The increasing power he gave to the clerics as political leaders of the Shi'a community as reflected in his writings cannot be viewed in isolation from the Iranian political context in which he operated. Among the religious scholars, Khomeini was the most vocal opponent of the Pahlavi state (1921–1979), whose rulers sought to limit the power of the clerics by various means. The regime's reliance on Western powers and its policy of controlling religious affairs and secularizing institutions traditionally under the control of the religious leaders diminished the power of the clerics immensely. In addition, Muhammad Reza Shah sent Khomeini into exile in 1963 after he openly criticized Shah's politics. Khomeini's concept of *velayat-e faqih* thus developed in dialogue with a political and social context which he believed was dismissive of the constitution, un-Islamic, unjust, immoral, and thus unacceptable for the community. Despite this, in his vision of an Islamic state, he adopted some Pahlavi national policies. But the Pahlavi regime was not the only opposition force against which Khomeini developed the concept of *velayat-e faqih*. Among religious scholars and lay Islamists, some of whom also envisioned an Islamic state as an ideal state, there were many who did not share Khomeini's vision of religious jurists' rule. Some, like the well-known Iranian Western-trained Islamist thinker 'Ali Shariati, argued that the clerics were actually the source of all the ill that has befallen Islam. In his view, the clerics were corrupt, obsessed with debating the correct form of some minor rituals, and thus were an obstacle in the way of "true Islam," which in Shariati's view already contained all aspects of modernity. According to Shariati, there was no need for the clerics to interpret the sources of Islam for the Muslims.

Following Khomeini, the duties of an Islamic state with jurists as both political and religious leaders of the community were several. Nevertheless, social justice, fighting foreign domination, continuing the mission of Muhammad, and supervising Muslims so they do not diverge from the Prophet's path represented the core of the state's duties. Khomeini envisioned a strong centralized government with a strong, effective army. Both would fight foreign domination and propagate Islam. In addition, taxes would be redistributed properly and a specific budget would be devoted to the needy. Corruption, considered by Khomeini a hallmark of the Pahlavi regime, would be prevented and punished.

The success of the Iranian Revolution, made possible through collective efforts of the left, the secularists, and a wide range of Islamist groups, enabled Khomeini to put his theories of the Islamic state and the rule of the jurisprudent to practice. After his death in 1989 Ayatollah 'Ali Khamenei took over the responsibility as a *vali*. This has created many controversies both within Iran and outside of Iran, as Khamenei does not have the required religious education to occupy such a position. According to earlier writings of Khomeini only the most senior religious scholars, and especially those with a focus on Islamic Law, could claim the position as guardian of the Muslim community. Thus while currently Khamenei serves as a leader (*rahbar*) of the Islamic Republic of Iran, in his official position as a *vali* he does not possess the quality as a source of emulation for Shi'as in Iran. In fact, in 1989 the Constitution of Iran was revised and the function of the leader and the *marja'* were separated. However, outside of Iran, among the powerful Shi'a party of Hezbollah in Lebanon, he is considered both a source of emulation as well as the *vali al-faqih*. In fact, prior to Ayatollah Khomeini's death, he made one final revision to the concept of the *velayat-e faqih* as he anticipated succession problems and was well aware of the opposition among many senior religious scholars to his interpretation of the concept. He then categorized the clergy into two groups, those most knowledgeable in religious scholarship and those who were most knowledgeable in current economic, social, and political affairs. It was the latter group he declared that should rule. Khomeini's interpretation of the concept of *velayat-e faqih* developed *vis-à-vis* the politics of the Pahlavi regime. However, when after the overthrow of the Pahlavi dynasty Khomeini became *vali* with its incorporation of political and religious power, he continued to adjust aspects of his theory of Islamic Government in light of the sociopolitical context of post-revolutionary Iran.

Suggested Reading

Abrahamian, E. 1993. *Khomeinism. Essays on the Islamic Republic.* Berkeley: University of California Press.

Martin, V. 2001. *Creating an Islamic State. Khomeini and the making of a new Iran.* London: I. B. Tauris.

Mavani, H. 2001. Analysis of Khomeini's proofs for al-Wilaya al-Mutalqa (comprehensive authority) of the Jurist, in Walbridge, Linda S., ed., *The most learned of the Shi'a. The institution of the Marja' Taqlid.* Oxford: Oxford University Press: 183–201.

ROSCHANACK SHAERY-EISENLOHR

✦ WEALTH AND POVERTY

Iran's GDP per capita of about $7,100 in 2005 (measured in Purchasing Power Parity U.S. dollars) places it firmly in the category of middle income countries. Iran is also known as a wealthy country thanks to its huge reserves of oil and natural gas. In 2006 its reserves of oil were estimated at about 130 billion barrels (or 10% of world reserves) and its natural gas at 27 trillion cubic meters (15% of world reserves and about 160 billion barrels of oil equivalent). This wealth, roughly 290 billion barrels of oil equivalent, valued at expected medium term price of $50 per barrel is about 14 trillion USD, or about $200,000 per person. The current annual income from this wealth, accrued in oil exports and domestic consumption, is about 80 billion per year, or about 1170 per person.

Iran's hydrocarbon wealth is entirely owned by the government, though access to this wealth is not equally shared. Rent seeking, which has been rampant since the 1970s, continues unabated and is a great obstacle for economic efficiency and growth. Much of privately held wealth was confiscated after the revolution, out of which numerous para-statal foundations have grown. It has grown substantially as a result of economic reforms of the 1990s, and is most likely unequally shared, though there is no data on private wealth distribution in Iran. The distribution of income is less equal than countries such as Egypt and India and about as unequal as that of China and the United States. Inequality has remained stable in recent years and is comparable to what it was before the revolution. The Gini coefficient of per capita expenditures ranged from 0.45 to 0.5 in the 1970s compared to about 0.43–0.45 in the last twenty years.

The Islamic Republic of Iran has been more successful in lowering poverty. According to the international two dollars per day poverty line (about $2.90 in 2005), Iran's poverty is one of the lowest in the Middle East and North Africa region, having declined from about 18% in 1995 to less than 9% in 2005. The minimum wage is set at about $12 per day (PPP dollars). Assistance to the poor is entrusted to the Ministry of Welfare and Social Affairs, which receives about 7,000 billion rials ($20 billion, PPP dollars) annually to provide health coverage for the poor. In addition, the semi-governmental charity Komiteh Emdad provides income assistance to about 8% of the poorest families.

Suggested Reading

Amuzegar, J. 2005. Iran's third development plan: An appraisal. *Middle East Policy*. 12: 46–64.

Esfahani, H. S. 2005. Alternative public service delivery mechanisms in Iran. *The Quarterly Review of Economics and Finance*. 45: 497–525.

Salehi-Isfahani, D. 2005. Human resources in Iran: potentials and challenges. *Iranian Studies*. 38: 117–147.

Salehi-Isfahani, D. 2006. Revolution and redistribution in Iran: inequality and poverty 25 years later." Working Paper, Department of Economics, Virginia Tech.

DJAVAD SALEHI-ISFAHANI

✦ WOMEN, STATUS OF

Women were the major losers of the Islamic Revolution in 1979, as they saw their legal status and social positions dramatically decline in the name of religious revival. Compulsory veiling, the ban on women singers, exclusion from political power, economic marginalization, and the return of unilateral divorce, polygamy, and temporary marriage characterized the first ten years of the Islamic Revolution. The second decade of the Islamic republic saw the emergence of policy shifts, new leadership, and rising societal expectations. Social change in family dynamics, educational attainment, cultural politics, women's social roles, and attitudes and values has occurred, though largely in spite of the state rather than due to progressive state initiatives. The promises of legal reform, the easing of cultural restrictions, and political liberalization, however, have not been realized, and in 2008 the women's movement faced repression similar to that experienced by the student movement in 1999.

WOMEN AND THE ISLAMIC REVOLUTION

Women were major participants in the Iranian Revolution against the Shah, which unfolded between 1977 and February 1979. Like other social groups, their reasons for opposing the Shah were varied and included economic deprivation, political repression, and identification with Islamism. The large urban street demonstrations included huge contingents of middle-class and working-class women wearing the veil as a symbol of opposition to what they perceived to be Pahlavi Westernized decadence. Many of the women who wore the veil as a protest symbol did not expect *hijab* (Islamic modest dress) to become mandatory. Thus when the first calls were made in February 1979 to enforce hijab, and Ayatollah Khomeini was quoted as saying that he preferred to see women in modest Islamic dress, many women were alarmed. Spirited protests and sit-ins were led by middle-class leftist and liberal women, most of them members of political organizations or recently formed women's associations. As a result of the women's protests, the ruling on hijab was rescinded—but only temporarily. With the defeat of the left opposition and the erstwhile liberal partners in 1980 and their elimination from the political terrain in 1981, the Islamists were able to make veiling compulsory and to enforce it harshly. What followed were years of repression, exacerbated by the harshness of a wartime economy.

During the first half of the 1980s, the Islamic Republic of Iran (IRI) banned women from acting as judges and discouraged women lawyers. It repealed legislation, known as the Family Protection Act of 1967 and 1973, which had restricted polygamy, raised the age of marriage for girls, and allowed women the right to divorce. The Islamic regime all but banned contraception and family planning. New policies excluded women from numerous fields of study, occupations, and professions—all in the name of new Islamic values and norms.

The effects of the Islamic Republic's preoccupation with cultural and ideological issues and with the definition of women's place in society were considerable. The full range of their social impact—which came to light when the results of the 1986 national census of population and housing were analyzed—included soaring fertility increases and population growth; a decline in female labor-force participation, particularly in the industrial sector; lack of progress in literacy and educational attainment; and a sex ratio that favored males. Clearly, Islamist politics had resulted in an extremely disadvantaged position for women—it had reinforced male domination, compromised women's autonomy, and created a set of gender relations characterized by profound inequality.

In time, however, the IRI reversed some of its most draconian policies on women, family, and gender relations, and a gradual improvement in social indicators could be observed. The changes occurred after the death of Ayatollah Khomeini and during the presidency of Hashemi Rafsanjani, in the context of a program for economic liberalization and integration into the global economy. During this time, Iranian civil society developed, and a lively women's press emerged. Further changes occurred during the two terms of President Mohammad Khatami, including the growth and vitality of Iranian civil society and a movement for political and cultural reform. Factors explaining these changes pertain to Iran's social structure, the end of war with Iraq (1980–1988), the increasing demand for female labor in the health and education sectors, and divisions within the political elite.

While the official discourse emphasized women's maternal roles, women were not legally banned from the public sphere; moreover, the regime rewarded Islamist women by allowing them to run for parliament and giving them jobs in the civil service. Islamist modernists within the regime recognized the need for women's participation and support. As early as the IRI's first parliament in 1980, there were four women members. Many of the women parliamentarians and women civil servants ("state feminists" or "Islamic feminists") later would make demands on the government for equality and greater opportunity.

Evidence of increasing fertility in a situation of declining government revenues, indebtedness due to the war with Iraq, and increasing unemployment and poverty alarmed the authorities. Thus, in the post-Khomeini era, the government reversed its opposition to family planning and embarked on a vigorous campaign to stabilize population growth, which was enthusiastically embraced by women. Family planning clinics throughout the country distribute contraceptives and family planning advice, frequently free of charge. By the year 2000, the total fertility rate had declined to 2.2 children per woman, one of the lowest rates in the Middle East. Surveys showed that the stated ideal was two children per family.

As a result of the advocacy of Islamic feminists/state feminists, restrictive barriers to women's educational achievement and their employment were removed in 1992. Women were encouraged to enter certain scientific and technical fields such as gynecology, pharmacology, midwifery, and laboratory work. While women still could not serve as judges, "women legal consultants" were permitted in the Special Civil Courts. A growing proportion of public sector employees were women, found mostly in the Ministries of Education and Health. In the academic year 2002–2003, women's university enrollments exceeded those of men for the first time since universities were established in Iran. A lively women's press emerged, with books, magazines, and women's studies journals taking on important political, cultural, religious, and social issues. In 2004, women constituted some 12% of publishing house directors and 22% of the members of the Professional Association of Journalists.

Political institutions remained almost exclusively masculine, but the 1995 and 2000 parliamentary elections not only resulted in more women members of parliament but also the appearance of several articulate and reform-minded advocates. Women's affairs offices were established in each ministry and government agency, and numerous non-governmental organizations dealing with women's concerns were formed.

The 1990s were thus characterized by a kind of quiet revolt by women and the emergence of a feminist pre-movement. Innovative ways of resistance to compulsory *hijab* could be observed, especially in the upscale neighborhoods of north Tehran. Women began to initiate divorce, even though divorce laws continued to favor men. The array of feminist periodicals and publishing collectives included books and articles criticizing the subordinate status of women in the Islamic Republic and calling for the modernization of family law. They also documented the array of social problems that Iran was experiencing: drug addiction, family violence, runaway teens, and prostitution. The "woman question" and urban social problems also appeared in the many creative and increasingly renowned films that were produced during this period and afterward.

In the 1990s, innovative and entrepreneurial characteristics of women's activism included the many feminist magazines and women's publishing collectives (e.g., *Zanan, Jens-e Dovvom, Farzaneh, Hoghough-e Zanan, Roshangaran Press*, and the Cultural Center of Women); academics forming women's studies courses or programs at their universities or writing on women's topics in the women's press; the growth of non-governmental organizations devoted to women's empowerment; legal campaigns on behalf of the rights of women and children; and the emergence in the 1990s of Islamic feminism, whereby believing women sought to frame their demands for women's rights in a religious idiom and to recover their religion from patriarchal interpretations. The role of *Zanan* magazine in the emergence and flourishing of Islamic feminism was studied extensively by expatriate Iranian feminist scholars.

Women, whose votes were crucial to the election of President Khatami in 1997 and in 2001 as well as to the formation of a majority reformist parliament in 2000, were strongly behind the reform movement. The Khatami years saw the easing of many cultural and social restrictions, and many women welcomed this. The struggle for human rights and women's rights in

Iran received international recognition when the 2003 Nobel Peace Prize was awarded to lawyer Shirin Ebadi. (Appointed as a judge prior to the revolution, she had lost her post afterwards but opened a law office that served political prisoners, women's rights activists, and advocates for children's rights.) And yet women were not given significant political or decision-making posts. Conservative members of parliament and the Council of Guardians blocked a bill to promote women's rights. A bill to raise the minimum age of marriage for girls from nine to fifteen was threatened with defeat; only a compromise decision on age thirteen saved the bill, though underage girls still could be given to marriage by parental permission.

WOMEN'S GRIEVANCES, COLLECTIVE ACTION, AND STATE REPRESSION

In the 1990s, the activist lawyer Mehrangiz Kaar had conducted a systematic analysis of Iran's laws pertaining to women's status in the family and society; her paper was widely distributed within Iran and in the Diaspora. A key objective of Iranian's women's rights activists, both secular and Islamic, became the modernization of family law and women's equal rights in matters of marriage, divorce, and child custody. Another concerned domestic violence, with many articles in the feminist press describing domestic violence as both a social problem and a violation of women's rights. A third concern was women's under-representation in formal politics and the need for greater participation in parliament, the local councils, and the highest political offices. Azzam Taleghani's self-nomination for president in 1997—and her disqualification on grounds of sex—brought the question of women and political participation to the fore. In 2001, some forty women sought the nomination, and all were summarily disqualified. Several documentary films were made on the subject of women's pursuit of the presidency.

At the start of the new millennium, the reform movement was in full swing in Iran, and there was much discussion—at home and abroad—of the secular nature of Iranian society, the growing visibility and advancement of Iranian women, and the distance between the clerical authorities and large segments of the population. However, two fundamental problems remained: the conservative faction of the Islamic regime was still firmly in charge and highly resistant to change, and women's subordinate legal status had not been overturned. Despite some reforms—such as the divorce amendments and employment policies of 1992—the legal framework remained very unfavorable to women, despite the reformist decade. In the run-up to the elections of 2005, feminists mobilized to take the call for women's equality in the family and society to the streets. For the first time since March 1979, public protests by women took place, in March and June 2005 and in March and June of 2006. Expatriate Iranian feminists extended much support and helped publicize the domestic activities; they also established contact between the domestic struggle and transnational feminist networks. Feminists in Iran were now openly demanding equality in the family, an end to stoning as a punishment for real or imagined sexual transgressions, and the ratification of the UN's Convention on the Elimination of All Forms of Discrimination Against Women (CEDAW) along with the abrogation of all gender-discriminatory laws in Iran.

But after the new and very conservative president, Mahmoud Ahmadinejad, took office in 2005, the authorities launched a crackdown on feminist protests. Women protestors were assaulted in 2006, 2007, and 2008 a number were arrested, jailed, and charged with undermining state security. Feminist leader Parvin Ardalan, who had received an international award for her human rights work, was refused permission to leave Iran to receive the Olaf Palme award in Stockholm. In January 2008, the authorities closed down the veteran women's magazine *Zanan*.

State repression forced the women's movement to devise a new strategy in 2006 for legal and policy change: the One Million Signatures petition campaign. This is a grassroots, door-to-door campaign to obtain signatures for the abrogation of all discriminatory laws and provide women with equality at home and in the society. At issue are the following legal provisions and social practices.

TEMPORARY MARRIAGE

Twelver Shiite Islam, the official version of Islam in Iran, allows temporary marriage, known as *muta'a* or *sigheh*. In the early 1990s, then-president Rafsanjani encouraged temporary marriage as an appropriate option for war widows. During the presidency of Khatami it was suggested that temporary marriage was a solution to the problems of young people who for different reasons (such as financial difficulties) were postponing permanent marriage. However, *sigheh* is a social taboo. The general reaction to *sigheh* is the stigmatization of women who engage in the practice. Historically, women who agree to *sigheh* do so out of financial need; in most cases the man is married and much older than the woman. A married/single man can have as many *sigheh* as he likes, while a woman is required to be unmarried and can only be *sigheh* of one man.

POLYGAMY

By law, a wife may obtain a divorce if her husband takes another wife without her permission or if the court agrees that he does not treat co-wives equitably. Polygamy is viewed negatively in Iranian society and is rarely practiced. Yet it remains legal and is sometimes encouraged by religious authorities.

OBEDIENCE, MAINTENANCE, AND GUARDIANSHIP

Under Iranian law, a husband must maintain his wife in return for his wife's obedience. A wife who is not *nashiza* (disobedient) may take the matter to court if her husband refuses to pay maintenance, and the court will fix a sum. In temporary marriage, the wife is entitled to maintenance only if the contract stipulates such. A husband may deny his wife the right to work in any profession "incompatible with the family interests or with the dignity of himself or of the wife." The husband also has the obligation to maintain his children, and as the guardian the father automatically takes custody of the children in the case of divorce. Only if the children are small are they able to remain with their mother; at puberty they are returned to the father.

POST-DIVORCE MAINTENANCE AND FINANCIAL ARRANGEMENTS

The 1992 amendments extended divorced wives financial rights, from maintenance during *idda* and deferred dower to the right to claim compensation for household services rendered to the husband during marriage. *Ujrat ul-mesl* (wages for house work) is considered one of the achievements of the advocates of women's rights in Iran. However, it is not clear how *ujrat ul mesl* is calculated. Moreover, *ujrat ul-mesl* is an option only if the wife is not initiating the divorce.

Women's social and economic rights in the IRI remain constrained in various ways. First, they make up only 13% of the non-agricultural salaried labor force, according to the most recent census data, but have unemployment rates that are disproportionately high and higher than those of men. Second, they are legally barred from being judges. Third, a woman does not have legal freedom of mobility—she needs the written permission of her husband or guardian to travel or obtain a passport, whether for business purposes or for pleasure. Fourth, in many cases, a woman needs the permission of her father or other male relative for work. Though a woman does not require her husband's permission to work, he can legally put limitations on the type of work she can or cannot do. Fifth, providing for the living expenses of the children lies with the husband, and the wife has no financial obligation toward her own children. This reinforces the notion that the mother is not the guardian of the children and is an economic dependant. The father, the paternal grandfather, and paternal great-grandfather all are more valid as a guardian than the mother herself. Such laws reinforce patrilineality and traditional gender roles (men's roles as breadwinners and women's roles as mothers and wives), in a kind of patriarchal gender contract that many women's rights activists find demeaning.

The contradictions between women's legal status and their social reality and aspirations, along with the blocked opportunities for employment and economic independence, have triggered a growing movement for women's rights. Activists demand an end to discrimination and the ratification of CEDAW. Iran's official position, however, is that it will not sign CEDAW because of its contradictions with Islamic law. It also has claimed that it is not bound by those international conventions that it has signed, where they contradict the *shari`a*.

Suggested Reading

Baghi, E. 2004. Hope for democracy in Iran. *The Washington Post*. October 25, p. A19.

Ezazi, S. 2000. Family violence. *Farzaneh*, Vol. 5. No, 10.

Mir-Hosseini, Z. 1996. Stretching the limits: a feminist reading of the Sharia in post-Khomeini Iran. In *Feminism and Islam: legal and literary perspectives*, ed. M. Yamani. New York: New York University Press: 285–319.

Mir-Hosseini, Z. 1996. Women and politics in post-Khomeini Iran: divorce, veiling, and emerging feminist voices, in Afshar, Haleh, ed., *Women and politics in the third world*. New York: Routledge: 142–169.

Moghadam, V. M. 1991. The reproduction of gender inequality in the Islamic Republic: a case study of Iran in the 1980s. *World Development*. 19: 1335–1350.

Moghadam, V. M. 2002. Islamic feminism and its discontents: toward a resolution of the debate. *Signs: Journal of Women in Culture and Society*. Vol. 27, no. 4.

Moghadam, V. M. 2003. *Modernizing women: gender and social change in the Middle East.* Boulder, Colo.: Lynne Rienner Publishers.

Najmabadi, A. 1998. Feminism in an Islamic Republic: 'years of hardship, years of growth.' In *Women, gender, and social change in the Muslim world*, eds. Y. Y. Haddad and J. Esposito. New York: Oxford University Press: 59–84.

Neshat, G, ed. 1983. *Women and revolution in Iran*. Boulder, Colo.: Westview Press.

Paidar, P. 1995. *Women in the political process in twentieth century Iran*. Cambridge, UK: Cambridge University Press.

Povey, E. R. 2001. Feminist contestations of institutional domains in Iran. *Feminist Review*. 69: 44–47.

Razavi, S. 2006. Islamic politics, human rights and women's claims for equality in Iran. *Third World Quarterly*. 27: 1223–1237.

Tabari, A., and N. Yeganeh, eds. 1982. *In the shadow of Islam: the women's movement in Iran*. London: Zed.

End Stoning Forever Campaign: http://www.meydaan.com/English/aboutcamp.aspx?cid=46

Change for Equality Campaign: http://www.change4equality.com/english/

Feminist School: http://feministschool.net/campaign/

VALENTINE M. MOGHADAM

Selected Bibliography

✦

Abrahamian, E. 1982. *Iran between two revolutions*. Princeton, NJ: Princeton University Press.

———. 1993. *Khomeinism: essays on the Islamic Republic*. Berkeley: University of California Press.

———. 1999. *Tortured confessions: prisons and public recantations in modern Iran*. Berkeley: University of California Press.

Adelkhah, F. 2000. *Being modern in Iran*. Jonathan Derrick, trans. New York: Columbia University Press.

Afkhami, G. R. 1985. *The Iranian revolution: Thanatos on a national scale*. Washington, DC: The Middle East Institute.

Afshari, R. 2001. *Human rights in Iran: the abuse of cultural relativism*. Philadelphia: University of Pennsylvania Press.

Agha, H. J. and A. S. Khalidi. 1995. *Syria and Iran: rivalry and cooperation*. New York: Council on Foreign Relations Press.

Ansari, A. M. 2000. *Iran, Islam and the democracy: the politics of managing change*. London: Royal Institute of International Affairs.

———. 2006. *Confronting Iran: the failure of American foreign policy and the next great conflict in the Middle East*. New York: Basic Books.

Amirahmadi, H. 1990. *Revolution and economic transformation: the Iranian experience*. Albany, NY: SUNY Press.

Arjomand, S. A. 1984. *The shadow of God and the hidden Imam: religion, political order, and societal change in Shi'ite Iran from the beginning to 1890*. Chicago: University of Chicago Press.

———, ed. 1984. *From nationalism to revolutionary Islam*. Albany, NY: SUNY Press.

———, ed. 1988. *Authority and political culture in Shi'ism*. Albany, NY: SUNY Press.

———. 1988. *The turban for the crown*. New York: Oxford University Press.

Azimi, F. 1989. *Iran: the crisis of democracy*. New York: St. Martin's.

Bakhash, S. 1985. *The reign of the Ayatollahs: Iran and the Islamic revolution*. London: I. B. Tauris.

Baktiar, B. 1996. *Parliamentary politics in revolutionary Iran: the institutionalization of factional politics.* Gainesville: University Press of Florida.

Bani-Sadr, A. H. 1991. *My turn to speak: Iran, the revolution, and secret deals with the U.S.* New York: Brassey's.

Bayat, A. 1997. *Street politics: poor people's movements in Iran.* New York: Columbia University Press.

Bill, J. 1988. *The eagle and the lion: the tragedy of American–Iranian relations.* New Haven, Conn: Yale University Press.

Bina, C., and H. Zangeneh, eds. 1992. *Modern capitalism and Islamic ideology in Iran.* New York: St Martin's Press.

Boroujerdi, M. 1996. *Iranian intellectuals and the West: the tormented triumph of nativism.* Syracuse, NY: Syracuse University Press.

Cottam, R. 1979. *Nationalism in Iran.* Pittsburgh, PA: University of Pittsburgh Press.

Dabashi, H. 1993. *Theology of discontent: the ideological foundations of the Islamic revolution in Iran.* New York: NYU Press.

———. 2001. *Close up: Iranian cinema, past, present and future.* London: Verso.

Dorraj, M. 1900. *From Zarathustra to Khomeini: populism and dissent in Iran.* Boulder, CO: Lynne Rienner.

Ehteshami, A. 1995. *After Khomeini: the Iranian second republic.* London: Routledge.

Esposito, J. L., ed. 1990. *The Iranian revolution: its global impact.* Miami: Florida International University Press.

Farson, S. K., and M. Mashayekhi. 1992. *Iran: political culture in the Islamic Republic.* New York: Routledge.

Fischer, M. M. J. 1980. *Iran: from religious dispute to revolution.* Cambridge, MA: Harvard University Press.

Fuller, G. E. 1991. *The center of the universe: the geopolitics of Iran.* Boulder, CO: Westview Press.

Gheissari, A. 1998. *Iranian intellectuals in the twentieth century.* Austin: University of Texas Press.

Gheissari, A., and N. Vali. 2006. *Democracy in Iran: history and the quest for liberty.* New York: Oxford University Press.

Ghods, M. R. 1989. *Iran in the twentieth century: a political history.* Boulder, CO: Lynne Rienner.

Graham, R. 1980. *Iran: the illusion of power.* New York: St. Martin's Press.

Hillman, M. C., ed. 1982. *Iranian society: an anthology of writings by Jalal Al-e Ahmad.* Lexington, Ky: Mazda.

———. 1976. *Literature East & West: major voices in contemporary Persian literature.* Volume XX.

Hiro, D. 1985. *Iran under the Ayatollahs.* London: Routledge, Kegan Paul.

Hunter, S. T. 1990. *Iran and the world: continuity in a revolutionary decade.* Bloomington: Indiana University Press.

Jahanbakhsh, F. 2001. *Islam, democracy and religious modernity in Iran (1953–2000).* Leiden: Brill.

Kamrava, M. 2008. *Iran's intellectual revolution.* Cambridge: Cambridge University Press.

———. 1990. *Revolution in Iran: the roots of turmoil.* London: Routledge.

Karim, P. M. and M. M. Khorrami. 1999. *A world between: poems, short stories, and essays by Iranian-Americans.* New York: George Braziller.

Karimi-Hakkak, A. 1995. *Recasting Persian poetry: scenarios of poetic modernity in Iran.* Salt Lake City, UT: University of Utah Press.

———. 1978. *An anthology of modern Persian poetry.* Boulder, CO: Westview Press.

Karsh, E., ed. 1989. *The Iran–Iraq war: impact and implications.* New York: St. Martin's.

Katouzian, H. 1981. *The political economy of modern Iran, 1926–1979.* New York: NYU Press.

Keddie, N. R., ed. 1983. *Religion and politics in Iran: Shi'ism from quietism to revolution.* New Haven, CT: Yale University Press.

Keddie, N. R., and R. Matthee, eds. 2002. *Iran and the surrounding world: interconnections in culture and cultural politics.* Seattle: University of Washington Press.

Kiarostami, A. 2002. *Walking with the wind: voices and the visions.* Translated by Ahmad Karimi-Hakkak and Michael C. Beard. Cambridge, MA: Harvard University Press.

Kurzman, C. 2005. *The unthinkable revolution in Iran.* Cambridge, MA: Harvard University Press.

Mir-Hosseini, Z., and R. Tapper. 2006. *Islam and democracy in Iran: Eshkevari and the quest for reform.* London: I. B. Tauris.

Nabavi, Negin. 2003. *Intellectuals and the state in Iran: politics, discourse, and the dilemmas of authenticity.* Gainesville: University Press of Florida.

———, ed. 2003. *Intellectual trends in twentieth century Iran: a critical survey.* Gainesville: University Press of Florida.

Najmabadi, A. 2005. *Women with mustaches and men without beards: gender and sexual anxieties of Iranian modernity.* Berkeley: University of California Press.

Pelletiere, S., and D. V. Johnson II. 1991. *Lessons learned: the Iran–Iraq war.* Carlise Barracks, PA: Strategic Studies Institute, U.S. Army War College.

Rahnema, S., and S. Behdad, eds. 1996. *Iran after the revolution.* London: I. B. Tauris.

Ramazani, R. K. 1990. *Iran's revolution: the search for consensus.* Bloomington: Indiana University Press.

Sanasarian, E. 1982. *The women's rights movement in Iran: mutiny, appeasement, and repression from 1900 to Khomeini.* New York: Praeger.

Schirazi, A. 1998. *The constitution of Iran: politics and the state in the Islamic Republic.* John O'Kane, trans. London: I. B. Tauris.

Sharbatoghlie, A. 1991. *Urbanization and the regional disparities in post-revolutionary Iran.* Boulder, CO: Westview Press.

Sick, G. 1985. *All fall down: America's tragic encounter with Iran.* New York: Penguin.

———. 1991. *October surprise: America's hostages in Iran and the election of Ronald Reagan.* New York: Times Books.

Soroush, A. 2000. *Reason, freedom, and democracy in Islam: essential writings of Abdolkarim Sorush.* Translated and Edited By Mahmood Sadri and Ahmad Sadri. New York: Oxford University Press.

Vahdat, F. 2002. *God and juggernaut: Iran's intellectual encounter with modernity.* Syracuse, NY: Syracuse University Press.

Wright, R. 2000. *The last great revolution: turmoil and transformation in Iran.* New York: Alfred A. Knopf.

Yaghmaian, B. 2002. *Social change in Iran: an eyewitness account of dissent, defiance, and new movements for rights.* Albany, NY: SUNY Press.

Zabih, S. 1982. *Iran since the revolution.* Baltimore, MD: The Johns Hopkins University Press.

About the Editors and Contributors

✦

MEHRAN KAMRAVA is Director of the Center for International and Regional Studies, School of Foreign Service in Qatar, Georgetown University. A political scientist, he is the editor of *The New Voices of Islam: Rethinking Politics and Modernity* (2006) and the author of *The Modern Middle East: A Political History Since the First World War* (2005), among other works.

MANOCHEHR DORRAJ is Professor of Political Science at Texas Christian University. He is the author of *From Zarathustra to Khomeini: Populism and Dissent in Iran* (1990) and the editor of *The Middle East at the Crossroads: Internal Dynamics and the Foreign Policy Challenges* (1999).

SIAVASH ABGHARI is Associate Professor of Business Administration at Morehouse College in Atlanta, Georgia.

ALI ABOOTALEBI is Professor of Political Science at the University of Wisconsin-Eau Claire.

ARSHIN ADIB-MOGHADDAM lectures in Politics and International Relations at the School of Oriental and African Studies, University of London.

KAZEM ALAMDARI is Adjunct Professor of Sociology at California State University, Northridge.

ROKSANA BAHRAMITASH is a research associate at McGill University Center for Developing-Area Studies.

LOIS BECK is Professor of Anthropology at Washington University, St. Louis, Missouri.

SOHRAB BEHDAD is Professor and John E. Harris Chair in Economics at Denison University in Granville, Ohio.

CYRUS BINA is Distinguished Research Professor of Economics and Management at the University of Minnesota, Morris Campus.

H. E. CHEHABI is Professor of International Relations at Boston University.

ALI DIZBONI is Assistant Professor in the Department of Politics and Economics at the Royal Military College of Canada.

NADER ENTESSAR is a professor and Chair of the Department of Political Science and Criminal Justice at the University of South Alabama in Mobile, Alabama.

FARIDEH FARHI is an independent researcher and Adjunct Professor of Political Science at the University of Hawai'i-Manoa.

HENGAMEH FOULADVAND is Executive Director of the Center for Iranian Modern Arts.

ROBERT O. FREEDMAN is Peggy Meyerhoff Pearlstone Professor of Political Science at Baltimore Hebrew University.

MOHAMMAD HOSSEIN HAFEZIAN is Assistant Professor of Political Science at Azad Islamic University in Karaj, Iran and a member of the Middle East and Persian Gulf Research Group of the Center for Strategic Research, located in Tehran.

AHMAD KARIMI HAKKAK is Director of the Center of Persian Studies at the University of Maryland.

HOUCHANG HASSAN-YARI is a professor and Head of the Department of Politics and Economics at the Royal Military College of Canada.

JULIA HUANG is in doctoral candidate in the Anthropology Department at Yale University.

YUKA KADOI is a lecturer in the Department of Architecture at the University of Edinburgh.

YAHYA KAMALIPOUR is a professor and Head of the Department of Communication and Creative Arts and Director of Center for Global Studies at Purdue University.

PERSIS M. KARIM is Associate Professor in the Department of English and Comparative Literature at San Jose State University.

SHAHLA KAZEMIPOUR is Assistant Professor and Associate Director for Research, Center for Population Studies and Research, Ministry of Science, Research & Technology, Tehran.

MASOUD KAZEMZADEH is Assistant Professor of Political Science at Utah Valley State College.

ROBERT E. LOONEY is Professor of National Security Affairs at the Naval Postgraduate School, Monterey, California.

PARDIS MAHDAVI is Assistant Professor of Anthropology at Pomona College in Pomona, California.

SHIREEN MAHDAVI is Adjunct Professor in the Department of History at the University of Utah.

MEHRDAD MASHAYEKHI is Visiting Assistant Professor in the Department of Sociology and Anthropology at Georgetown University, Washington D.C.

YASUYUKI MATSUNAGA is a Fellow at the Center for Interdisciplinary Study of Monotheistic Religions, Doshisha University, Kyoto, Japan.

VALENTINE M. MOGHADAM is Professor of Sociology and Director of Women's Studies at Purdue University.

MAJID MOHAMMADI is Adjunct Professor of Near Eastern Studies at Binghamton University.

MAHMOOD MONSHIPOURI is Assistant Professor in the International Relations Department at San Francisco State University.

FARHAD NOMANI is a professor and Co-chair of the Department of Economics at the American University of Paris.

FIROOZEH PAPAN-MATIN is Assistant Professor of Persian Literature at the University of Washington, Seattle.

ORLY RAHIMIYAN is a Ph.D. candidate in the Middle Eastern Studies Program of Ben-Gurion University and a Research Fellow at the Ben Zvi Institute in Israel.

FARHANG RAJAEE is Associate Professor of Humanities at Carlton University in Ottawa, Canada.

EVA PATRICIA RAKEL is a lecturer in Political Science at the University of Amsterdam.

SOHI RASTEGAR is Director of the Emerging Frontiers In Research and Innovation Program at the U.S. National Science Foundation.

GHOLAM HOSSEIN RAZI is Professor of Political Science at the University of Houston.

JALIL ROSHANDEL is Associate Professor of Political Science at East Carolina University.

MAHMOUD SADRI is Professor of Sociology at Texas Women's University.

DJAVAD SALEHI-ISFAHANI is Professor of Economics at Virginia Polytechnic Institute and State University.

MEHDI SEMATI is Associate Professor of Communication Studies in Eastern Illinois University.

ROSCHANACK SHAERY-EISENLOHR is a lecturer in Persian in the Department of Asian and Near Eastern Studies at the University of Chicago.

MAJID SHARIFI is Assistant Professor of Government at Eastern Washington University.

FAEGHEH S. SHIRAZI is Associate Professor of Middle Eastern Studies at the University of Texas at Austin.

HADI SULTAN-QURRAIE is Assistant Professor at the Defense Language Institute.

NAYEREH TOHIDI is a professor and Chair of the Department of Women Studies at California State University, Northridge.

SANAM VAKIL is Assistant Professor of Middle East Studies at Johns Hopkins University, Baltimore, Maryland.

MEHRDAD VALIBEIGI teaches economics at the American University, Washington D.C.

HAMID ZANGENEH is Professor of Economics at Widener University in Chester, Pennsylvania.

Index

✦